THE GENERAL THEORY AND AFTER

A SUPPLEMENT

The Collected Writings of John Maynard Keynes

P. Sraffa, J. M. K., and D. H. Robertson at Tilton, 1927

THE COLLECTED WRITINGS OF
JOHN MAYNARD KEYNES

VOLUME XXIX

THE GENERAL THEORY
AND AFTER

A SUPPLEMENT

EDITED BY
DONALD MOGGRIDGE

MACMILLAN
CAMBRIDGE UNIVERSITY PRESS
FOR THE
ROYAL ECONOMIC SOCIETY

Published for the Royal Economic Society
throughout the world, excluding the U.S.A. and Canada, by

THE MACMILLAN PRESS LTD
London and Basingstoke
Associated companies in Delhi Dublin Hong Kong Johannesburg
Lagos Melbourne New York Singapore Tokyo

THE SYNDICS OF THE CAMBRIDGE UNIVERSITY PRESS
32 East 57th Street, New York, NY 10022, U.S.A.

Printed in Great Britain
at the University Press, Cambridge

British Library Cataloguing in Publication Data

Keynes, John Maynard, *Baron Keynes*
The collected writings of John Maynard Keynes

Vol. XXIX: The 'General theory' and after
A supplement
1. Economics
I. Moggridge, Donald. II. Royal Economic Society
330.15'6 HB171
ISBN 0-333-24173-8

Library of Congress Cataloguing in Publication Data

Keynes, John Maynard, 1883–1946.
The collected writings of John Maynard Keynes.

Vol. XXIII has imprint: New York, Cambridge University Press,
for the Royal Economic Society.
CONTENTS: v. 1. Indian currency and finance.—
v. 2. The economic consequences of the peace.—
v. 3. A revision of the treaty. [etc.]
1. Economics—Collected works.
I. Royal Economic Society, London.
HB171.K44 330.15'6'08 76-13349
ISBN 0-521-22949-9

This book is sold in the U.K. subject to
the standard conditions of the Net Book Agreement

CONTENTS

GENERAL INTRODUCTION

This new standard edition of *The Collected Writings of John Maynard Keynes* forms the memorial to him of the Royal Economic Society. He devoted a very large share of his busy life to the Society. In 1911, at the age of twenty-eight, he became editor of the *Economic Journal* in succession to Edgeworth: two years later he was made secretary as well. He held these offices without intermittence until almost the end of his life. Edgeworth, it is true, returned to help him with the editorship from 1919 to 1925; Macgregor took Edgeworth's place until 1934, when Austin Robinson succeeded him and continued to assist Keynes down to 1945. But through all these years Keynes himself carried the major responsibility and made the principal decisions about the articles that were to appear in the *Economic Journal,* without any break save for one or two issues when he was seriously ill in 1937. It was only a few months before his death at Easter 1946 that he was elected president and handed over his editorship to Roy Harrod and the secretaryship to Austin Robinson.

In his dual capacity of editor and secretary Keynes played a major part in framing the policies of the Royal Economic Society. It was very largely due to him that some of the major publishing activities of the Society—Sraffa's edition of Ricardo, Stark's edition of the economic writings of Bentham, and Guillebaud's edition of Marshall, as well as a number of earlier publications in the 1930s—were initiated.

When Keynes died in 1946 it was natural that the Royal Economic Society should wish to commemorate him. It was perhaps equally natural that the Society chose to commemorate him by producing an edition of his collected works. Keynes himself had always taken a joy in fine printing, and the Society, with the help of Messrs Macmillan as publishers and the Cambridge University Press as printers, has been anxious to give Keynes's writings a permanent form that is wholly worthy of him.

The present edition will publish as much as is possible of his work in the field of economics. It will not include any private and personal correspondence or publish many letters in the possession of his family. The edition is concerned, that is to say, with Keynes as an economist.

Keynes's writings fall into five broad categories. First there are the books which he wrote and published as books. Second there are collections of articles and pamphlets which he himself made during his lifetime (*Essays in Persuasion* and *Essays in Biography*). Third, there is a very considerable volume of published but uncollected writings—articles written for newspapers, letters to newspapers, articles in journals that have not been included in his two volumes of collections, and various pamphlets. Fourth, there are a few hitherto unpublished writings. Fifth, there is correspondence with economists and concerned with economics or public affairs. It is the intention of this series to publish almost completely the whole of the first four categories listed above. The only exceptions are a few syndicated articles where Keynes wrote almost the same material for publication in different newspapers or in different countries, with minor and unimportant variations. In these cases, this series will publish one only of the variations, choosing the most interesting.

The publication of Keynes's economic correspondence must inevitably be selective. In the day of the typewriter and the filing cabinet and particularly in the case of so active and busy a man, to publish every scrap of paper that he may have dictated about some unimportant or ephemeral matter is impossible. We are aiming to collect and publish as much as possible, however, of the correspondence in which Keynes developed his own ideas in argument with his fellow economists, as well as the more significant correspondence at times when Keynes was in the middle of public affairs.

Apart from his published books, the main sources available to those preparing this series have been two. First, Keynes in his will made Richard Kahn his executor and responsible for his economic papers. They have been placed in the Marshall Library of the University of Cambridge and have been available for this edition. Until 1914 Keynes did not have a secretary and his earliest papers are in the main limited to drafts of important letters that he made in his own handwriting and retained. At that stage most of the correspondence that we possess is represented by what he received rather than by what he wrote. During the war years of 1914–18 and 1940–6 Keynes was serving in the Treasury. With the opening in 1968 of the records under the thirty-year rule, many of the papers that he wrote then and between the wars have become available. From 1919 onwards, throughout the rest of his life, Keynes had the help of a secretary—for many years Mrs Stephens. Thus for the last twenty-five years of his working life we have in most cases the carbon copies of his own letters as well as the originals of the letters that he received.

There were, of course, occasions during this period on which Keynes wrote himself in his own handwriting. In some of these cases, with the help of his correspondents, we have been able to collect the whole of both sides of some important interchange and we have been anxious, in justice to both correspondents, to see that both sides of the correspondence are published in full.

The second main source of information has been a group of scrapbooks kept over a very long period of years by Keynes's mother, Florence Keynes, wife of Neville Keynes. From 1919 onwards these scrapbooks contain almost the whole of Maynard Keynes's more ephemeral writing, his letters to newspapers and a great deal of material which enables one to see not only what he wrote but the reaction of others to his writing. Without these very carefully kept scrapbooks the task of any editor or biographer of Keynes would have been immensely more difficult.

The plan of the edition, as at present intended, is this. It will total thirty volumes. Of these the first eight are Keynes's published books from *Indian Currency and Finance*, in 1913, to the *General Theory* in 1936, with the addition of his *Treatise on Probability*. There next follow, as vols. IX and X, *Essays in Persuasion* and *Essays in Biography*, representing Keynes's own collections of articles. *Essays in Persuasion* differs from the original printing in two respects: it contains the full texts of the articles or pamphlets included in it and not (as in the original printing) abbreviated versions of these articles, and it also contains one or two later articles which are of exactly the same character as those included by Keynes in his original collection. In *Essays in Biography* there have been added a number of biographical studies that Keynes wrote both before and after 1933.

There will follow two volumes, XI–XII, of economic articles and correspondence and a further two volumes, already published, XIII–XIV, covering the development of his thinking as he moved towards the *General Theory*. There are included in these volumes such part of Keynes's economic corres-pondence as is closely associated with the articles that are printed in them. A supplement to these volumes, XXIX, prints some further material relating to the same issues, which has since been discovered.

The following thirteen volumes deal with Keynes's *Activi-ties* during the years from the beginning of his public life in 1905 until his death. In each of the periods into which we divide this material, the volume concerned publishes his more ephemeral writings, all of it hitherto uncollected, his correspondence relating to these activities, and such other material and correspondence as is necessary to the understanding of Keynes's activities. These volumes are edited by Elizabeth Johnson and Donald Moggridge, and it has been their task to trace and interpret Keynes's activities sufficiently to make the material fully intelligible to a later generation. Elizabeth Johnson has been responsible for vols. xv–xviii, covering Keynes's earlier years and his activities down to the end of World War I reparations and reconstruction. Donald Moggridge is responsible for all the remaining volumes recording Keynes's other activities from 1924 until his death in 1946.

The present plan of publication is to complete the record of Keyne's activities during World War II with a group of two volumes. A further group of three volumes will cover his contributions both in the Treasury and at Bretton Woods and elsewhere to the shaping of the post-war world. It will then remain to fill the gap between 1923 and 1939, to print certain of his published articles and the correspondence relating to them which have not appeared elsewhere in this edition, and to publish a volume of his social, political and literary writings.

Those responsible for this edition have been: Lord Kahn, both as Lord Keynes's executor and as a long and intimate friend of Lord Keynes, able to help in the interpreting of much that would be otherwise misunderstood; the late Sir Roy Harrod as the author of his biography; Austin Robinson as Keynes's co-editor on the *Economic Journal* and successor as Secretary of the Royal Economic Society. Austin Robinson has acted throughout as Managing Editor; Donald Moggridge is now associated with him as Joint Managing Editor.

In the early stages of the work Elizabeth Johnson was assisted by Jane Thistlethwaite, and by Mrs McDonald, who was originally responsible for the systematic ordering of the files of the Keynes papers. Judith Masterman for many years worked with Mrs Johnson on the papers. More recently Susan Wilsher, Margaret Butler and Leonora Woollam have continued the secretarial work. Barbara Lowe has been responsible for the indexing. Susan Howson undertook much of the important final editorial work on the wartime volumes. Since 1977 Judith Allen has been responsible for seeing the volumes through the press.

EDITORIAL NOTE

During the winter of 1975–6, after Lady Keynes had gone into a nursing home, members of the Keynes family began sorting out the contents of Tilton, Keynes's country house in Sussex. Much to everyone's surprise, they discovered a considerable quantity of additional Keynes papers, which had been missed in the original assembly of the papers after 1946. One result of this discovery was the large laundry hamper full of papers which greeted the editor on his return to Cambridge in May 1976. In this hamper was a substantial amount of economic correspondence and manuscripts from the year of Keynes's illness 1937–8, plus some earlier material relating to the *General Theory*.

Although many of the new papers could easily be incorporated into the appropriate Activities volume (*JMK*, vol. XXI), a large amount defied this treatment. For in the new find was material closely related to that previously published in Volumes XIII and XIV of the Collected Writings. Given the volume of this material, the Managing Editors decided to present it as a supplement to these volumes. We also decided to take advantage of this supplement to pick up one or two pieces that we had inadvertently left out of these volumes and to prepare a list of corrections to them. Finally, given the recent discovery of the letters from Maynard to Lydia Keynes, which throw some light on the composition of *A Treatise on Money*, we have added a brief note on that subject.

In this, as in all the similar volumes, in general all of Keynes's own writings are printed in larger type. Keynes's own footnotes, as well as those of his correspondents, are indicated by asterisks or other symbols to distinguish them from the editorial footnotes indicated by numbers. All introductory matter and all writings by others than Keynes are printed in smaller type. The only exception to this general rule is that occasional short quotations from a letter from Keynes to his parents, his wife, or a friend, used in introductory passages to clarify a situation, are treated as introductory matter and are printed in the smaller type.

Most of Keynes's letters included in this and other volumes are reprinted from the carbon or manuscript copies that remain among his papers. In most cases he has added his initials to the copy in the familiar fashion in which he signed to all his friends. Except in cases where we have obtained the top copy from the papers of friends or colleagues, we have no certain means of knowing whether the top copy sent to the recipient of the letter carried a more formal signature.

PART I
PREPARATION

Chapter 1

FROM THE *TRACT* TO THE *TREATISE*

Keynes began working on the *Treatise* during the summer of 1924 at Tilton. Dennis Robertson was there for a visit during the early stages.

For the period 1924–5, we know no more about the development of Keynes's ideas than from the material presented in Volume XIII (pp. 15–43) until he began his long series of letters to Lydia. Written almost daily whenever they were apart, these run from October 1925 until his illness in 1937. They form the basis of the statements in this section. In the first, dated 18 October, he mentioned receiving the final version of Robertson's *Banking Policy and the Price Level*. The next day, he said that it would probably be another fortnight before he got back to his book, but there was no mention of his doing anything beyond 'some philosophical passages about love of Money'[1] (6 November) until the end of the next month.

From a letter to LYDIA KEYNES, *27 November 1925*

This morning I had nothing to do!—so I took out the basket where my book lives and admired its table of contents.[2] Then I read the first chapter. This needed a reference to my manuscript on ancient currencies.[3] But when that was taken out, I was a lost man and spent the rest of the morning trying to remember my theories about Greek and Babylonian affairs. I feel drawn to waste a little more time over these things.

And 'waste time' he did. The next day he reported working on ancient currencies until two in the morning, the following day until 1.30 and the next for five hours in the afternoon. The next six letters all referred to further work on the subject and included a vow not to allow himself more than a week's dissipation on the work. There were no further references

[1] See *JMK*, vol. VI, p. 258, n. 1.
[2] See *JMK*, vol. XIII, p. 42.
[3] See *JMK*, vol. XIII, p. 43.

to progress on the book beyond references to ancient currencies on 14 February and 7 March, until 25 April 1926.

From a letter to LYDIA KEYNES, *25 April 1926*

Yesterday I finished going through so much of my book on Money as I have written. It is wonderful how I forget. There is more of it than I thought and I had the pleasure of reading it through as though it was someone else's. But I am appalled by the hard work which is still needed to finish it. I suppose I must begin seriously to-day, or soon.

The letters to Lydia recorded no further work on the book that term, although one draft table of contents exists from two days later and another followed one month later.[4] However, as reported in Volume XIII (pp. 43, 45–6) the summer vacation of 1926 seems to have been a productive one. But this was followed by a long gap until 21 January 1927, when Keynes reported that he had actually managed to begin writing again 'after more than three months' interval'. The next week saw two more references to writing, but a gap followed while Keynes waited to collect more earlier drafts which he had left at Tilton. In fact, there were no further references in the letters to writing the *Treatise* until 20 May, when there began a series of references, supported by tables of contents already printed in Volume XIII (pp. 47–8), until 8 June 1927, when the correspondence ended until October.[5]

When term and the letters began again in October 1927, Keynes reported lecturing from the draft book, but made no references to progress. It was January 1928 before further references occurred. On 20 January he reported that he had spent the morning 'absorbed on my book'. He continued the next day, although he felt 'a little stale at it'.

I still work hard at my book. Dennis [Robertson] came in last night and we had a long talk about the new theory. I think it will do, and that it is very important. But it owes a great deal to him.

A week later came a further report:

This morning beautiful sunshine, and I worked speedily at my egg, finishing the first draft of 'The Pure Theory of the Credit Cycle'—60 pages of Basildon, so I felt very cheerful.

[4] See *JMK*, vol. XIII, pp. 43–4.
[5] One more draft table of contents dated 22 September appear in *JMK*, vol. XIII, pp. 48–50. This presumably reflects his summer's work.

The next Sunday's letter reported completion of that chapter, now eighty-two pages in length, and its dispatch to the typist. During the rest of February there was no mention of the book, but on 2 March he spent two hours with Piero Sraffa discussing the chapter and made necessary corrections two days later. The progress continued during the next term and by 20 May 1928 he was ready to send five chapters to the printer.

During this period, his evolving theoretical views appear to have begun to affect his policy views. When Sir Richard Hopkins of the Treasury consulted Keynes about R. G. Hawtrey's view that Bank rate should fall from 4 to 3 per cent and that the Treasury should promise the Bank that they would suspend the limit of the fiduciary issue if that was necessary to maintain cheap money, Hopkins reported as follows:[6]

> I asked Mr Keynes his general views on this. While differing of course from our currency system and attaching importance to more abundant credit, he said he was much less interested in Bank rate (indeed he saw no harm in a high rate if credit were adequate) than in the initiation of new schemes of capital development (housing etc.) as a means of correcting the state of trade and employment.

For the rest of 1928 we know relatively little as to the progress of the book, for all that survive are a note from Frank Ramsey, a single chapter of proof dated 6 October 1928 and another table of contents from the same date—all reprinted in Volume XIII (pp. 78–83). The same lack of new information continues through the first half of 1929, for beyond a reference to working on his book on 17 January and the statement of 5 May, 'I am putting in a little time at my book now and again', we know nothing. However, the surviving evidence in Volume XIII (pp. 83, 113–18) suggests that the summer was a period of considerable activity.

Keynes's decision of the summer of 1929 to re-cast the *Treatise* in two volumes brought two comments from colleagues. The first was from Dennis Robertson.

From a letter from D. H. ROBERTSON, *30 August 1929*

I'm sorry you are having so much trouble with your tome, but I expect it is worth it. The 2-volume idea sounds rather attractive. But you will soon be bothered with the desire to bring your illustrations up to date with 1928 figures before publishing!

The second came from Richard Kahn.

[6] Public Record Office, T176/16, Sir Richard Hopkins to Chancellor of the Exchequer, 27 March 1928. I am indebted to Dr S. K. Howson for this document.

From a letter from R. F. KAHN, *29 September 1929*

My first thoughts on receiving your letter[7] were, if I may say so, of your great courage. But on partaking of the first fruits that were enclosed I realised to the full how altogether right you were. The point, I suppose, is that the logical and time sequences which are appropriate to the conception of ideas are not always the best adapted for the purposes of exposition. In particular, the modification in the treatment of the Fundamental Equations that you have now introduced right at the outset carry, so it appears to me, big advantages.

I must apologise for the delay in replying. I have held back this letter in the hope of being able to enclose the proofs. But I know find that my work is rather behindhand, and, unless there is a particular hurry, I should prefer to wait until next week, when I shall, perforce, have completed my own share of the Adam Smith Prize[8] work. I have read the proofs and I have not much to say; but it would take some time to set it out.

With the Michaelmas term of 1929, Keynes began lecturing from galley proofs of the *Treatise*[9] to an audience which included, on 14 October at least, Dennis Robertson. During the term, matters moved more quickly and by 24 November he felt able to report that 'it looks as if my proof sheets are going to get through the criticisms of Dennis and Pigou without any serious damage'.

Robertson's comments from this period appear in Volume XIII (pp. 118–19). Pigou's comments appear below.

Fragments from A. C. Pigou's comments on the *Treatise*, autumn 1929.

...indicate this weakness of the Snyder index when used for your purposes.

81. Ref. to me. My sentences were not directed at all to this controversy. I have always thought that what you call the Jevons–Edgeworth index is rot. I was discussing the conditions in which a *sample collection* may be used to represent a total collection which is a perfectly distinct thing—your composite commodity—but for which we can't get figures.

113. I think you neglect unduly this point. When p is just < 1 and $1/q$ much > 1, it is reasonable to say the purchasing power of a £ has *probably* gone

---

[7] This has not survived.
[8] A prize essay competition in Cambridge. Kahn won the prize in 1929.
[9] R. S. Sayers, *The Bank of England, 1891–1944* (Cambridge, 1976), Vol. I, p. 366.

down. In my chapter I argue that any plausible mean is useful for this purpose, and that Fisher's mean has technical merits. I think you ought at least to indicate there is a problem arising when one of your limits indicates a fall and the other a rise in purchasing power, and discuss in what, if any, conditions one can then say whether a rise or fall (i.e. whether a £ will purchase more or less utility for a representative man of fixed tastes) is more probable.

Bank rate I'm not sure that I fully understand this section. But does what you argue imply, in the analysis, that changes in Bank rate cannot affect E or O. I don't see why they shouldn't, and, if they do, Bank rate won't *only* act there but [I] realise it puts up both I and S. Anyway ought there not to be some argument to show that E/O stands unaffected? What happens if O alters e.g. that real incs. and/or attend. technique or population changes?

A £ *does* buy a units of composite A in period I
    would buy a' „ „   „   „ „   „   II
    does buy b' „ „   „ B in period II
    would buy b „ „   „   „ „   „   I

I then get: 'The larger is $[(b'/b) \div (a/a')]$, *the more likely it is* that a £ brings more satisfaction in period II than in period I.'[10]

But it does *not* follow and I can't get without illicit ratio probabilities: 'When $[(b'/b) \div (a/a')] > 1$ (or indeed greater than any assigned finite quantity), it is more likely than not that a £ buys more satisfaction in period II than in period I.' I think your room will be all right tonight, but I should like to go about 10. Would it be a fearful punishment for people not to smoke?[11]

A. C. P.

p. 2 Profits of 'entrepreneurs'
    Ought not ordinary share-holders in companies to be mentioned.
p. 6 I don't think this does justice to Marshall. His purpose was to link up
    value of money and general theory of value.
Printing You always leave a wide gap between P. R. Ought not the letters to be closer together?

---

[10] The following pencil comments by Keynes appeared here: Is there any virtue of this formula over $b'/b + a'/a$ or any other mean function of the two?

[11] Presumably this refers to Pigou's paper to Keynes's Monday evening Political Economy Club on 25 November 1929.

Ch. 1 & 2   I think it would be much clearer if you put early on

$$E+Q = \text{total expenditure}$$
$$= PR+P'C$$
$$= PR+I$$
$$= E-S+I$$
$$\therefore Q = I-S$$

Ordinarily one thinks of income and total expenditure as identical, and it is difficult to accustom oneself to definitions that do not allow this. I should *begin* by emphasising

$$E = \text{income as now defined}$$
$$Q = \text{profit as now defined}$$
$$\therefore E+Q = \text{total expenditure}$$

Of course this is only a point as to *form*. I did not see the start of ch 2 till I had worked it out.

Early in the Lent term of 1930 Keynes arranged for Richard Kahn to do the index to the book and he reported to Lydia that he himself was working quite hard on it.[12] By 3 February he had started working through volume II of the *Treatise*. Despite other commitments, most notably his private 'evidence' before the Macmillan Committee, he continued to make good progress during this and the following term. By 19 May he was talking to Cambridge booksellers as to the best price for the book and six days later he was planning the final Book of the *Treatise*. At this stage, the references to the book in his letters to Lydia ended, as did the term. However, from 26 May one fragment survives.

It is impossible to raise the real earnings of labour if there is no rise in efficiency and no spontaneous change in the supply schedules of the other factors of production.

An examination of this problem under conditions, as it were, of barter and without express reference to money, tacitly assumes, in effect, that we are dealing with a closed system of which the banking system acts at all costs so as to stabilise the price level.

Now if under these conditions money wages are raised by

[12] Letter to Lydia of 27 and 31 January 1930.

fiat, the postulate that prices shall nevertheless not rise, i.e. that real wages shall rise to the same extent as money wages, makes it necessary that the banking system should adopt deflationary measures, i.e. raise the rate of interest. This deters investment, so that business losses ensue and entrepreneurs discharge their men. The rate at which they discharge them depends on the rate at which they can disentangle themselves from their existing commitments in the shape of contracts, fixed plant, etc.

Since the high rate of interest stimulates saving rather than otherwise, this tends to accentuate the disequilibrium between savings and investment. Moreover business men find their interest costs as well as their labour costs raised, whereas their product sells at an unchanged price.

The logical conclusion is that eventually the whole population is unemployed and starves to death.

I offer this as an illustration of the awkwardness of discussing problems of distribution without reference to the mechanism of money.

26.5.30   J. M. K.

This concludes the additional material relating to the composition of the *Treatise on Money*. The book was finished before the beginning of the Michaelmas term of 1930.[13]

[13] For the remaining, surviving correspondence prior to publication see Volume XIII, pp. 118–39, 173–6.

Chapter 2

ARGUING OUT THE *TREATISE*

Among the letters of comment Keynes received after the publication of the *Treatise* was one from Bertil Ohlin.[1] Keynes's reply is of some interest.

To PROFESSOR B. OHLIN, *5 January 1931*

Dear Professor Ohlin.

Thanks very much for your letter of December 31. I am most happy that you find matters of interest in my book. My own feeling is that now at last I have things clearer in my own head, and I am itching to do it all over again. I am sorry that my ignorance of Swedish should have kept me in ignorance of the work of Davidson and others. As to your point that reparations cause a shift in the demand curve of the receiving country, irrespective of any rise in the price level of that country, I do not think I disagree with you.[2]

On the matter of the Wicksell essay,[3] I am rather horrified to contemplate such a long further delay. Is it a matter which would really take you much time once you settled down to it? A delay of six months I should not mind. But a delay of a full year, and even then some measure of uncertainty, seems to me rather formidable. Could you not consider whether this might not be slipped in, now that you have got your book[4]

[1] Ohlin was then in Geneva working for the League of Nations on an investigation of the depression. The results of the investigation were published under the title *The Course and Phases of the World Economic Depression* (Geneva, 1931).

[2] The reference here is to Keynes's debate with Ohlin in the *Economic Journal* for 1929. See J. M. Keynes, 'The German Transfer Problem', March; B. Ohlin, 'The Reparation Problem: A Discussion, I, Transfer Difficulties, Real and Imagined', June; J. M. Keynes, 'The Reparation Problem: A Discussion, II, A Rejoinder', June; B. Ohlin, 'A Rejoinder', September; J. M. Keynes, 'A Reply', September.

[3] The reference here is to the introduction to the translation of Wicksell's *Interest and Prices* (London, 1935), then in hand by R. F. Kahn.

[4] Presumably *Interregional and International Trade* (Cambridge, Mass., 1933).

out of the way, along with your work for the League of Nations? As for Dr. Lindahl, I am, unluckily, quite ignorant of his personality and his qualifications. If, however, you think it is impossible to do the work yourself in the course of 1931, I do think we should consider whether it should not be handed over to him. Will you let me know how you feel on further consideration?

Yours sincerely,
J. M. KEYNES

Keynes also received a comment on the book from Professor F. W. Taussig.

From a letter from F. W. TAUSSIG, *4 March 1931*

I must not fail to add a word about your *Treatise on Money*. I have dipped into it, and of course I shall want to read it all,—or at least all that I can follow. Being in the throes of getting out a book of my own, I let other things, even the most important, go for the moment. But I have read enough to appreciate the masterly character of your work. You have done much more than put together a theory of money. You deal not only with the mechanism of exchange, but with the most difficult questions of the organization of production, and the dynamics of the sort of community we live in (I dislike 'dynamics', but you will see what I mean). Not least, you face the new and highly intricate form which the working of the whole business has taken during the last decade. The book will have plenty of reviews, but you must be prepared to have very few that show a real following of your work. It will probably take years before it is fully understood and before critical comment will be made deserving your careful attention. It is the sort of thing that people will turn to again and again and which cannot fail to influence the thought even of the most discerning and well equipped. I cannot express too highly my admiration.

To Taussig's comment, Keynes replied.

From a letter to F. W. TAUSSIG, *21 March 1931*

I have appreciated immensely what you write about my book. It will make me all the more interested to know how you feel about the fundamental conceptions when you have given them further consideration.

When I wrote the book many of the ideas were still too fresh in my mind for me to have thought of the clearest, most accurate or most convincing ways of expressing them. The result is, I find, that many readers find it slow and difficult work to get into complete contact with what I am trying to say. Before long I shall make an effort to express more fundamentally parts of the argument in another way.

Meanwhile your letter is very encouraging; for there is no one whose good opinion of my book I would rather have than yours.

Two additional items have come to light concerning the Keynes–Hawtrey correspondence over the *Treatise*. The first piece is Keynes's letter to Hawtrey on receiving the final version of the latter's criticism of the book prepared as a working paper for the Macmillan Committee. It should appear before the introduction to the letter dated 30 January 1931 on page 169 of Volume XIII. [5]

To R. G. HAWTREY, *16 February 1931*

My dear Ralph,

I felt enormously honoured by the final version of your *opus* on me and the trouble you had taken. It is very seldom indeed that an author can expect to get as a criticism anything so tremendously useful to himself.

I made a good many notes on points which I should like to discuss with you, though, particularly in the first 12 pages, there is comparatively little from which I dissent. But this

---

[5] The meeting referred to in the previous letter (p. 169) took place on Sunday 14 December 1930.

must wait a little as influenza has put me fearfully behindhand with my drafting for the Macmillan Committee. I will write to you about it again a little later on. I only wanted to say before too much time had elapsed how grateful to you I am for it.

Yours sincerely,

J. M. KEYNES

Keynes passed Hawtrey's comments over to Richard Kahn. His reaction came in a letter dated 25 March (the references are to paragraphs in Hawtrey's piece).

From R. F. KAHN, *25 March 1931*

My dear Maynard,

As I promised in my last letter, I am returning Hawtrey's thing. I am very grateful to have been allowed to see it and am only sorry that I have not anything important to say about it. There really is extraordinarily little in the way of criticism that is at all fundamental in the thing, and it is pleasant to see that H. has understood the *Treatise* so very well.

The question of stocks seems to me to have only a secondary importance so far as the general theory is concerned. It is mainly a question of time lags, but in connection with the Credit Cycle, which is so much a question of time lags, I feel a little sympathy for Hawtrey's attitude, though I think that he is misguided on the major issues.

On the possibility of output altering as a result of a change in savings or investment you could, of course, admit the justice of H.'s contribution.

All the later sections that deal with stock-exchange investment and new issues are terribly hard to follow. While in § 130 H. recognises that profits are available to take up new issues, one feels that he is forgetting this a lot of the time. But I do feel that an attempt ought to be made to investigate the conditions of equilibrium in the stock exchange markets on some such lines as H. attempts. I myself still feel rather confused about the whole thing.

I enclose a few odd notes.

Yours

R. F. K.

36–39. I am afraid I cannot follow this, but I feel rather suspicious.

43. I cannot see that the effect of a fall in demand on the price of an intermediate product depends on its distance from the consumer.

48.   So long as output does not alter (and windfalls are not partly spent), the criticism fails. But if output can alter, savings are not purely cause but partly effect (in the extreme case—e.g. production everywhere at constant *prime* cost—the difference between *net* savings and investment may be unalterable. But the causal force of an *attempt* to alter savings still remains).

67.   I cannot see this.

77.   The price would move to an equivalent extent—and I agree with your comment.

87.   How do lines 7 to 11 tally with §74?

150.   H. seems to be misunderstanding the meaning of natural rate?

160.   I cannot follow.

179.   The word 'investment' has two meanings.

185.   The fact that a rise in rates of interest increases β even before wages curve down is obvious but important.

187–97. I too find this very unintelligible.

198   This is a point that I have often mentioned to you and with which I feel considerable sympathy.

201.   What an extraordinary blunder!

For the period of the 'Circus' discussions of the *Treatise*, we have very little new material. Keynes mentions on 20 April 'talking for hours' with Piero Sraffa and Richard Kahn and on 10 May he mentions arguments on purchasing power with Kahn and Joan Robinson, but beyond that all the new material we have is a note to Kahn.[6]

To R. F. KAHN, *17 April 1931*

RFK

Not only is the *total* income of entrepreneurs as defined by me a function of their output, but also their *rate* of income per unit of output. For as output falls the reward per unit of output which leaves them under no incentive to *change* their output falls also (assuming the supply schedule is upward).

Thus as output falls, the income of entrepreneurs falls *faster* than output. Thus when O is falling, unless entrepreneurs' expenditure on consumption falls faster than O, there is a *reduction* of saving.

[6] This should appear following Kahn's note of 17 April in Volume XIII (p. 207).

In other words, if $O.f(o)$ is the amount of entrepreneurs' income when output is o, $O.f(o)$ will fall faster than O and there will only be an increase of saving if entrepreneurs' expenditure falls faster than $O.f(o)$.

(Please return)   J. M. K.
20.4.31

The December 1931 issue of the *Economic Journal* carried a note by H. Somerville entitled 'Interest and Usury in a New Light'. In it he suggested that the *Treatise* provided a vindication of the Canonist attitude to interest and usury. This note led to a symposium on 'Saving and Usury' in the next issue with contributions from Edwin Cannan, B. P. Adarkar and B. K. Sandwell. At the end of the symposium, Keynes summed up.

From The Economic Journal, *March 1932*

IV. SAVING AND USURY

There is naturally much to agree with in the preceding notes. Nevertheless, I should like on one main issue to come to the support of Mr Somerville.

On p. 126 above Prof. Cannan agrees with Mr Somerville that if saving is conceived as mere refraining from expenditure, or if it is conceived as saving up money, 'the case against interest as a consequence of saving is black'. But, he continues, 'the answer is that interest is not, in fact, obtained in consequence of saving in either of these two senses. No one gets a penny of interest in consequence of merely refraining from expenditure; no one gets a penny of interest in consequence of having merely saved up money.' I wish I could agree with him in attributing this natural justice to the economic system, but I am sure that it is not so. Prof. Cannan has, I think, overlooked a vital aspect of the argument in my

Treatise on Money wherein it differs from what I was brought up to believe and continued to believe until recently.

The point is this. The answer to the question whether there is an increment of wealth corresponding to the savings of an individual seldom depends, as Prof. Cannan claims, on what he does with the money which represents that part of his income which he refrains from spending on current consumption. In particular, the answer does *not* depend, as Prof. Cannan seems to suggest, on whether he 'hoards' the money by increasing his cash or uses it to buy a security or some other capital asset. He may use his savings to buy a bond, and yet there may be no increment of capital wealth coming into existence as a result of his saving. I have argued in my *Treatise* that the causes which determine the increment of capital wealth are only contingently and indirectly connected with those which determine the amounts of individual savings. If an increment of saving by an individual is *not* accompanied by an increment of new investment—and, in the absence of deliberate management by the central bank or the government, it will be nothing but a lucky accident if it is—then it *necessarily* causes diminished receipts, disappointment and losses to some other party, and *the outlet for the savings of A will be found in financing the losses of B.*

Thus when an individual saves, his savings *must* be balanced by the creation either of an asset or of a debt (or a loss paid for by an asset changing hands). But, as a rule, it lies entirely outside the power of the individual saver to determine which it is to be, and whether the result, or rather the accompaniment, of his saving is to be an asset or a debt. What he has done is to make possible the creation of an asset without a rise in the price level. But failing a simultaneous increment of new investment, either by good management or by a lucky accident, then his act of saving will *cause* an equal loss to someone else; a debt will be created or an asset will change hands, but there will be no increment of wealth.

Does Prof. Cannan hold that if an individual increases his bank deposit by 'saving up' money out of income, there necessarily results an increment of wealth to the community? If so, this is a view with which I have tried to join issue in my *Treatise on Money*; if not, he has failed to meet the point.

Now when an act of saving merely results, however unintentionally, in a loss to someone else, it is of an anti-social tendency, and the subsequent payment of interest to the saver—for, *pace* Prof. Cannan, debts have to pay interest just as much as assets—is a burden which, if it accumulates with time, may become insupportable.

That is why, without contesting anything in Mr Adarkar's note, I nevertheless agree with Mr Somerville that it is this social evil, to the possibility and theoretical explanation of which I drew attention in my *Treatise*, which probably lay behind the doctrine of the Canonists. Mr Adarkar is, of course, perfectly right that the Canonists did not not see the point accurately and that the distinction which they drew between interest and profit does not logically coincide—or, at least, would not in a modern community—with the distinction between interest on savings represented by debts and interest on savings represented by assets. For one thing, it is impossible to earmark any particular savings against particular debts or assets. Yet as moralists they were trying to devise general rules which would be applicable to the actual circumstances of experience. May not Mr Somerville be right that the social evil of usury, as conceived by the Canonists, was essentially due to the fact that in the circumstances of their time saving generally went with the creation not of assets but of debts? In the Middle Ages the economic circumstances and the magnitude of the risks did not favour capital enterprise, and the annual increment of capital wealth was negligible, zero or negative. Except where it was closely and directly associated with business or with real estate (exceptions which they admitted), saving almost always had its counterpart in debt and not in assets; so that interest was generally 'usury'. The rate of interest at that time (as it is throughout the world today) was too high to permit an amount of enterprise on a scale equal to the current amount of positive saving. Consequently individual saving was mostly balanced by losses and the incurring of debt; for he who inadvertently incurs a debt through the disappointment of his expectations has to pay whatever he is asked.

Personally I have come to believe that interest—or, rather, too high a rate of interest—is the 'villain of the piece' in a more far-reaching sense than appears from the above. But to justify this belief would lead me into a longer story than would be appropriate in this place.

J. M. KEYNES

The remaining new material from the period of arguing out the *Treatise* relates to the 1933 Robertson–Keynes discussion of savings and hoarding. The discussion opened with a letter from Robertson and early drafts of Robertson's 'A Note on the Theory of Money'[7] and 'Saving and Hoarding'.[8] The work planned for the future appeared as 'Industrial Fluctuation and the Rate of Interest'.[9] This letter and the two letters and note following should appear before the material already available on page 306 of Volume XIII.

From a letter from D. H. ROBERTSON, *1 April 1933*

The enclosed is a bye-product of revising my lectures on index-numbers. I have not succeeded in getting the point made in §3 clear in my mind before, though it has long been latent. The rest is, more or less, an old story, though it hasn't appeared in print. Do you think it of sufficient interest to print in the *Journal*, with a reply?

I have also written a longish article (20 pages like this) trying again to make clear what I mean by saving, hoarding, etc. It is purely methodological, but intended to be the first of a pair, of which I hope to get the

---

[7] *Economica*, August 1933.
[8] *Economic Journal*, September 1933.
[9] *Economic Journal*, December 1934.

second, dealing with the trade cycle and the natural rate of interest, done by the end of next term. But I don't think the *Journal* ought to be flooded with this sort of stuff, and perhaps I will try it on Robbins for *Economica*.

I hate always to appear in print as a controversialist with you, but it is because of the inexhaustible suggestiveness of the *Treatise*! And I don't see how progress is better made in these fundamental matters than by public discussion between the ½ dozen people who are wallowing in them.

I know I shall never reconvert you to the old K-and-V method;[10] but I can't refrain from suggesting how much stronger they make the *prima facie* case for public works. For on your and Kahn's s[hort] p[eriod] method, all new money inevitably becomes completely inert in the end, and most of it pretty quickly. Hence your arguments can do nothing to allay the objections of those who urge that the budgets *of future years* will be burdened by the interest charges on the loan. But surely *prima facie* money once effectively introduced into circulation may be expected to stay there, and to circulate (thus affecting prices or employment as the case may be) with a velocity approximating to that of existing money, unless and until it is withdrawn by taxation, deflation, etc.

Also I am concerned about the foreign balance,—at any rate as put so precisely in the expanded version. I can't see why a public works campaign should be *pro tanto* stymied if foreigners send us £1m worth of business, but not if they send us £1m of securities!

But that is another story.

I enjoyed *Essays in Biography* enormously, especially re-reading Edwin Montagu, which I think is the best thing in that genre that you have ever done.

To D. H. ROBERTSON, *3 May 1933*

My Dear Dennis,

I have now read the two enclosed papers carefully and my reflections on them are as follows.

The paper on Saving and Hoarding is, I think, very interesting and precise, and I should like to have it for the *Journal*.[11] There is only one passage in it where, in my judgement, you are inconsistent with yourself. My criticisms are, first, that I cannot concede to you the claim that you are

---

[10] The old quantity theory of money.
[11] It appeared in the issue for September 1933.

using the term 'Saving' nearer to common-sense than I am! Indeed, however wild my definition may be, yours seems to me still wilder! But the main point is that I cannot discover what you gain by your 'days', which seem to me to stand in the way of dealing with a period as a whole. I have set forth these criticisms in more detail in the enclosed paper.

The other document is, to me in my present state of mind, much less interesting. I would rather, on the whole, that you sent it somewhere else than to the *Journal*. If it appeared in the *Journal*, it would seem natural for me to write some rejoinder, but I would really rather not publish a rejoinder to it; because this is a case—my fault not yours—where you are addressing yourself to one of the deader of my dead selves. I think there is a good deal in what you say, though I think I should still stick to my own view. In my present state of mind, however, I doubt that either version of the Cambridge equation is of any serious utility, and I can't remember that I have ever come across a case of anyone ever using either of them for practical purposes of interpretation. Thus, whether my version is slightly better than yours, or whether I ought to yield to your criticisms, I am not prepared to put up a serious case in defence of either. All this section is really a survival of the time when I was trying to make some practical use of the Cambridge equation, an attempt I have long since given up.

One can of course write down quite a number of equations of this type, stating the *de facto* relationship of some one thing to some other. But are they of any use for causal interpretation? All the versions of the quantity theory, which make no distinction between swops and intermediate transactions and genuine production–consumption transactions, seem to me to tell one nothing.

One point of detail, when at the top of page 2 you argue that saving deposits are potentially spendable, the same is of course true for an individual of the whole of his Stock Exchange securities and other assets.

Yours ever,

[copy initialled] J. M. K.

I

The definition of hoarding on page 3 relates the change in the money stock during the day to the *disposable* income, i.e. to the previous day's income. But the argument at the bottom of page 4 and many subsequent passages relates hoarding to the *actual* day's income.

If we stick to the definition of hoarding on page 3, the hoarding of some must always be exactly equal to the dishoarding of others; and there can never be any *net* hoarding or dishoarding.

II

On either definition of hoarding, the paradoxical result follows that a man, who had reduced his stock of money to *nil*, may nevertheless be hoarding. For this will always be the plight of an entrepreneur who is making a loss, i.e. whose income is negative.

III

At the end of a year a man cannot ascertain how much he has saved during the year by calculating by how much his income during the year has exceeded his expenditure. For let us suppose that the technical 'day' is equal to one month, and that his income, which two months before the end of the previous year was 14, has been falling by one a month; and let us suppose further that he spends each month an amount equal to his income, not of the previous month, but of that month. The result is then as follows:—

Month	Actual income	Disposable income	Expenditure	Savings (on D.H.R.'s definition)
1	14	?	14	?
2	13	14	13	1
3	12	13	12	1
4	11	12	11	1
5	10	11	10	1
6	9	10	9	1
7	8	9	8	1
8	7	8	7	1
9	6	7	6	1
10	5	6	5	1
11	4	5	4	1
12	3	4	3	1
13	2	3	2	1
14	1	2	1	1

Thus the man's total savings during the year are 12 units in spite of his having spent during this period the whole of his income.

IV

But it is worse than this. For not only are his savings different from the excess of his income over his expenditure, but it is impossible for him to know how much he has saved until he has sent up to the Central Statistical Bureau and ascertained the velocity of circulation of money.

For suppose that the technical 'day' turned out on enquiry to be, not one month, but two months, the table could then be as follows:—

Months	Actual income	Disposable income	Expenditure	Savings
1, 2	27	?	27	?
3, 4	23	27	23	4
5, 6	19	23	19	4
7, 8	15	19	15	4
9, 10	11	15	11	4
11, 12	7	11	7	4
13, 14	3	7	3	4

Thus it now turns out that, although his income and expenditure have both been exactly the same as before, namely equal to one another, he has now saved, not 12 units, but 24 units.

The above difficulties arise whenever income is supposed capable of changing.

V

The same sort of difficulty arises in connection with automatic lacking. Let us suppose that prices are rising 1 per mil per diem. Then if a technical 'day' *is* a day, he will suffer automatic lacking of 1 per mil of his daily income, i.e. in 1,000 days he will have automatically lacked altogether an amount equal to one day's income.

But if a technical 'day' is 100 days, he will suffer automatic lacking of 50*/1,000. 100 of his daily income, i.e. in 1,000 days he will now have automatically lacked the equivalent, not of one day's income, but of 50 days' income. Yet for the man himself the two cases are indistinguishable.

* 50, because the *average* rise of price during the 100 days is 50 per unit.

VI

Another illustration is the following. There is no investment and the public save *s* every day. The entrepreneurs neither save nor dissave, but always spend their disposable incomes. Consequently every day the entrepreneurs spend *s* more than their income. Thus a point comes when they haven't a bean left, but they have never dissaved! And not only so. It is probable that the poor devils will, at some time during the process, have laid themselves open to the accusation of hoarding!

VII

There seems to me a confusion, or at any rate a lack of explanation, between an entrepreneur's gross expenditure on his business for which he mainly needs cash, and his net expenditure on himself. He may have to sell securities to keep up cash for the former, even though he cuts the latter to *nil*. But this may be a minor point.

VIII

The argument on pp. 8 and 9 may be open to objection. We cannot suppose it possible for the public to buy new instrumental goods produced on that day as a result of increased saving on that day. Thus within the day we must consider ourselves as dealing with a given volume of investments.

I should say, therefore, that the price of securities will have to rise until someone turns 'bearish' and prefers cash to securities at the new price. But this means that cash changes hands between persons who are more or less bearish, not that there is any *net* change of hoarding.

IX

My fundamental reason for feeling that the division into water-tight days is not useful, is because it diverts attention from what seems to me to be the main issue, namely the effect of A's spending on B's income.

4·5·33   J. M. K.

From a letter from D. H. ROBERTSON, *4 May 1933*

Very many thanks for taking so much trouble about my things. I have today been finishing a bit of work for Chatham House, and am off to Oxford (to stay with Meade) for the week-end, so I shan't settle down to study your comments till next week. I don't know at all whether I [shall] find I have an answer! But I think probably in any case I shall like the article to appear in the *Journal* as an *attempted* solution of a beastly classic problem! And I am entirely content for the little index-no. thing not to do so,—I may try to dispose of it elsewhere.

Robertson's more extended reply came with a letter on 19 May.[12]

From D. H. ROBERTSON, *19 May 1933*

My dear Maynard,

I have now carefully considered your criticisms, for which again many thanks, and enclose some notes on them. So far as I can see, I don't feel impelled by them to withdraw the thing or modify it in essentials: nor at present do I see any way of making it clearer, though I *might* see a way of putting some of the points more clearly when I see it again after an interval in proof.

I should be grateful if I might have, in due course, about 3 proofs,—I should like to try it on the Prof. before publication and on my one faithful disciple Maurice Allen.[13]

Yours,

D. H. R.

[12] This should appear at the top of p. 307 of Volume XIII.
[13] Then a Fellow of Balliol College, Oxford, later Assistant Director of Research, International Monetary Fund, 1947–9; Adviser, Bank of England, 1950–64, Executive Director, 1964–70.

I

Here is a fundamental matter on which I have failed to make myself plain. In my own view, the definition of Hoarding on p. 3 is (i) not open to the objection you bring, (ii) adhered to on p. 4 and (so far as I can see) throughout.

(i) If by tucking money away I reduce your income and money stock, I can't see that my definition carries the implication that you are dishoarding as much as I am hoarding. You have not 'taken steps' to alter your proportion,—I have.

(ii) Bottom of p. 4. My reason for saying that entrepreneurs have neither hoarded nor dishoarded is not that $(M_1b/R_1b) = (Mb/Rb)$,—this happens to be true in the simplified case when $K = 1$, but is not true in the more general case (analysed on p. 15) in which K is >1. My reason for the statement is that they have been purely passive,—they have 'taken no steps' to make M_1b/R_1b different from Mb/Rb; if it becomes difficult (as it does in the general case where K is >1) it is owing to the actions of other people.

II and VII

I must admit that I have evaded certain complexities by confining myself to cases in which entrepreneurs' income, while sinking below normal, remains positive. To consider the cases where it becomes negative would involve taking account of the way in which the income of Class A reaches them through the hands of Class B, and immensely complicates the algebra. I doubt whether it raises any new principle, though I concede it produces some mathematical oddities. Consider the following story, which is one of progressive Hoarding initiated and maintained by entrepreneurs.

Phase 1

Public's stock	= 1000,	public's income = 1000	$K_a = 1$
Entrepreneurs'		entrepreneurs'	
stock	= 2000,	income = 500	$K_b = 4$
Total stock	= 3000,	total income = 1500	$K = 2$

i.e. we can arrive at K by weighting K_a and K_b according to the proportion of total income received by the two classes ($K = 1 \times 2/3 + 4 \times 1/3 = 2$)

Phase 2

Public's stock $= 1000$, public's income $= 1000$ $K_a = 1$

Entrepreneurs' $= 2000$, entrepreneurs' $= 0$ $K_b = \dfrac{2000}{0}$
stock income

Total stock $= 3000$, total income $= 1000$ $K = 3$

$$K = 1 \times 1 + \frac{2000}{0} \times \frac{0}{1000} = 1 + 2 = 3$$

Phase 3

Public's stock $= 1000$, public's income $= 1000$ $K_a = 1$

Entrepreneurs' $= 2000$, entrepreneurs' $= -500$ $K_b = \dfrac{2000}{-500}$
stock income

Total stock $= 3000$, total income $= 500$ $K = 6$

$$K = 1 \times 2 + \frac{2000}{-500} \times \frac{-500}{500} = 2 + 4 = 6$$

I do not know whether this is orthodox mathematics (there are infinities of different sizes, I think, nowadays, aren't there?), but it seems to give quite sensible results. I should certainly say that entrepreneurs are hoarding all the time they are making K_b pass through all values between 4 and -4 via infinity and $-$infinity!

III and VI

I don't find this paradoxical,—I suppose because I have got used to the idea! At any rate I still plead that my result is *less* paradoxical than yours, acc. to which, if a man is an entrepreneur with a normal income of 14, he will during the year have saved $2+3+\ldots+13 = 90$ (!) in spite of his having spent during this period the whole of his income.

I dare say I should have been wiser to stick out, as I did in my book, against using the word Saving at all, and continuing to call my activity Spontaneous Lacking,—in which case nobody's preconceptions of what the word ought to mean could have been offended! But the

$$\text{`Savings} \begin{Bmatrix} \text{exceeding} \\ \text{falling short of} \end{Bmatrix} \text{Investment'}$$

phrase is so attractive for expressing what we both want to convey that one longs to find some definition of the words which will enable one to use it without straining the meaning of either word unbearably.

25

IV, V

I can't help thinking you have been misled by the simplification adopted on p. 1 to avoid plaguing the reader with too many complexities at once, and quite definitely removed on p. 15. The 'day' is, by definition, quite a different entity from the period of circulation of money against income, which quite certainly in real life is many 'days' long. The 'day' is an atomic unit of time: income may be different on one 'day' from what it was on the 'day' before, but it cannot change during the 'day', i.e. be greater on the second half of a 'day' than on the first (this disposes of §IV). Hence if the income-flow is greater, and the level of prices higher on each solar day than on the preceding one, that *proves* that the technical 'day' does not exceed the solar day in length (this disposes of §v).

It may be true that the individual does not distinguish between the privation which he suffers through Automatic Lacking, and that which he suffers from past contracts being doctored in his disfavour: but the reasons for the economist to distinguish them are set out on p. 18, first paragraph of §12.

VIII

Pp. 9–10 are intended to deal with this. Surely we must, as always, visualise a *continuous* chain of economic processes,—in equilibrium, on any 'day', the public is buying old securities, the professionals are buying new ones, the promoters are buying investment goods.

If, when *A* saves more, *B* is tempted to part with securities in exchange for money, *B is* according to my definition, committing an act of Hoarding,—see p. 3, end of last paragraph but one, and p. 9, last sentence.

IX

This apparatus is *intended* to concentrate attention on this very issue! See bottom of p. 1.

The additional material in the exchange concluded with a short note from Keynes.

To D. H. ROBERTSON, *20 May 1933*

D.H.R.

Is the technical day the same for everyone?—e.g. for weekly wage-earners and salaried people paid quarterly?

About how long do you believe it to be in practice?

J.M.K.

When Keynes sent Robertson a copy of the reply he intended to make to Robertson's article[14] Robertson replied to Tilton.[15]

From a letter from D. H. ROBERTSON, *22 July 1933*

Thank you for your letter and criticisms. I don't find any objection *per se* to your comment appearing in the same number as my article, rather than 3 months later: indeed, if that is to be the end of the matter, I think it would be much more convenient to the reader that it should.

The question of substance, as always, is who is to have the last word! I feel I should like to put up a defence against your main criticism on the enclosed lines: while you, no doubt, will feel that you could reply to this! I expect these things get rather boring to the reader if they go on for ever (like Taussig and Pigou on railway rates).[16] But perhaps your No. 1, my enclosed No. 2,[17] and any further reply you may wish to make, might appear together in the Dec. *Journal*; and I would then be content to leave it at that.

Alternatively I might incorporate this in the second instalment which I hope to write: but I don't know whether that will get done before the March *Journal*, and it would be better to clear up this part of the story before that, if possible.

The continuation of the Robertson–Keynes correspondence on this matter, and Pigou's *Theory of Unemployment*, is also now more nearly complete. The letter from Keynes beginning on p. 310 of Volume XIII was finally sent off to Robertson dated 10 September. The letter followed that printed with the exception of an additional sentence following the last line of page 312, where Keynes added the following: 'On his assumptions dx and $d(w'/\pi)$ vanish throughout and are always zero.' The letter was signed 'Yours ever, J. M. Keynes'.

Robertson's copy of the letter carried a series of Robertson's annotations to particular points of Keynes's. These ran as follows (all references being to the version printed in Volume XIII, pp. 310–13):

Page 310, 14th line of letter: This seems to me all right. The real wage is

---

[14] The final *Economic Journal* version of December 1933 appears in Volume XIII, pp. 327–30. The original version and the covering letter have not survived.

[15] This letter should appear at the bottom of p. 309 of Volume XIII.

[16] A. C. Pigou, *Wealth and Welfare*, (New York, 1912), ch. XII; F. W. Taussig, 'Railway Rates and Joint Costs Once More', *Quarterly Journal of Economics*, February 1913; 'Railway Rates and Joint Costs', *ibid*, May 1913; 'Railway Rates and Joint Costs', *ibid*, August 1913; A. C. Pigou, 'Railway Rates and Joint Cost', *ibid*, May 1913; 'Railway Rates and Joint Costs', *ibid*, August 1913.

[17] This has not survived.

expressed in terms of wage goods, and so is the 'currency' which labour is bought with.

Page 311, line 11: No, not same as $F(x)$ on p. 35.

Page 311, line 12: Robertson replaced the word 'supply' with 'demand'.

Page 311, lines 13–14: Presumably aggregate paid ('total revenue').

Page 311, line 31 to page 312 line 2: Surely it is not true to say that ACP assumes P/π invariable. The whole of Part III is concerned with forces which change the demand function (in terms of wage-goods) for labour, thus altering the ratio of π to P. (The possibility of this ratio altering is explicitly discussed on p. 102.)

Page 312, line 16: I agree with the argument of p. 102, but think he *underestimates* it, for he assumes that K is obliterated, whereas it *may* be transferred to non-wage-earners and remain in circulation. On the other hand, I concede there *may* be reasons for thinking that the wage reduction will be associated with an increase of hoarding by non-wage-earners.

Page 312, lines 20–21: I don't see this at all!

Page 313, line 7: The *cet. par* is a very big one: he argues as strongly as anyone that the demand function (in terms of wage goods) may be raised by low interest rates, Gov^t action etc.

Page 313, lines 8–9: No, I don't agree!

The correspondence on Pigou's *Theory of Unemployment* continued with the two letters from Robertson, reproduced on pp. 313–15 of Volume XIII before the three further documents printed below appear.

From a letter from D. H. ROBERTSON, *25 September 1933*

I have looked at the Prof's book again, with your criticism. I don't *think* I agree with the main drift of the latter. It seems to me that the Prof. *does* take account of the variability of P/π in the place where it is relevant, viz, in discussing—not the elasticity but—the *variability* of the demand for labour.

I enclose corrected proof of our discussion,—the ink corrections definitive—you will see my complex coming out in the note!—the pencil ones for your consideration.[18] Perhaps best leave all as it is: I expect I am to blame for my laziness in rushing into articles, instead of slowly hatching a book. But I do hope you will consider whether in your new formulation you can do something to meet the criticism that your 'saving' tangles up causes and results. I quite agree that the reduction and obliteration of

[18] These have not survived.

28

non-entrepreneur incomes can be tacked on to the *Treatise* analysis without great difficulty: but I still don't see that there is *any* reason to suppose it* will be substantial enough to make my Saving a negligible aggregate: and I still think that to make the causal sequence clear *my* Saving *must* be disentangled from its uncomfortable position as a minor (quantitative) element in *your* Saving!

To D. H. ROBERTSON, *2 October 1933*

D.H.R.

The Prof. p. 102, §4

N_1 labour employed in   wage-good industries

N_2 ,,   ,,   ,, non -   ,,   ,,

X reduction of money wages

In non-wage-good industries receipts are initially unchanged, whilst costs are reduced by N_2X. Thus profits increase by N_2X and they are stimulated to expand.

In wage-good industries, however, receipts are reduced by $N_1X + N_2X$ and costs reduced by N_1X. Thus their profits *decrease* by N_2X and they are stimulated to contract.

The net result may be either greater or less employment, and either lower or higher real wages, according to circumstances. It is easy to show that either result is possible, though to work out the answer for the most general possible case is hideously complex.

2.10.33   J.M.K.

From D. H. ROBERTSON, [*October 1933*]

I have been looking again at Pigou, book II, and I still cannot grasp your objections

I   The elasticity of demand for labour in terms of wage goods, E_d (p. 40)

(a) In dealing with an individual industry, Pigou seems to me to make it quite clear that E_d depends *both* on the elasticity of demand for the product in terms of wage goods (E_f, p. 45) *and* on the productivity function of labour in the industry in question (η, p. 45). I.e. *neither* does he assume that the price of one product in terms of all others is invariable, *nor* does

* The reduction.

he fail to use the fundamental theorem of employment,—which are the two things you accused him of doing!

(b) Similarly, in dealing in ch IX with industry as a whole, he takes (p. 92) as a limiting case that in which the elasticity of demand, in terms of wage goods, for non-wage goods is actually zero: and reaches his final optimistic result in spite of taking account of this case.

If you want to dispute his results, you must, I think, either dispute his view about the magnitude of η on p. 91, which is obviously a matter of judgement, not of analysis, or find some flaw in the detail of the analysis of ch IX. I cannot see that the general method of analysis is open to the objections which you have brought against it.

II   Money wages and real wages, p. 102

It seems to me that the argument is valid, and that it is you who, in the attached criticism,[19] are neglecting the fundamental theorem of employment! In accordance with this theorem, entrepreneurs in the wage-good industries must be supposed to be carrying output and employment to the point at which the marginal prime cost, i.e. marginal labour-cost, of wage-goods is equal to their price. When now the rate of wages is reduced from W to $W-K$, the marginal labour-cost is reduced to $(W-K)/W$ times the old level, while the price is only reduced to $[Q_1+N(W-K)]/Q_1+NW$ times its old level, where Q_1 is the amount of non-wage-earners incomes spent on wage-goods and N is the total number of wage-earners. There is therefore a prime profit being made on the marginal unit of output, and therefore an inducement to expand output in the wage-good industries, as well as in the non-wage-good industries.

The correspondence continued with a letter from Keynes. As was frequently the case, Robertson made marginal pencilled notes on his copy. These appear here as numbered footnotes to the letter.

To D. H. ROBERTSON, *19 October 1933*

Dear Dennis,

I have arranged with Hawtrey to put off his visit until next week, as I find that it suits him just as well, if not better.

Your note in reply to mine about the Prof. is very interesting indeed. On the first point I withdraw my criticism, at any rate for the form in which I made it. My difficulty has

[19] Above, p. 29.

been to discover what assumptions the Professor was depending on. I now think I have found a way of rationalising what he has done, and what you write confirms this. The result is, however, to make me believe more firmly than before that his argument requires assumptions which are only valid when involuntary unemployment, in the sense in which I use that term, is absent. That is to say, his argument requires that any reduction in the real equivalent of the ruling money wage will lead to a curtailment of the employable supply of labour. Granted this, the rest, I am now prepared to concede, probably follows. But this on my view excludes the case of unemployment of the depression type, when the above condition cannot be assumed to be satisfied.

What has interested me most, however, is your reply to the second point about the effect on employment of altering money wages. What you say is perfectly true and extremely important, and I should not have overlooked it. It does not, however, help the Professor, since it is inconsistent with his assumptions. So long as one was trying to work within the ambit of his peculiar assumptions, my previous criticism was right. But what I ought to have noticed, and what follows from your point, is that his assumptions are really incapable of fulfillment except in some extraordinary limiting case.

Your argument shows that the reduction of cost at the margin will cause a tendency for prices to fall in such a manner that[20] the aggregate margin left over for entrepreneurs declines, i.e. the fall in aggregate sale proceeds will be greater than the aggregate fall in labour cost. But this is another way of saying that the inevitable result of a reduction of money wages is to cause a decline in entrepreneurs' incomes as well as wage incomes, and this infringes the Professor's condition[21] that entrepreneurs' incomes and expenditure are exactly as they were before.

[20] In the wage good industries.
[21] He never asserts this of any group of industries only of industry as a whole.

The Professor's condition can only be fulfilled if the reduction in efficiency at the margin due to diminishing returns in the short period proceeds at a rate just sufficient to compensate your point that prices are reduced by less than labour cost per unit of labour;—which is, in truth, impossible for a substantial reduction in money wages.

If we were to take the reasonable simplification which I gather you are doing, of assuming constant returns,[22] then all incomes must in virtue of your argument fall in the same degree as money wages, so that the equilibrium position is exactly that it was before, and there is no change in employment either way. This is the criticism I ought to have made.

J. M. K.

From a letter from D. H. ROBERTSON, *22 October 1933*

(1) Here is some more about the Prof.[23]

(2) I'm taking to [the] typist tomorrow a draft reply to you (i.e. your No. 1) and Hawtrey,[24] and will send you 2 copies, (one for transmission to him), with his article, as soon as ready. I have some hopes *he* will agree with the first part of my reply, and *you* with the second!...

I'm still utterly mystified by your objections!

I. In Part II ACP is making no assumption whatever about the nature of the supply function of labour, and is not called on to. He is discussing *elasticity* of demand for labour, i.e. what will happen to demand *if* the real supply price of labour changes.

In Parts III and IV he *is* making the assumption that the real supply price of labour is held constant, and not till Part V ch IX does he explicitly state the possibility that *money* wages will be held constant, i.e. that if the real wage is reduced through inflation the supply of labour will not contract. You may say if you like that this is an unrealistic method of procedure: but such an objection has nothing whatever to do with the analysis of Part II.

[22] No, I'm assuming short period increasing marginal cost. With short period constant cost there couldn't be any non wage incomes to start with, and *cadit quaesito.*

[23] The I and II of the attached comment deal respectively with paragraphs 2 and 3–6 of Keynes's letter of 19 October.

[24] R. G. Hawtrey had also submitted a comment on Robertson's 'Saving and Hoarding'. The two comments with Robertson's reply appeared in the *Economic Journal* for December 1933.

II. Certainly, if we divide into wage-good industries and others, aggregate prime profit will in the first instance be diminished by $N_b K$ in the former and increased by $N_b K$ in the latter, where K is the reduction in wage rate and N_b is the number employed in the non-wage-good industries. I.e. aggregate prime profit in industry as a whole will remain unchanged, which is what ACP states.

But even in the wage-good industries, while aggregate prime profit is less than it was before the wage cut, it is also less than it can be made by expanding output, since prices have not fallen so much, as marginal prime costs. I.e. the conclusion remains valid, that in *both* groups of industries there will, as a result of the wage cut, be an incentive to expand output.

In point of fact I think the Prof. *under*states his case! For the natural assumption to start with seems to me to be that either the aggregate wage bill is reduced from NW to $N(W–K)$, the NK is not obliterated but transferred to entrepreneurs, so that non wage incomes rise from Q to $Q+NK$.

The correspondence then resumes as printed in volume XIII (pp. 315–22).

The final additional letter relating to this chapter is another comment on Keynes's letter on Pigou's *Theory of Unemployment*. It is a letter from Gerald Shove, which should appear at the top of p. 326 of Volume XIII. The other fragments of the correspondence have not survived.

From G. F. SHOVE, *27 September 1933*

My dear Maynard,

Thank you very much. Lunch on Saturday will suit me very well and I will be with you at 1 o'clock.

About the Prof. I *did* mean that wage goods are money for all purposes. (See e.g. the very curious passage at the bottom of p. 154 and top of 155 where, if 'real income' is transferred from one set of non-wage earners to another who cannot immediately find an outlet for it in 'consumption or capital goods attractive to them', the 'wage goods['] which would have been used by the first set in putting labour to work on non-wage goods are '*piled up by the transferers in idle stocks* or used by them in buying foreign securities'.)

But I do not think he has any idea that he is making such an assumption or that it affects his conclusions (see Part IV ch 1 §1 p. 185).

And your fundamental objection to the apparatus (at any rate as regards output as a whole and the general rate of wages) remains, doesn't it?

I am not sure whether I have spotted the *non-sequitur* on p. 102. But there would seem to be other ways of removing the 'disequilibrium' referred to towards the end of §4 besides an *increase* of employment.* (I don't think I understood what you said about this matter in your letter to Dennis, and I should like you to expound it when we meet.)

Yours

GERALD

---

* e.g. transfers from wage goods to non-wage goods.

Chapter 3

TOWARDS THE *GENERAL THEORY*

The first additional material directly relating to the composition of the *General Theory*, other than the one additional 'Circus' document reprinted above (p. 12), concerns Keynes's lectures in the spring of 1932. On 11 February, he reported to Lydia that he was discussing their contents with Richard Kahn. When he gave his first lecture on 25 April, he reported that Kahn, Piero Sraffa and Joan and Austin Robinson were there to 'spy' on him. This first lecture, which Keynes thought had 'passed off comfortably' appears to have derived from the following materials.

Typed and handwritten fragments from which Keynes appears to have lectured, 25 April 1932.

NOTES ON FUNDAMENTAL TERMINOLOGY

I

The difficulty of choosing convenient terminology is partly due to the circumstance that so many useful economic expressions are strongly tinged with the implications of long-period equilibrium economics. It is, therefore, a difficult question for the modern student of short-period economics how far he shall use the familiar expressions, endeavouring to break down their present long-period associations. The object of the terminology proposed below does not differ from the object of the slightly different terminology which I employed in my *Treatise*. I have been led to adopt it partly as the result of experience as to what the reader in fact finds troublesome and partly out of a resolve to use language which is more unequivocally adapted to short-period problems.

One observation of a general character may, perhaps, be

35

useful. Critics often argue as if *logical* points were involved in definitions where in fact none such are present. Provided definitions are used *consistently* in a given context, each set will lead to perfectly accurate Fundamental Equations. For example, there are various ways in which we can split up the gross receipts of entrepreneurs and we can reach a Fundamental Equation corresponding to each of these ways. No one of these equations is more 'logical' than any other. The choice between them depends upon which is most useful and significant in its applications. Moreover, there is a further point which critics are still more liable to overlook—and one of very great practical importance to anyone who essays to write an intricate work on economics. A definition can often be *vague* within fairly wide limits and capable of several interpretations differing slightly from one another, and still be perfectly serviceable and free from serious risk of leading either the author or the reader into error, provided that *any* of the alternative definitions will do so long as it is used consistently within a given context. If an author tries to avoid all vagueness and to be perfectly precise, he will become so prolix and pedantic, will find it necessary to split so many hairs, and will be so constantly diverted into an attempt to clear up some other part of the subject, that he himself may perhaps never reach the matter in hand and the reader certainly will not. I believe, therefore, that it is necessary in writing economic theory for one's language to be less generalised than one's thought. It is often impracticable to discuss the most generalised case; and the author selects, therefore, a fairly typical case out of the genus which he is in fact discussing, and talks in terms of this,—satisfied in his own mind the same argument applies *mutatis mutandis* to the other members of the genus, and that the task of mutating the mutanda is a merely routine one as soon as the argument in the particular case discussed has been fully grasped by the reader. This means, of course, intelligence and goodwill on the part of the reader.[1] But an author is entitled to presume these qualities. At any rate if he tries to dispense with them by endeavouring to concoct a legal document which he is prepared to stand by literally and to suffer deprivation of rights if any case or contingency can be discovered for which he has failed to provide strictly and explicitly beforehand,- -then, I am afraid, he will never, if he has a thorough mind, reach the stage of publication.[2]

There is another problem of exposition which frequently faces the economist. How far is it worthwhile to anticipate objections or difficulties which will only be raised by someone who has not really followed the argument or taken in the point? Where such further explanations may help to clarify the argument itself, yes. But beyond that, no. For there is no reasonable limit to the objections which can be raised by someone, who has misunderstood the argument, and an author is unlikely to be successful if he tries to anticipate beforehand what points will be taken by a critic whose mind is really running on another track.

Thus theoretical economics often has a formal appearance

---

[1] See *JMK*, vol. XIII, p. 243.

[2] At an earlier stage of drafting, the material included in the 'lecture notes' had run down to the words 'stage of publication' above. Then, instead of continuing in the form that appears to have been adopted in the lecture, the manuscript, subsequently crossed out, continued:—

'With this preamble let me proceed to my proper task.

'Let us designate by E' the gross receipts of entrepreneurs, meaning by this the money-value or sale proceeds of the community's current output of goods and services. This is the quantity which most economists have had in mind when they speak of aggregate *Income*. In my *Treatise on Money* I found it convenient, for reasons which will become plain later on, to depart from this use of words. But I admit that my departure from common usage in this respect has caused confusion; and I am willing for the future to mean by *Income E'*.

'The gross receipts of entrepreneurs, representing the value of output O, are conveniently analysed into three parts,—namely, what we may call (1) their prime costs of production, (2) their fixed costs, and (3) their profits.

'The precise definition of prime cost, or, as I should prefer to call it, of *variable cost*, I must leave to those who are dealing with this concept in detail. Put shortly, C may be said to be the prime or variable cost of producing output O, if O is the sum of component items O_1, O_2 etc. and C is the sum of components C_1, C_2 etc., such that it is necessary for the production of O_2 that entrepreneurs should have the expectation of gross receipts from the disposal of O_2 at least equal to C_2.'

where the reality is not strictly formal. It is not, and is not meant to be, logically watertight in the sense in which mathematics is. It is a generalisation which lacks precise statement of the cases to which the generalisation applies.

Thus it is exceedingly dependent on the intelligence and goodwill of the reader or hearer, whose object should be to catch the substance, what the writer is at. Those writers who try to be *strictly* formal generally have no substance.

This is [the] explanation of pernickitiness of economists under criticism. We are all open enough to criticism, heaven knows, but the critic disagreeing is not infrequently one who has missed the point and then justifies his criticism by taking logical points.

Example of Marshall

Prof. Pigou and debating points.

On the other hand, this often leads one when criticised to think things are debating points when they really are substantial.

I hope that in these lectures I shall show that I am not obstinate and can take advantage of criticism on substantial points of argument and exposition.

Free digressions

Money and prices will not be mentioned for several lectures.

Keynes thought that his second lecture was less good and it certainly raised problems. For from it came a 'manifesto' from Richard Kahn and Austin and Joan Robinson. The covering letter for the 'manifesto' appears in Volume XIII (p. 376) with some of the ensuing correspondence. Now we can add to it. Below we print four documents: the first appears to be the draft material for the lecture, which started the discussion; the second is the 'manifesto' with Keynes's pencilled comments in numbered footnotes at the appropriate points and the authors' original footnote in the usual format; the third is Keynes's reply, while the fourth is Joan Robinson's reply to Keynes. The correspondence then continues with the second Joan Robinson note on page 376 of Volume XIII.

Typed and handwritten fragments from which Keynes appears to have lectured, 2 May 1932.[3]

III

It is, I think, characteristic of a normal economic community that ΔO and $\Delta E'$ are never of opposite signs and that $\Delta E' - \Delta F$ and $\Delta E'$ are never of opposite signs.

This means in plain language that decreased output never leads to increased income, and that, whenever there is a change in income, there will be a change in expenditure the same in direction but less in amount. It is not inconceivable that circumstances should exist in which these conditions are not fulfilled;—for example, the first condition might fail if new opportunities for monopoly were being simultaneously introduced, or in the event of peculiar provisions governing the rate of earnings. Nevertheless it is reasonable in general to assume that these conditions will be fulfilled.

Then since $\Delta I = \Delta E' - \Delta F$, and since we are assuming that $\Delta E' - \Delta F$ has the same sign as $\Delta E'$, and that $\Delta E'$ has the same sign as ΔO, it follows that ΔI has the same sign as ΔO. That is to say O and I increase together, i.e. the volume of output and the volume of investment go up and down together; or, in more familiar language, the volume of employment directly depends on the amount of investment. Only if our initial assumptions are unfulfilled—and a little reflection will show how difficult it is to conceive circumstances in which they are not fulfilled—need we doubt the direct reaction of changes in investment on the volume of output and employment.

I have said that it is difficult to devise an example in which the above generalisation does not hold good. If, however,—to

---

[3] We have no means of telling directly the exact meanings attached to the symbols used in this lecture. They may follow the *Treatise* or they may follow other definitions such as those on pages 37n2 or 65 below.

give such an example—the state were to decree, or if trade unions were to insist, that, whenever there was an increase in investment, there should also be such an increase in rates of earnings that the increase in aggregate earnings on the basis of the old output was greater than the increase in investment, and if earners were to save these increased earnings whilst entrepreneurs maintained their expenditure at their previous level, then every increase in investment would be associated with a decrease in profit and therefore in output.

Thus we are left with the remarkable generalisation that, in all ordinary circumstances, the volume of employment depends on the amount of investment, and that anything which increases or decreases the latter will increase or decrease the former.

The following is a further example of the practical utility of these distinctions. Since *cet. par.* I and E are both likely to fall with Q, and F to fall with $E+Q$, it follows that any given position of O is one of unstable equilibrium, in the sense that any movement away from O in either direction will tend to aggravate itself by stimulating a further movement in the same direction, until a point is reached where the fall in E is sufficiently in excess of the fall in F to offset the fall in I (and similarly *mut. mut.* with an upward movement). Thus if we preach and practise open-handedness when I is rising and economy when I is falling, (as unfortunately we generally do) we run the risk of aggravating the upward and downward movement as the case may be.

These examples illustrate how, if we introduce a few simple assumptions based on general knowledge of the outside world, we can galvanise our truisms into being generalisations of far-reaching practical importance. Indeed, I believe, that any man who has thoroughly grasped the truism

$$\Delta Q = \Delta I + \Delta F - \Delta E$$

and has allowed this colourless and in itself inoperative liquid to enter his marrowbones, will never be, in his outlook on the practical world, quite the same man again!

The general upshot of this and the previous chapter seems to be that the fluctuations of output and employment for a given community over the short period, within the ranges of fluctuations which certainly occur, depend almost entirely on the amount of current investment—not indeed with logical necessity but with a high degree of probability in practice. This goes beyond the contention of my *Treatise*, where it was meant to depend on the amount of Investment *relatively* to Saving—which has the advantage of logical necessity, apart from the results of temporary miscalculation or of a.policy which deliberately ignored considerations of profit.

This less restricted generalisation is the result of taking account of the probable effect on saving of a *change* in the amount of investment. This is a development of a point made in my *Treatise* that changes in the general situation are most often initiated by changes in the amount of investment, and that given the existing level and distribution of real incomes corresponding to a given level of output, there is not likely to be a spontaneous change in the propensity to save. If, then, we regard changes in investment as being normally the causative factor, *i.e.* the factor, changes in which most often initiate changes in the other factors, then the presumption is that the induced change in saving will not be sufficient to offset, and may sometimes be of such a character as to accentuate, the effects of the change in investment on profit and on output. Thus whilst we cannot deduce from observing changes in investment the exact *amount* of the changes in other factors, we can infer with a degree of probability approaching to certainty the *direction* of these other changes.

It is reasonable, at any rate over the short period, to assume that entrepreneurs' unit costs will increase with increasing output, which is another way of saying that with increasing output earnings will increase more than in proportion. Thus we have to superimpose on the probable effects of changes in O, the probable effects of changes in k in the same direction as the changes in O.

The typed 'manifesto' ran as follows with Keynes's comments appearing as numbered footnotes.

From JOAN AND AUSTIN ROBINSON AND RICHARD KAHN, *May 1932*

PREAMBLE

In your last lecture you challenged us to find exceptions to the various assumptions which you lay down as necessary to the proof that an increase in I increases O. Our difficulty however is not so much that we doubt your conclusion (to which it would be difficult to object on grounds of common sense) as that the method of formal logic which you pursued appears to hedge it round with restrictions which detract unnecessarily from its generality without increasing its plausibility.

Moreover the conditions suggested by your formal proof do not appear to have an obvious relevance to the problem.

I

THE FORMAL PROOF

Conditions laid down
   (a) $\Delta E'$ and ΔO have the same sign.
   (b) $\Delta E' - \Delta F$ and $\Delta E'$ have the same sign.

Proof
$$\Delta E' - \Delta F = \Delta I$$
$\therefore$ ΔI and ΔO have the same sign

We first *criticise condition (b)*
   This condition means that if income increases, expenditure will not increase by as much. Now it is surely obvious that if this condition is not fulfilled, i.e. if expenditure increases by more than income increases, the

presumption in favour of your assertion that I and O move together is actually strengthened.[4]

The fact of the matter is that condition (b) is necessary, not to show that I and O move together but to ensure that there shall be stable equilibrium. If expenditure were to increase by more than income, equilibrium would be unstable and any small increment in investment would cause output to rise either to infinity or to the point where condition (b) came into operation, whichever happened first.

Criticism of condition (a)

The implication of this condition is that your proof would break down if an increase in output were accompanied by a fall in its value. It is quite true that this is extremely unlikely to occur, but if it *were* the case that an increase in output was accompanied by a very great fall in prices, the presumption in favour of the proposition that I and O move together would surely once again be increased, not diminished.[5]

But it has of course to be accepted that your proof is formally correct, and that since condition (b) *must* be fulfilled, any breakdown (as for instance in the exception which you gave in [the] lecture) must be traced to a failure of condition (a).

Let us grant for the sake of argument that an increase in O will be accompanied by an increase in E'. It does not follow that an increase in E' will be necessarily accompanied by an increase in O, for an increase in E' may (as in your exceptional case) be accompanied by such a large increase in cost of production that O declines.

II

THE SIMPLE-MINDED PROOF

The problem seems to us to be susceptible to treatment by the method of Supply and Demand. For the truth of the proposition that an increase in I will lead to an increase in O, the two following conditions appear to us to be sufficient, though not necessary:

(a) That an increase in I will lead *per se* to a rise in the demand for consumption goods, i.e. that the demand for consumption goods on the part of producers of capital goods will increase when the value of their output increases.[6]

---

[4] Are you not confusing income with earnings? This does not seem to provide against the case where earnings are increasing faster than income.

[5] I am not clear why: could this be developed?

[6] Is this the same thing as that ΔI and ΔF have the same sign? If so, it follows from my condition (b). For condition (b) may be rewritten ΔI and $\Delta I + \Delta F$ have the same sign.

(b) That the conditions of supply of consumption goods are not affected by a change in I.[7]

When these conditions are fulfilled, an increase in I will lead to a rise in the demand curve for consumption goods without raising the supply curve, and so must lead to an increase of output of consumption goods, and *a fortiori* to an increase in total output.

When these conditions are not fulfilled, it is still possible that output may increase unless they break down to a sufficient extent. If (a) is not fulfilled there is no *increase* in R, but there will be an increase in C (except in the case where the increase in I is entirely due to a rise in P'), and unless there is actually a (sufficient) *reduction* in R, O will increase.

(b)$_1$ It is only if the increase in I brings about a *sufficient* rise in the supply curve of consumption goods that their output will be diminished, and the rise will have to be still greater if the decline in R is to offset the increase in C. Moreover it has to be borne in mind that any rise in cost of production is almost certain to be accompanied by a rise in the demand for consumption goods on the part of the factors of production which are responsible for the increase in cost.

It may be concluded therefore that it is extraordinarily unlikely that an increase in investment should ever fail to increase output.

III

THE EXCEPTIONAL CASE

The exceptional case which you gave in the lecture can be treated in these terms. You start off by assuming that an increase in investment leads to no increase in the demand for consumption goods. It then follows that if the increase in investment raises the cost of producing consumption goods by any amount, no matter how small, there will be a decline in R.

Whether this diminution in R will be sufficient to offset any increase in C which the increase in I may comprise will depend on the amount by which costs increase, but it is impossible to lay down any *a priori* rule.

It is to be assumed that your line of approach was as follows:

[7] This is a condition, exceptions to which are fairly easy to think of, isn't it. Is it not a little less general than my conditions? Also it is not included in my conditions? Your (b) looks to me the same as saying that ΔO and ΔI are of the same sign. This, taken in conjunction with your (a), namely that ΔI and ΔF have the same sign, gives ΔO and $\Delta I + \Delta F$ of the same sign, i.e. ΔO and $\Delta E'$ of the same sign which is my (c).

$$Q = I + F - E$$
$\therefore$ if F is constant, $\Delta Q = \Delta I - \Delta E$.
$\therefore$ if $\Delta E > \Delta I$,
ΔQ is negative *if* ΔI is positive.
Now $\Delta Q_2 = \Delta I - \Delta E_2$
But $\Delta Q = \Delta I - \Delta E$
$\therefore \Delta Q_1 = \Delta E_1$

$\therefore$ if cost of producing consumption goods increases, their output will decline, by an amount depending on the increase of cost.

Any possible case lies between the two following extremes:—

(1) Where there is no increase in C, and the whole increase in I is due to an increase in P'. Then any increase in the cost of producing consumption goods, no matter how small, will reduce total output. The increase in cost given in your example is unnecessarily great: There is no need to offset the increase in the profit on capital goods (Q_2) since here the increase in profit is not associated with an increase in output.

(2) Where the price of capital goods remains equal to their cost of production and their output (C) increases. Then the cost of producing capital goods increases by ΔI.* What therefore follows from your assumption that total costs increase by more than ΔI is that R declines, but in order that the decline in R shall offset the increase in G, it is necessary that the increase in total costs exceed ΔI by a large amount that cannot be determined *a priori*.

It thus appears that in case (1) your assumption is unnecessarily strong, and in case (2) not strong enough, to ensure that an increase in I will lead to a decline in O.

J.R.

E.A.G.R.

R.F.K.[8]

---

* In case (2) the assumption that an increase in I is unaccompanied by any increase in the demand for consumption goods is even more unplausible than in case (1). In order that it shall be fulfilled it has to be supposed that the additional factors of production employed in producing capital goods spend no more than they spent when they were unemployed.

[8] Your conditions boil down to
(a) ΔI and ΔF have the same sign
(b) ΔO and ΔI have the same sign
except that they are a little more stringent (and, therefore, more open to exception) than these.

I am not quite clear whether these are more or less stringent than my (a) and (b), but I think more stringent, for I can deduce my (a) and (b) from them, but not, on first sight, the other way round.

Indeed your (b) possibly begs the whole question, because it is practically what one sets out to prove.

1. The exceptional case infringes the first condition. For it is an example of $\Delta E > \Delta E'$. Consequently $\Delta E'$ and ΔQ are of opposite signs. Therefore, since ΔQ and ΔO have the same sign,* ΔO and $\Delta E'$ are of opposite signs which infringes the first condition. E.g. on the conditions postulated, whenever investment increases producers of consumption goods will find their cost rising and their receipts stationary, and will therefore reduce their output.

2. The following case infringes the second condition. The University of Cambridge pursues sound finance. That is to say, when it builds a laboratory, it always meets the cost out of the year's income by economising on other outlay and also, in addition, sets on one side out of current income a sufficient sum to cover the cost of the upkeep of the laboratory in subsequent years.

In other words ΔI and $\Delta I + \Delta F$ are of opposite signs which can be rewritten $\Delta E' - \Delta F$ and $\Delta E'$ are of opposite signs which infringes the second condition.

3. If we imagine a community which pursues the same species of sound finance as the University of Cambridge and is also imbued with the spirit of justice, in the sense that men come before machines, so that every act of investment has to be accompanied with an increase in the rate of wages of the kind postulated in the first exceptional case both conditions are infringed.

The increase of investment has reduced expenditure on two tickets, the reduction under each head being separately greater than the increase of investment, and being additive to one another to give the effect on profit.

---

* The only exception to this, which I am deliberately excluding at this stage of the argument, arises if industries have different (Q, O) supply curves and ΔQ is associated with a redistribution of Q between industries.

From JOAN ROBINSON [*May 1932*]

My dear Maynard,

I am sorry I did not make myself clear. Could we have another word perhaps during the weekend?

But meanwhile I take up your challenge.

(1) On your method the condition you give that ΔI and ΔO should fail to move together in the first exceptional case (not the University one) is definitely erroneous except on a special assumption about the elasticity of supply of capital goods and consumption goods.

(2) I quite agree that there is no reason to divide goods in[to] capital and consumption and say that their elasticities are likely to be different, but at the same time you are unnecessarily tying your hands by adopting a method which forces you to assume that the elasticities are related in one particular way.

(3) Our method can go one step further than yours (I don't want to make any grander claim for it than that). You begin by increasing I. Now, I say, tell me the elasticity of supply of capital goods i.e. how much increase in *output* does this ΔI entail. Then I will tell you for any set of conditions of supply of consumption goods what increase in E would be necessary to prevent O from increasing and so turn this into an exceptional case.

In this sense I consider our method more general than yours. You announce in advance that yours only works when ΔQ and ΔO have the same sign. Ours is designed to overcome that limitation.

Therefore I still maintain that ours says (a little) more than yours. The point of dividing R goods and C goods is not that their elasticities are *likely* to be different, but simply that you know C has increased, and you want to find out if R has diminished sufficiently to offset the increase in C, in order to see whether you have got an exceptional case.

Further I hope to convince you that you really were using a supply curve in your lecture, but I will leave that point in the hope of seeing you and having it out by word of mouth.

I think our method is much less different from yours than you suppose and it would be worthwhile finding out if there is really a substantial difference, or merely a verbal one.

Forgive me if I appear pig-headed. It does seem to me important to get this cleared up.

Yours unrepentantly,

JOAN

47

Keynes talked with Kahn and with Kahn and Joan on 8 May 1932. The argument took all day, but Keynes told Lydia that he thought they had solved the problem amicably in the end. There followed Keynes's letter of 9 May reprinted on p. 377 of Volume XIII.

The only other new handwritten note from this period of lectures appears to have reflected Keynes's future lecturing plans after the above exchange (see also Volume XIII, pp. 294–301).

Restatement of Conditions

ΔE and ΔQ same sign (ii)
ΔQ and ΔO ,,   ,,   (iii)
ΔI and $\Delta I + \Delta F$,,   ,,   (i)

Investment and income increase together (i)
Income and profits don't (ii)
Profits and output   ,, (iii)

Walker's point[9]
2nd exceptional case
Same thing as if we substitute ΔF for ΔI

Mercantilism
Protection
$\Delta I + \Delta F$ Disbursement
DHR holds that increased disbursement involves decreased hoarding

For the rest of 1932, we have four new additional pieces of material. First we have two very early tables of contents, the second being a simple re-working of the first. Then we have two fragments of drafts, which follow closely students' lecture notes for 10 October and 14 November 1932.[10]

---

[9] Edward Ronald Walker (b. 1907); Australian economist and diplomat; research student in Cambridge, 1931–3; Ph.D., 1933.
[10] Those of R. B. Bryce and L. Tarshis.

TOWARDS THE GENERAL THEORY

Earliest surviving draft table of contents, 1932

The Monetary Theory of Production

INTRODUCTION. CHAP. I. FUNDAMENTAL DEFINITIONS AND IDEAS

BOOK I THE INTERRELATIONS OF INVESTMENT, EXPENDITURE, PROFIT AND OUTPUT

Chapter 1 The relation of Disbursement to Profit
2 The relation of Profit to Output
3 The relation of Earnings to Disbursement
4 The relation of Disbursement to Output
5 The relation of Investment to Foreign Trade
6 Generalisations
7 Historical Retrospect

BOOK II THE RATE OF INTEREST

BOOK III THE DETERMINATION OF PRICE

Chapter 1 The Differential of Consumption-goods and Capital-goods
2 The meaning and consequences of 'Bearishness'
3 The relation of Price to Cost of Production
4 The relation of Price to the Quantity of Money

BOOK IV THE CONTROL OF THE RATE OF DISBURSEMENT

Second earliest draft table of contents [1932]

BOOK I INTRODUCTION

BOOK II THE MONETARY THEORY OF PRODUCTION

Chapter 1 The relation of Disbursement to Profit
2 The relation of Profit to Output
3 The relation of Earnings to Disbursement
4 The relation of Disbursement to Output
5 The relation of Investment to Foreign Trade
6 Generalisations
7 Historical Retrospect

[The intervening chapter numbers do not appear in the original.]

Typed and handwritten fragment of material from which, to judge from students' lecture notes, Keynes appears to have lectured, 10 October 1932

II

In the case of a machine, we assume that when it is in over-supply those of its utility-giving powers which evaporate with time will accept anything rather than go to waste. Consequently its short-period supply price is equal to the discounted long-period price of those of its qualities which will 'keep', and drops like a stone, as soon as it is in over-supply, from its long-period price to the equivalent of the extra depreciation involved in using it over not using it. We do not make any allowance for the machine *disliking work*, i.e. for the disutility, as distinct from the depreciation, arising out of work.

But when we come to labour, we are not so free to make a corresponding assumption. We cannot assume that a labourer regards any reward as better than none, or that he will be worked whenever the value of his service is greater than the excess of his 'running cost' over his cost on a 'care-and-maintenance' basis. We have to remember, on the contrary, (a) that there is a disutility in work, and also (b) that, unlike a machine, he can often insist on a care-and-maintenance basis of cost, even when his value if in work would be greater than the excess of his running cost over what he costs the community on a care-and-maintenance basis.

Accordingly whilst the short-period supply price of a machine is almost vertical, the short-period supply price of labour is nearer horizontal;—prime cost being arrived at by combining these two supply curves.

Now suppose that the short-period supply price of labour was just like that of a machine; what would happen then? Prime cost would be next door to zero. There could be much more violent changes in relative prices and relative wages without affecting output. And the result would be that relative supply prices could, in general, change to a sufficient extent for relative elasticity of demand to come to the rescue before unemployment ensued. Relative prices would change sufficiently *to force expenditure along the old channels* pending the gradual redistribution of the forces of production in accordance with a new long-period equilibrium. Thus there would be no need for unemployment even during severe transitions. Meanwhile as machines wore out and as work-people died and retired, the force of the disparities between relative prices and wages would be gradually shifting the economic system to a new position of long-period equilibrium in which the disparities no longer existed.

Thus, if we assume that the short-period supply price of labour is determined on the same principles as that of machines under free competition and that prime cost (in terms of money) is next door to zero, it follows that there will be no unemployment in the short period any more than in the long. Indeed the short period will not be so very unlike the long, and a foot-note here and there will be sufficient to deal with the important differences between the two. The net advantages of different employments of capital and labour will be unequal in the short period, whereas they are equal in the long period. This will be the only important difference, and this very difference will be gradually transforming the short period into the long with the lapse of time, failing fresh sources of disturbance, by reason of its effect on the direction in which as yet unspecialised resources are specialised.

These conditions would be satisfied in a socialist or a communist state, or, indeed, in any state in which employers were equally responsible for the maintenance of their men as they are for the maintenance of their machines, whether they are employing them or not. But not only so. It seems to me that this is that state of affairs generally postulated in Marshall's *Principles of Economics* and it is the behaviour of an economic system thus governed which he is discussing. The rare passages in which the possibility of unemployment is envisaged are really blemishes on the logicality and consistency of the main structure.

III

There is, however between these postulates and those of a Monetary Economy, a half-way house, which permits the existence of unemployment in the short period, and is therefore a much more plausible representation of the real world. I am not sure that Marshall ever occupied this half-way house, but it is, I think, the habitation of Prof. Pigou.

We have assumed above, not only that there is no lower limit to the money wages which labour will accept rather than be unemployed, but also that there is no lower limit to the real wages which they will accept. If we differentiate between these two cases, as it is highly reasonable to do, we distinguish at the same time between the case where the disturbance provoking the short-period conditions is due to a change in relative demand and supply, and the case where it is due to a change in demand as a whole relatively to supply as a whole due to deficient disbursement.* For in the former case the factors of production employed in an industry which has declined in relative attractiveness will have to accept lower *real* wages as well as lower money wages, if they are to avoid unemployment, during the interval before there has been time for the industry to contract or disappear. This is equally the case whether there is a change in the relative prices of different consumables or in those of consumables compared with investments. But in the latter case where there is a *general* falling off of demand for all purchasable things alike, whether consumables or investments, if everyone accepts a reduced money income, no one—it seems at first sight—need suffer a reduction of real rates of income.

Now in Prof. Pigou's half-way house the short-period supply price of labour is not determined like that of a machine. Some elasticity is presumed, but it is an elasticity which is responsive to the real wage offered, not to the money wage offered. Consequently it allows for unemployment of the first category due to changes in the direction of demand but not for unemployment of the second category due to deficient disbursement in the aggregate. Or, rather, in so far as it allows for unemployment of the second category, it is as a qualification of the normal case due to the unreasonableness of labour (and of other factors of production) in not being content with their former real wages. And it naturally follows that it is inclined to seek the solution for unemployment of this character in a suitable reduction of money wages and money rewards generally. Thus at first sight it seems plausible to suppose that the underlying assumption of the Real-Wage Economy relates to the fluidity of money

* For the meaning of this expression see p.   below. It is the same thing as what in my *Treatise on Money*, I have called an excess of saving over investment.

wages and money rewards generally. Let us, therefore, begin by pursuing this line of thought.

We must clearly assume, if we follow this line

[Here the manuscript ended.]

Typed and handwritten fragment from which Keynes appears to have lectured, 14 November 1932

Is the distinction between the Monetary Economy and the Real-Wage Economy partly the same as that between short-period economics and long-period economics, the fundamental assumption of the Real-Wage Economy being one which is in fact satisfied in the 'long period'? The answer to this question is complicated by the doubt as to just what we mean, in this context, by 'long-period equilibrium',—a matter which Marshall has not explicitly settled for us. For there are three suggestions conveyed by the term, which are differently dominant on different occasions of its use. The first suggestion conveyed by the term 'long-period' is that it relates to a position towards which forces spring up to influence the short-period position whenever the latter has diverged from it. The second suggestion conveyed is that the long-period position differs from short-period positions in being a stable position capable *cet. par.* of being sustained, whilst short-period positions are *cet. par.* unstable and cannot be sustained. The third suggestion is that the long-period position is, in some sense, an *optimum* or ideal position from the point of view of production, i.e. a position in which the forces of production are disposed and utilised to their best possible advantage.

Nevertheless, whilst the answer is complicated by these ambiguities, we may endeavour to reach it without exploring them further. For the root of the objection which I find to the theory under discussion, if it is propounded as a long-period theory, lies in the fact that, on the one hand, it

54

cannot be held that the position towards which the economic system is tending or the position at which it would be at rest or the *optimum* position (i.e. *optimum* competitively with other given circumstances), whichever of these tendencies we have in view, is entirely independent of the policy of the monetary authority; whilst, on the other hand, it cannot be maintained that there is a unique policy which, in the long run, the monetary authority is bound to pursue.

Thus I conclude that this theory is not really dealing with a generalised doctrine of the long period, but is concerned, rather, *with a special case*; i.e. with a long-period position corresponding, in some or all of the senses of this term, to a *particular* assumed policy on the part of the monetary authority.

On my view, there is no unique long-period position of equilibrium equally valid regardless of the character of the policy of the monetary authority. On the contrary there are a number of such positions corresponding to different policies. Moreover there is no reason to suppose that positions of long-period equilibrium have an inherent tendency or likelihood to be positions of optimum output. A long-period position of optimum output is *a special case* corresponding to a special kind of policy on the part of the monetary authority. This conclusion will be developed in subsequent chapters.

[although the pagination is consecutive, some words are missing at this point]

...monetary authority consists in keeping the quantity of money constant?* In this case, if, starting from a position of equilibrium with saving and investment equal, the price level stable and the factors of production fully employed, there occurs a change which causes the rate of interest existing at

* It would make no material difference to the argument if we were to assume (e.g.) that the stock of money increases by a regular annual increment.

that moment to become such as to cause saving to be in excess of investment, prices will fall, rates of earnings will fall, and output will fall, in accordance with the argument in my *Treatise on Money*. Consequently the demand for money in the active circulation will fall, which in turn will affect the state of liquidity preference so that there will be a lowering *cet. par.* of the rate of interest corresponding to the given quantity of money. As a result of this, therefore, we can reckon on a fall in the rate of interest which will retard saving (in my sense) and stimulate investment until they are once again restored to their former equality. Thus it might seem that, whilst a diminished propensity to spend may have a depressing influence in the short period; nevertheless forces are automatically set in motion (subject to our initial assumptions) which will eventually restore equality between saving and investment with both of them at a higher absolute level than before and the factors of production again fully employed.

Now I should agree that there is a large class of possible monetary policies—indeed all or most of those in which the total supply of money is not perversely correlated with the demand for money in the active circulation, a perverse correlation in this case being a tendency for the former to change in the same direction as the latter and perhaps at a faster rate—where a divergence between saving and investment tends to set up forces which ultimately tend, failing new sources of disturbance, to bring them together again to equality. In other words neither prices nor output will fall forever; and they will, after the introduction of some disturbing change in the fundamental economic factors, come to rest again at some position from which they will have no further tendency to depart (though the position of equilibrium may not be a very stable one), so long as no new sources of disturbance intervene. But this is quite a different thing from concluding that the long-period position of equilibrium corresponding to the new situation is the same as the original position, both being positions of optimum output of the factors of production. For the decline in output may be itself one of the factors which had, by reason of its retarding effect on saving, produced the new equilibrium, so that the fact of the level of output being below the optimum may be in itself one of the conditions of the maintenance of equilibrium. Thus, even on the assumption of a constant stock of money, this assumption merely determines which of the large number of conceivable positions of long-period equilibrium corresponding to the different possible levels of output will be actually occupied by the economic system or towards which the economic system will tend.

I conclude that the generalised long-period theory is considerably more complicated than the traditional theory, which is best regarded as applying to a class of cases; and that a clear distinction between *the rate of interest* as the expression of liquidity preference, *the expectation of quasi-rent*, and *the state of time preference* as expressing the relation between the level and distribution of income and the propensity to spend, as being three different and separate concepts, is as important to a satisfactory long-period theory as it is to a short-period theory.

During the Christmas vacation of 1932, Keynes read Colin Clark's *The National Income 1924–1931* (London, 1932). On reading it, he wrote to the author.[11]

[11] Keynes had recommended Clark's manuscript to Daniel Macmillan on 2 December 1931. At the time, he had said 'that Clark's work, on this and allied subjects, is quite outstanding, and that he is likely to become the recognised authority, in the course of time...Clark is, I think, a bit of a genius:—almost the only economic statistician I have ever met who seems to me quite first class.' See also *JMK*, vol. XIII, p. 413 for the use Keynes made of Clark's work.

To COLIN CLARK, *2 January 1933*

My dear Colin,

I have just finished reading your book carefully, which I hadn't time to do in term time. I think that it is *excellent.* An enormous step forward. I hope it is selling all right.

You have quite convinced me that *gross* output, gross investment, gross savings, etc. is the natural way to work and not with the net, and I have been re-writing my definitions and equations on these lines. I am sure it is an improvement.

There is one interesting possibility suggested by your tables in the last chapter. You will remember that Kahn suggested that secondary employment might be about as large as primary employment, i.e. that additional investment x increases output by $2x$. If one tries this hypothesis on your figures, it works out surprisingly well, as follows:—

Work in terms of 1924 price level.

Assume a normal increment of 120 p.a. about 3 per cent non-cumulative. Normal output with saving and investment equal, would then have been as follows

	1924	1925	1926	1927	1928	1929	1930	1931
	4,054	4,174	4,294	4,414	4,534	4,654	4,774	4,894
Subtract, to get the actual, double the excess of saving over investment	54	22	344	−66	94	88	326	522
Computed output in actual savings–investment circs.	4,000	4,152	3,950	4,480	4,444 [*sic*]	4,566	4,448	4,372
Your actual fig. of output reduced to 1924 prices	4,000	4,148	3,956	4,508	4,560	4,788	4,640	4,360

which for so rough a formula is very close.

Yours ever,

J. M. KEYNES

P.S. The above is on the figs. of p. 136. It comes out even better if one works with the figs. of p. 134 and takes normal increment of 110 p.a. (116 p.a., which [? illegible] beginning and end would be a little closer yet.

Assumed normal	4,079	4,189	4,299	4,409	4,519	4,629	4,739	4,849
Deduct for deficient inv.	−102	+30	−354	+76	−138	+136	−314	−562
	3,977	4,219	3,945	4,485	4,381	4,765	4,425	4,287
Your actual	3,977	4,118	3,923	4,458	4,527	4,754	4,606	4,329

P.P.S. Taking figures of p. 134 and assuming a normal increment of 2½ per cent per annum we have

Normal	4,079	4,181	4,286	4,393	4,503	4,616	4,732	4,851
Correct for investment	−102	+30	−354	+76	−138	+136	−314	−562
Computed output	3,977	4,211	3,932	4,469	4,365	4,752	4,418	4,289
Actual	3,977	4,118	3,923	4,458	4,527	4,754	4,606	4,329
% computed to actual	100	102	100	100	97	100	96	99

Keynes's calculations and Colin Clark's reply entered into the correspondence with Richard Kahn that has already appeared in Volume XIII (pp. 412–13).

From COLIN CLARK, *16 January 1933*

Dear Maynard,

Sorry for delay in answering your letter. I have been watching the grass grow in Devon and owing to a misunderstanding no letters were forwarded.

This really is rather fascinating. It certainly beats Physics.

I have calculated the appropriate figure for the upward trend of O at £157m per annum at 1924 prices. This I have done by fitting the line of least squares in the data for 1924–9 omitting 1926. I think it is best to use these data because you will remember I have assumed that $\Sigma Q = O$ over this period.

	O^{12} (Prices of 1927–9)	Wages	Total E	E/O	P (1927–9 = 100)	π (1927–9 = 100)	I	Q	O computed
	(£ million per qr)						(£ million per qr)		
1927 i	1,064	447	64	1·000	102·9	105·9	207	+63	1,156
ii	1,056	451	1,070	1·013	101·8	104·6	169	+35	1,114
iii	1,069	453	1,076	1·007	101·5	102·4	163	+18	1,091
iv	1,065	453	1,079	1·013	100·0	100·5	170	−9	1,048
1928 i	1,074	453	1,082	1·007	100·2	100·5	167	−2	1,071
ii	1,068	452	1,083	1·014	99·6	100·2	171	−13	1,058
iii	1,062	451	1,085	1·022	100·2	99·5	180	−29	1,035
iv	1,071	453	1,089	1·017	99·8	100·0	219	−18	1,066
1929 i	1,102	455	1,094	0·993	99·6	99·9	186	+7	1,125
ii	1,120	461	1,102	0·984	98·1	97·9	86	−6	1,108
iii	1,132	464	1,106	0·976	97·0	96·8	209	−9	1,111
iv	1,133	463	1,107	0·977	96·7	96·6	199	−12	1,119
1930 i	1,109	456	1,096	0·988	96·1	96·5	195	−25	1,095
ii	1,074	446	1,083	1·008	94·6	95·8	165	−54	1,044
iii	1,059	443	1,077	1·017	93·9	95·9	162	−62	1,035
iv	1,035	437	1,066	1·030	92·3	95·4	149	−79	1,008
1931 i	1,014	429	1,052	1·038	91·2	95·9	171	−50	1,017
ii	1,002	427	1,041	1·039	90·1	94·8	157	−91	1,000
iii	987	423	1,028	1·042	88·8	93·5	124	−106	975
iv	993	430	1,035	1·042	89·1	94·1	123	−100	998
1932 i	1,000	424	1,030	1·030	88·7	92·9	133	−101	1,001
ii	993	420	1,027	1·039	88·7	93·5	153	−98	1,018
iii	986	417	1,025	1·040	87·9	92·5	136	−113	993

[12] The symbols in the column headings are from Clark's book, which in turn uses those of the *Treatise on Money*.

This gives results not different from yours.

But I have been able to get an even more striking confirmation, brought up to date, from my quarterly figures from mid-1927 to date. I use this same trend and deduct $2Q$ and get the results shown in the diagram. The broken red line I get by the refinement of expressing Q, not in 'current money', but dividing by π.

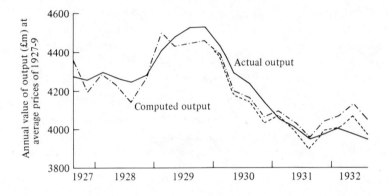

The agreement is all the more remarkable when one remembers that I have not been able to 'pivot' these curves by making their bases equal over the period. The 'computed output' still depends on the trend calculated from the data of 1924–9. The probable error is only 1½ % and the largest single error is only 3 %.

I enclose also the relevant data [see p. 60], because I know you fight shy of diagrams.

Please ring me up when you come to Cambridge, ∴ inter alia I want to discuss that London & Cambridge memorandum.[13]

Yours,

COLIN

During the first three months of 1933, Keynes's other activities, most notably work on *Essays in Biography*[14] and *The Means to Prosperity*,[15] reduced the time in Cambridge that he could spend directly on his book. From late

---

[13] Presumably what eventually appeared as *Special Memorandum No. 38* of the London and Cambridge Economic Service, C. Clark, 'Investment in Fixed Capital in Great Britain', September 1934.

[14] *JMK*, vol. x.

[15] *JMK*, vol. ix, vi (i).

April, however, there were regular reports to Lydia of such work and he seems to have made good progress for the rest of the Easter term.

The summer vacation brought its usual burst of activity, despite the distractions of the World Economic Conference, and work on the book seems to have gone on quite well. After his return to Cambridge for the new term, he reported to Lydia on 15 October

Alexander has just been to give his criticism on the latest version of my first three chapters—I got off much lighter than usual.

Five days later he reported a 'tremendous burst of activity of writing...scribble, scribble, scribble for 3½ hours, 19 pages'. Later in the term, once the King's Audit was over, he reported more activity and on 3 December discussions with Piero Sraffa on the manuscript.

Piero of course made some exhausting difficulties, but nothing of real consequence, I am glad to say.

From these activities during 1933 many more documents survive than we had thought at the time of compiling Volume XIII. First we have two more tables of contents, which would appear to antedate that reprinted on pp. 421–2 of that volume.

First draft table of contents, 1933

The Monetary Theory of Employment

BOOK I

BOOK II

The second draft table of contents follows the first after Book I, but the book's title and early chapter headings were re-worked.

The General Theory of Employment

From these two new draft tables of contents, plus the one already reprinted in Volume XIII (pp. 421–2), fragments of several chapters survive.

First we have a typed fragment of what was probably Chapter 6 of the first 1933 table of contents on p. 62.

6 A SUMMARY OF THE ARGUMENT SO FAR

We conceive the economic organisation of society as consisting, on the one hand, of a number of firms or entrepreneurs possessing a capital equipment and a command over resources in the shape of money, and, on the other hand, a number of workers seeking to be employed. If a firm decides to employ workers to use the capital equipment to produce output, it must have enough command over money to pay the wages of the workers and to purchase those goods which it has to purchase from other firms during the period which must elapse before the output can be, conveniently and economically, sold for money. This period we call the *accounting period* for the output in question. A firm will give employment if it expects the sale proceeds at the end of the accounting period to exceed the variable costs which it will have incurred during the period, both items in the calculation being sums of money.

The firm may be producing goods for consumption or for investment. Goods are for consumption if they will enter into consumption at a date sufficiently soon after the commencement of the accounting period for interest charges on them to be a comparatively negligible factor. Otherwise they are for investment.

The firm's expectations as to the sale proceeds of consumption goods will depend on ideas as to the prospective consumption of the public in relation to the prospective production of such goods. Its expectations as to the sale-proceeds of investment goods will depend on factors which we have not yet analysed.

The aggregate amount of employment offered will depend, broadly speaking, on the amount by which the sale proceeds of output as a whole are expected to exceed their variable cost,—though, when we come to details, we must not overlook the fact that the nature of the distribution of the aggregate expectation of quasi-rent between different firms will probably affect the volume of employment, since the supply and cost functions (*vide infra*) of different firms are not uniform.

We have shown that this is the same thing as to say that

the amount of employment will depend on the expectations of disbursement, which in turn depends on the amounts of prospective investment and consumption.

Thus the amount of employment will be determined by a set of simultaneous equations which relate together employment (N), prospective quasi-rent (Q), prospective variable cost (E), prospective investment (I) and prospective consumption (C), as follows:—

$$N = f_1(Q)$$
$$E = f_2(N)$$
$$C = f_3(D)$$
$$D = E + Q = I + C$$

where f_1, to be investigated in detail later, may be called the Supply Function, f_2 the Cost Function, and f_3 depends on the propensity to save. If we assume f_1, f_2, and f_3 to be known, we still require a knowledge of I before N is determinate. The determination of I, therefore, must be the subject of our next enquiry. If, however, we suppose the entrepreneur firms to know the supply function f_1, the cost function f_2, the propensity of save f_3 and the prospective investment I, then the amount of employment N which they will offer will be determinate.

It follows from this that, given the supply and cost functions and the propensity to save, the amount of employment will entirely depend on the prospective investment.

The commencement of the next accounting period will find the firms in possession of a different capital equipment, modified from the previous equipment by wastage and obsolescence on the one hand and the new investment on the other hand. Thus we are supposing, in accordance with the facts, that at any given time the productive processes set on foot, whether to produce consumption goods or investment goods, are decided in relation to the then existing capital equipment. But we are not assuming that the capital equipment remains in any sense constant from one accounting period to another.

If we look at the productive process in this way, we are, it seems to me, in the closest possible contact with the facts and methods of the business world as they actually exist; and at the same time we have transcended the awkward distinction between the long and the short period.

Above all, however, we are basing our conclusions about employment on the proper criterion, namely whether it is expected to *pay* a firm in possession of a capital equipment to spend money on incurring variable costs; i.e. whether the result of spending money on employment and of selling the output is expected to result in a larger net sum of money at the end of the accounting period than if the money had been retained. Other criteria, such as the relation between the real output which a given employment will yield and the disutility or real cost of that employment, or the relation between the real wages of a given employment and the amount of its marginal output, are not appropriate to the actual nature of business decisions in a world in which prices are subject to change during an accounting period, such changes being themselves a function *inter alia* of the amount of investment during the period.

We must now turn to an examination of the factors which determine the amount of current investment.

Second, we have a typed and handwritten fragment from what was probably the first chapter of the second 1933 draft table of contents (above p. 63), an early draft of what became chapter 5 of that table of contents and a fragment of the chapter on Capital.

A fragment of the first chapter of the second 1933 draft table of contents

I define a *barter economy* as one in which the factors of production are rewarded by dividing up in agreed proportions the actual output of their co-operative efforts. It is not necessary that they should receive their share of the output *in specie*;—the position is the same if they share the sale-proceeds of the output in agreed proportions. Since this economy does not exclude the use of money for purposes of transitory convenience, it might perhaps be better to call it a *real-wage economy*, or a *co-operative economy* as distinct from an *entrepreneur economy*. In a barter (or co-operative) economy only miscalculation or stupid obstinacy can stand in the way of production, if the value of the expected real product exceeds the real costs. But in a monetary (or entrepreneur) economy this is not so;—the volume of output which will yield the maximum value of product in excess of real cost may be 'unprofitable'.

The classical theory, as exemplified in the tradition from Ricardo to Marshall, appears to me to presume that the conditions of a neutral monetary economy are fulfilled; i.e. that we are dealing with an entrepreneur economy which is made to behave in the same way as a co-operative economy.

More recently many endeavours have been made towards constructing a theory of a generalised monetary economy,--though not, I think, with a sufficiently clear consciousness of the exact nature of the system which they are attempting to handle. Malthus, as a contemporary of Ricardo, and Wicksell as a contemporary of Marshall, are obviously to be cited as the leading accredited economists who were discontented with the limitations of the classical theory as an explanation of the real world and laboured towards extending its boundaries. But there are few names to be joined to theirs in the hundred years from the death of Ricardo,—though the classical theory has been subjected, throughout that period, to a barrage of dissatisfaction from practical men on the one side and from cranks on the other.

It is to the theory of a generalised monetary economy, i.e. of an economy in which, through the fault or the inaction or the impotence of the monetary authority, the conditions laid down above for a neutral economy are not fulfilled, that this book will attempt to make a contribution.

We shall find that we need to approach many familiar notions from a new angle and with the aid of a new terminology. One is immensely hampered—the author of this book scarcely less than his readers—by the hold which the preconceptions of the classical theory have upon us as the result of education and long habit. However dissatisfied the plain man may have felt with the conclusions of the classical theory regarded as practical precepts, the thinking of politicians and civil servants and the gentlemen who write to the newspapers is saturated by the presuppositions of this theory and admits with extreme reluctance any ideas which go beyond them. I fancy that the whole matter will be much simpler than it now appears when we are thoroughly used to it. The ensuing chapters of this book are indeed much simpler now than in their first draft. But the theory will not be written as clearly and simply as it should be, except by one who has been brought up on it. Meanwhile we must plunge in, with such apologies as are appropriate, for still talking the new language haltingly and without elegance.

An early typed and handwritten draft of what eventually became chapter 5 of the second 1933 draft table of contents (above p. 63).

7 CERTAIN FUNDAMENTAL EQUATIONS

I

Our fundamental equations consist of nothing but the truisms which result from the equality between aggregate Income (Y) which is the sum of Earnings (E) and Quasi-rents (Q), and aggregate Disbursement (D) which is the sum of Consumption-expenditure (C) and Investment (I), so that we have

$$Y = E+Q = C+I = D$$

whence $$Q = D-E = I-(E-C)$$

It will often be convenient to designate the amount of *change* in any factor between one position and another by putting Delta Δ in front of the letter denoting the factor. Thus ΔQ stands for the change in quasi-rent, ΔD for the change in disbursement and so on.

$E-C$, the excess of earnings over consumption corresponds to what I called *Saving (S)* in my *Treatise on Money*. It is not identically the same concept, since it does not include the normal return to capital equipment which I then included in earnings. Since, however, this 'normal' [return] is constant for a given capital equipment, it follows that $\Delta(E-C)$ is for a given capital equipment, identically the same as ΔS. Whilst I still think that $\Delta(E-C)$ is the important concept for us to isolate, I have been in great perplexity whether to continue to call it the change in *Saving*. For the reasons given in the next chapter, I have decided to give up doing so. Nevertheless we shall need some name for $\Delta(E-C)$, i.e. for the decrease in spending after allowing for any decrease in earnings. I propose to call it the amount of *Economising*, designated by S'. Thus the community is economising, if it reduces its consumption by more than its earnings.

Let us, therefore, define Saving S (both individual and aggregate) as the excess of income over consumption, so that

$$S = Y-C = E-C+Q$$

and $$\Delta S = \Delta(E-C)+\Delta Q$$
$$= \Delta S'+\Delta Q$$

Thus defined, aggregate current saving S is, of necessity, exactly equal to aggregate current investment I, so that

$$\Delta Q = \Delta S-\Delta S'$$
$$= \Delta I-\Delta S'$$

That is to say quasi-rent increases or decreases according as the community is increasing or decreasing its investment more than it is increasing or decreasing its economising.

[a page is missing from the manuscript at this point]

in the volume of output from a given capital equipment. Thus we have

II. ΔN and ΔQ have the same sign.

Further, since $\Delta Q = \Delta I - \Delta S'$, we have

III. ΔN and $\Delta I - \Delta S'$ have the same sign.
That is to say, employment will increase or decrease according as the community is increasing or decreasing its investment more than its economising.

It is, I surmise, a conclusion of the Classical Theory that, given the amount of capital equipment and the supply schedule of labour in terms of output, the volume of output and hence the ratio of aggregate quasi-rent to the price of output tends to be *constant*. I cannot point to any passage where this is stated. For the classical theory is primarily concerned, not with the *amount* of the aggregate quasi-rent, but with its distribution between the different firms, with the efforts of the firms to maximise their share of it relatively to their capital equipment, and with the reaction of these things on the kind of capital equipment which is newly erected from time to time; and it is not so clear what assumption is made concerning either the aggregate of quasi-rent or the aggregate of output. But the above must, I think, be considered as following from the second postulate. Output will be pushed to the point at which the utility of the marginal product is equal to the disutility of the marginal employment; and aggregate quasi-rent in terms of output must, therefore, be such [an] amount as corresponds, given the supply function of the capital equipment (i.e. the quantity of output corresponding to the application of any given quantity of employment to the given capital equipment), to the quantity of output. If this is correct, then it is the case that, given the capital equipment and the supply schedule of labour, aggregate quasi-rent, divided by the price of output, is constant. It is only when we waive the second postulate that aggregate quasi-rent, divided by the price of output, can be supposed to fluctuate, apart from changes in capital equipment or in the supply schedule of labour in terms of output.

This is fundamental. For it is the fluctuations of aggregate quasi-rent, such as the classical theory has not contemplated as possible, which lead to fluctuations in employment, in spite of there being no change either in the supply function of the capital equipment or in the supply schedule of labour in terms of product.

III

If we assume that we are able to overcome, sufficiently for our purpose, the difficulties in the way of measuring an aggregate of non-homogeneous output, then O being the quantity of current output thus measured and P the expected average price of each unit of current output, we have $D = O.P$. Therefore, since $E = N.W$ where W is the rate of wages and N the amount of employment, we have

$$O.P = N.W + Q$$

$$= N.W + I - (E - C)$$

so that

$$P = \frac{N}{O}\,W + \frac{I - (E - C)}{O}$$

I introduce this equation of price here, not because I propose to pursue it further at this moment, but to help readers of my *Treatise on Money* to see at once the relationship between the method of exposition now adopted and that with which they are already familiar. My present definitions are not identical with those I gave formerly, but they deal with substantially the same concepts which I was then driving at. In particular, the reader should notice that E no longer includes an allowance for 'normal' quasi-rent, with the result that a quantity equal to Q'/O, where Q' is the long-period expectation of the return to capital, has been subtracted from the first term of the equation, as set forth in my *Treatise on Money*, and added to the second term. This means that the second term no longer vanishes in long-period equilibrium but becomes equal to the 'normal' return to capital per unit of output. The first term is now the part of the price which goes to reward employment, and the second term is the part of the price which goes to reward capital equipment. This is, I think, a clearer and more useful dichotomy than that which I adopted previously; and it is equally adapted to long-period and to short-period analysis.

Since the item which I am transferring is constant for a given capital equipment, *changes* in the two terms are the same as before, so long as we are considering the position in relation to the same equipment. On this assumption, therefore, the quantity of employment increases or decreases, as before, according as the second term is increasing or decreasing.

For small changes in price and output we have*

$$\Delta P . O + P . \Delta O = N \Delta W + W \Delta N + \Delta Q.$$

But for small changes $P . \Delta O = W \Delta N$, i.e. the value of the marginal product is equal to its variable cost, so that

$$\Delta P = \frac{N}{O} \Delta W + \frac{\Delta Q}{O}$$

or
$$\Delta P = \frac{N}{O} \Delta W + \frac{\Delta I - \Delta S'}{O}$$

* Assuming the standard case of the theory of the individual firm, i.e. perfect competition, etc.

which is substantially the same as the fundamental price equation in my *Treatise on Money*.

It is to be observed that the concept of an average price per unit of output, as distinct from the 'forward' price of output as a whole, raises precisely the same difficulties as to a quantitative measure of a non-homogeneous complex, as does the measurement of real output itself.

Thus the price equation given above cannot be employed, strictly speaking, except in those special cases where we can overcome the difficulty of measuring real output. Nevertheless as an approximate description, especially where small changes over consecutive intervals of time are in view, it is, of course, good enough for most practical purposes. It is a familiar truth that all our statements about changes in the price level of output as a whole are subject to the difficulties of defining a price index which is strictly applicable to both of two different situations.

I find it, however, a matter of considerable intellectual satisfaction that these partly insoluble difficulties of quantitative description do not arise in our causal analysis, which is *strictly logical* in itself and is subject, in practice, not to essentially insoluble difficulties, but only to the actual imperfections of our knowledge.

A typed fragment of the chapter on Capital of the second 1933 draft table of contents (above, p. 63)

7 DEFINITIONS AND IDEAS RELATING TO CAPITAL

I

The Concept of an Accounting Period

There are two kinds of forecast which an entrepreneur has to make and two kinds of production period which he must have in view. The first forecast is that which he has to make when he decides to spend money on setting up a capital equipment; and the period which he must have in view in making it is equal to the prospective length of life of the capital equipment which he is setting up. The second forecast is when, being in possession of a capital equipment, he decides how much variable cost to incur in working it, i.e. (broadly speaking) how much employment to provide and how much output to aim at; and the period which he must have in view is equal to the time which must elapse between the decision which will lead him to incur variable cost and the date when he will recoup himself by selling the resultant output.

The phrase 'production period' is not unambiguous in common usage, but it has been generally applied, I think, to the first and longer of these periods. I have, therefore, thought it convenient to use the phrase 'accounting period' for the second and shorter of the two periods. They correspond, broadly speaking, to the length of life of fixed and working capital respectively. The accounting period applies just as much to the production of capital goods as to that of consumption goods. That is to say, the distinction, in the case of capital goods, between the latter period and the former is the same as the distinction between the time it takes to produce capital goods and the time it takes to wear them out.

The importance of the accounting period lies in the fact that *all* decisions to employ labour depend on expectations covering this period; though some of these expectations, depend in turn on expectations covering the longer period. For example the decision to employ labour in manufacturing a steel rail depends on what price the manufacturer expects to get for the steel rail when he is ready to deliver it; but this expectation will depend in turn on some one else's expectation (or even, perhaps, on his own) of what will happen

74

during the period between the delivery of the steel rail and its being worn out by use.

It might be possible to invent border line cases where it would be something of a conundrum to distinguish between the two types of period. But the distinction between the production of capital goods and the use of capital goods is, in general, one of the easiest and clearest of distinctions to make.

The two types of forecast correspond to those made by the producer or manufacturer and the investor or capitalist respectively. It is the former who employs labour; he produces goods for sale either to the consumer or the investor; his goods are for sale as soon as they are finished; and his forecast relates to the period which elapses between his decision to employ labour and the sale of his output. The latter does not employ labour but must be conceived as hiring out his capital goods to a producer from one accounting period to the next, or, where his goods are consumption capital such as dwelling houses, to the consumer. His forecast relates to the hire which he expects to get during each accounting period until the goods are worn out or scrapped. It leads, in my opinion, to a great confusion to merge the two periods together and to regard the whole period from the first employment of labour until the goods are finally worn out as constituting a single period of production. It does not correspond to the facts of business calculation and is not convenient for economic analysis, whilst its appearance of logical completeness is illusory since a period of production in this sense never, strictly speaking, begins and never ends in all those cases where capital goods are employed in the production of capital goods in an indefinite succession.

The two periods distinguished above might, perhaps, be termed the Employment Period and the Investment Period.

Our first fundamental proposition, namely

N and Q have the same sign,

can then be expressed:— the quantity of employment and the expectation of quasi-rent during the employment period increase and decrease together.

Third we have typed drafts of chapters 2 and 3 from the draft table of contents printed on pp. 421–2 of Volume XIII. The second of these chapters is a re-worked version of a draft intended for the previous draft table of contents (above p. 63).[16]

A draft of chapter 2 from the last 1933 draft table of contents.

2 THE DISTINCTION BETWEEN A CO-OPERATIVE ECONOMY AND AN ENTREPRENEUR ECONOMY

It may help us to understand both the origins of the Classical Economics and the essence of the distinction between the classical theory and the more generalised theory which I shall here try to develop, if we consider in what conditions the postulates of the classical theory would be satisfied.

I

The Classical Economics presupposes that the factors of production desire and receive as the reward of their efforts nothing but a predetermined share of the aggregate output of all kinds which they can produce, both the demand and the supply of each factor depending upon the expected amount of their reward in terms of output in general. It is not necessary that the factors should receive their shares of the output in kind in the first instance;—the position is substantially the same if they are paid in money, provided

[16] The re-working was fairly minor, except for the removal of a section II and rather extensive re-drafting of footnote * on page 90. As a result, we print the later version of the chapter and provide only the excised section II as an addendum.

they all of them accept the money merely as a temporary convenience, with a view to spending the whole of it forthwith on purchasing such part of current output as they choose. Nor is it necessary that current output should comprise the whole of wealth;—the position is still substantially the same if the factors of production swap their wage in respect of current output for other forms of wealth, provided that those with whom they swap intend to employ the whole sum forthwith to purchase some part of current output. It may even be the case that the supply function of a factor, in terms of what it can produce, varies according to the value of what it can produce in terms of something which it cannot produce. The essential point is that by whatever roundabout methods every factor of production ultimately accepts as its reward a predetermined share of the expected current output either in kind or in terms of something which has an exchange value equal to that of the predetermined share.

It is easy to conceive of a community in which the factors of production are rewarded by dividing up in agreed proportions the actual output of their co-operative efforts. This is the simplest case of a society in which the presuppositions of the classical theory are fulfilled. But they would also be fulfilled in a society of the type in which we actually live, where the starting up of productive processes largely depends on a class of entrepreneurs who hire the factors of production for money and look to their recoupment from selling the output for money, provided that the whole of the current incomes of the factors of production* are necessarily spent, directly or indirectly on purchasing their own current output from the entrepreneurs.

The first type of society we will call a *real-wage* or *co-operative*

---

* This statement is incomplete as it stands and is subject to certain assumptions as to the expenditure of the entrepreneurs themselves which will be explained later in the argument.

economy. The second type, in which the factors are hired by entrepreneurs for money but where there is a mechanism of some kind to ensure that the exchange value of the money incomes of the factors is always equal in the aggregate to the proportion of current output which would have been the factor's share in a co-operative economy, we will call a *neutral entrepreneur economy*, or a *neutral economy* for short. The third type, of which the second is a limiting case, in which the entrepreneurs hire the factors for money but without such a mechanism as the above, we will call a *money-wage* or *entrepreneur economy*.

It is obvious on these definitions that it is in an entrepreneur economy that we actually live to-day.

The law of production in an entrepreneur economy can be stated as follows. A process of production will not be started up, unless the money proceeds expected from the sale of the output are at least equal to the money costs which could be avoided by not starting up the process.

In a real-wage and co-operative economy there is no obstacle in the way of the employment of an additional unit of labour if this unit will add to the social product output expected to have an exchange value equal to 10 bushels of wheat, which is sufficient to balance the disutility of the additional employment. Thus the second postulate of the classical theory is satisfied. But in a money-wage or entrepreneur economy the criterion is different. Production will only take place if the expenditure of £100 in hiring factors of production will yield an output which it is expected to sell for at least £100. In these conditions the second postulate will not be satisfied, except in the limiting case of a neutral economy.

Nevertheless the greater part of the classical analysis has been usually applied without compunction or qualification to an entrepreneur economy, with the tacit assumption that the criterion, as stated above, for starting up production in an entrepreneur economy is substantially equivalent to the criterion, as stated above, for starting up production in a co-operative economy. Now it is not impossible, as we shall see subsequently, for an entrepreneur economy to be made to behave in the same manner as a co-operative economy:—this is simply the peculiar and limiting case of the ways in which an entrepreneur economy can behave, which we have termed a *neutral economy*. The classical theory, however, as exemplified in the tradition from Ricardo to Marshall and Professor Pigou, appears to me to presume that the conditions for a Neutral Economy are substantially fulfilled in general; —though it has been a source of great confusion that its assumptions have been *tacit*, so that you will search in vain for any express statement of the simplifications which have been introduced or for the relationship of conclusions demonstrated for a Neutral Economy to the facts of the real world.*

Yet it is easy to show that the conditions for a Neutral Economy are not satisfied in practice; with the result that there is a difference of the most fundamental importance between a co-operative economy and the type of entrepreneur economy in which we actually live. For in an entrepreneur economy, as we shall see, the volume of employment, the marginal disutility of which is equal to the utility of its marginal product, may be 'unprofitable' in terms of money.

* One can infer what the implicit beliefs of the classical economists must have been, but it is extraordinarily difficult to find any passage to quote expressed in black and white. The following from Marshall's *Pure Theory of Domestic Values*, p. 34, found for me by Mrs Robinson, is an unusually categorical statement:— 'The whole of a man's income is expended in the purchase of services and of commodities. It is indeed commonly said that a man spends some portion of his income and saves another. But it is a familiar economic axiom that a man purchases labour and commodities with that portion of his income which he saves just as much as he does with that which he is said to spend. He is said to spend when he seeks to obtain present enjoyment from the services and the commodities which he purchases. He is said to save when he causes the labour and the commodities which he purchases to be devoted to the production of wealth from which he expects to derive the means of enjoyment in the future.' [This quotation appeared on p. 19 of the final version of *The General Theory* (*JMK*, vol. vii).]

II

The explanation of how output which would be produced in a co-operative economy may be 'unprofitable' in an entrepreneur economy, is to be found in what we may call, for short, *the fluctuations of effective demand*.

Effective Demand may be defined by reference to the expected excess of sale proceeds over variable cost (what is included in variable cost depending on the length of the period in view). Effective demand fluctuates if this excess fluctuates, being deficient if it falls short of some normal figure (not yet defined) and excessive if it exceeds it. In a co-operative or in a neutral economy, in which sale proceeds exceed variable cost by a determinate amount, effective demand cannot fluctuate; and it can be neglected in considering the factors which determine the volume of employment. But in an entrepreneur economy the fluctuations of effective demand may be the dominating factor in determining the volume of employment; and in this book, therefore, we shall be mainly concerned with analysing the causes and consequences of fluctuations in effective demand interpreted in the above sense.

From the time of Ricardo the classical economists have taught that supply creates its own demand;—which is taken to mean that the rewards of the factors of production, must, directly or indirectly, create in the aggregate an effective demand exactly equal to the costs of the current supply, i.e. that *aggregate* effective demand is constant; though a want of balance due to temporary miscalculation as to the strength of *relative* demands may bring losses in certain directions balanced by equal gains in other directions, which losses and gains will tend in the long run to guide the distribution of productive resources in such a way that the profitability of different kinds of production tends to be equalised.

For the proposition that supply creates its own demand, I

shall substitute the proposition that expenditure creates its own income, i.e. an income just sufficient to meet the expenditure. This, we shall find, is a more general proposition than the former. For whilst the former must be taken to mean that a change in the aggregate cost of production will be balanced by an equal change in aggregate expenditure, the latter is consistent with inequality between changes in the cost of production and changes in expenditure.

The doctrine that supply creates its own demand has dominated classical theory during the century since Ricardo established it. Malthus's powerful arguments against this theory were completely forgotten, partly—

...[A page of manuscript is missing at this point]...

III

The distinction between a co-operative economy and an entrepreneur economy bears some relation to a pregnant observation made by Karl Marx,—though the subsequent use to which he put this observation was highly illogical. He pointed out that the nature of production in the actual world is not, as economists seem often to suppose, a case of $C-M-C'$, i.e. of exchanging commodity (or effort) for money in order to obtain another commodity (or effort). That may be the standpoint of the private consumer. But it is not the attitude of *business*, which is a case of $M-C-M'$, i.e. of parting with money for commodity (or effort) in order to obtain more money.* This is important for the following reason.

---

* Cf. H. L. McCracken, *Value Theory and Business Cycles*, [New York, 1933] p. 46, where this part of Marx's theory is cited in relation to modern theory. The excess of M' over M is the source of Marx's *surplus value*. It is a curiosity in the history of economic theory that the heretics of the past hundred years who have, in one shape or another, opposed the formula $M-C-M'$ to the classical formula $C-M-C'$, have tended to believe *either* that M' must always and necessarily exceed M *or* that M must always and necessarily exceed M', according as they were living

The classical theory supposes that the readiness of the entrepreneur to start up a productive process depends on the amount of value in terms of product which he expects to fall to his share; i.e. that only an expectation of more *product* for himself will induce him to offer more employment. But in an entrepreneur economy this is a wrong analysis of the nature of business calculation. An entrepreneur is interested, not in the amount of product, but in the amount of *money* which will fall to his share. He will increase his output if by so doing he expects to increase his money profit, even though this profit represents a smaller quantity of product than before.

The explanation of this is evident. The employment of factors of production to increase output involves the entrepreneur in the disbursement, not of product, but of money. The choice before him in deciding whether or not to offer employment is a choice between using money in this way or in some other way or not using it at all. He has the command of £100 (in hand or by borrowing), and he will use it if by so doing he expects, after deducting his variable costs including interest on the £100, to turn it into more than £100. The only question before him is to choose, out of the various ways of employing £100, that way which will yield the largest profit in terms of money. It must be remembered that future prices, in so far as they are anticipated, are already reflected in current prices, after allowing for the various considerations of carrying costs and of opportunities of production in the meantime which relate the spot and forward prices of a given

in a period in which the one or the other predominated in actual experience. Marx and those who believe in the necessarily exploitatory character of the capitalist system, assert the inevitable excess of M'; whilst Hobson, or Foster and Catchings, or Major Douglas who believe in its inherent tendency towards deflation and under-employment, assert the inevitable excess of M. Marx, however, was approaching the intermediate truth when he added that the continuous excess of M' would be inevitably interrupted by a series of crises, gradually increasing in intensity, or entrepreneur bankruptcy and underemployment, during which, presumably, M must be in excess. My own argument, if it is accepted, should at least serve to effect a reconciliation between the followers of Marx and those of Major Douglas, leaving the classical economists still high and dry in the belief that M and M' are always equal!

commodity.* Thus we must suppose that the spot and forward price structure has already brought into equilibrium the relative advantages, as estimated by the holder, of holding money and other existing forms of wealth. Thus if the advantage in terms of money of using money to start up a productive process is increased, this will stimulate entrepreneurs to offer more employment. It may be true that employment will be greater in one situation than in another, although the larger money profit in the first case corresponds to a smaller quantity of product than does the smaller money profit in the second case. For the entrepreneur is guided, not by the amount of product he will gain, but by the alternative opportunities for using money having regard to the spot and forward price structure taken as a whole.

Thus the classical theory fails us at both ends, so to speak, if we try to apply it to an entrepreneur economy. For it is not true that the entrepreneur's demand for labour depends on the share of the product which will fall to the entrepreneur; and it is not true that the supply of labour depends on the share of the product which will fall to labour. It is these fundamental divergencies at the outset which make it impracticable to start with the classical theory and then, at an advanced stage of the argument, to adapt its conclusions to the vagaries of an Entrepreneur Economy.

IV

The theory of 'appreciation and interest', as it is usually called, chiefly associated with the name of Professor Irving Fisher but first originated by Marshall, is, I think, vitiated by the same considerations. Suppose that £100 rises in value by 10 per cent over a year and is lent out at 5 per cent for the same period, then it is said that the 'real' rate of interest is

---

* For an examination of this *vide* my *Treatise on Money*, Vol. II [*JMK*, vol. VI], Chapter 29.

15 per cent; whilst if it falls in value by 10 per cent, the 'real' rate of interest is *negative* by 5 per cent. No wonder, it has been usual to conclude, that entrepreneurs are eager to borrow for productive purposes when prices are rising and reluctant when they are falling; and the plausibility of this reasoning has been reinforced by its apparent* conformity with the facts of experience.

Nevertheless the reasoning is not sound. If the change in the value of the £100 is not expected and takes the market by surprise, obviously an event which was not foreseen cannot have affected the volume of employment. In this case the 'real' rate of interest merely expresses a statistical fact *ex post facto*, and it cannot be one of the influences which determined the business expectations which decided the volume of employment.

If, on the other hand, we suppose that the change in the value of money is foreseen, then it must be already exerting its influence on present prices as well as on future prices; and an anticipation of such a price change can only exist if the technical market conditions are present which permit a spread of 10 per cent between spot and forward prices in one direction or the other. But in this event there is no reason why either the borrower or the lender need take account of the 'appreciation' as distinct from the 'interest'. The borrower is only interested in the prospect of an excess of his money receipts over his money outgoings; whilst the lender has no means whatever open to him whereby he can avoid the prospective gain or loss arising through the expected change in the value of money, since the prices of all the things which he could buy already reflect it. An individual can only speculate to his own supposed advantage on a forthcoming event if there is sufficient doubt about it for different people to take different views.

* It is not really in conformity with experience. For lenders and borrowers are presumably equally well able to look after themselves; yet there is no observable tendency for more stability in the real rate of interest than in the money rate.

In short, it is not the prospect of rising prices as such which stimulates employment, but the prospect of an increased margin between sale proceeds and variable costs.

V

It is pertinent to ask the question whether the fluctuation of effective demand can be properly described as a *monetary* phenomenon. Obviously it is not a necessary result of using money. For a co-operative economy and a neutral economy can equally well use money. The question must be, therefore, whether the fluctuations could occur in the absence of money.

The difficulty of answering this question is partly due to the ambiguity or obscurity as to what exactly is meant by 'using money'. I should prefer to say, as I have said above, that the fluctuation of effective demand is a characteristic of an entrepreneur economy as distinguished from a co-operative economy. Could then such an entrepreneur economy exist without money?

It is of the essence of an entrepreneur economy that the thing (or things) in terms of which the factors of production are rewarded can be spent on something which is not current output, to the production of which current output cannot be diverted (except on a limited scale), and the exchange value of which is not fixed in terms of an article of current output to which production can be diverted without limit. It is not necessary that the thing in which the factors of production are rewarded should be the same for all, provided that the above conditions are fulfilled. Nor is it necessary that the means of remuneration should be no part of current output, provided there are strict limits to the extent to which output can be diverted to it. In actual fact under a gold standard gold can be produced, and in a slump there will be some diversion of employment towards gold mining. If, indeed, it were easily practicable to divert output towards gold on a sufficient scale

85

for the value of the increased current output of gold to make good the deficiency in expenditure in other forms of current output, unemployment could not occur; except in the transitional period before the turn-over to increased gold-production could be completed.

What, then, in the light of this, is the answer to our original question? Money is *par excellence* the means of remuneration in an entrepreneur economy which lends itself to fluctuations in effective demand. But if employers were to remunerate their workers in terms of plots of land or obsolete postage stamps, the same difficulties could arise. Perhaps anything in terms of which the factors of production contract to be remunerated, which is not and cannot be a part of current output and is capable of being used otherwise than to purchase current output, is, in a sense, money. If so, but not otherwise, the use of money is a necessary condition for fluctuations in effective demand.

So far there is nothing in our criterion for money to suggest that the fluctuations in effective demand are more likely to be in excess or in deficit. I fancy, however, that there is a further feature of our actual monetary system which makes a deficiency of effective demand a more frequent danger than the opposite; namely the fact that the money in terms of which the factors of production are remunerated will 'keep' more readily than the output which they are being remunerated to produce, so that the need of entrepreneurs to sell, if they are to avoid a running loss, is more pressing than the need of the recipients of income to spend. This is the case because it is a characteristic of finished goods, which are neither consumed nor used but carried in stock, that they incur substantial carrying charges for storage, risk and deterioration, so that they are yielding a negative return for so long as they are held; whereas such expenses are reduced to a minimum approaching zero in the case of money. If it were not for this consideration, the effective demand at a given moment would be governed by more permanent considerations concerning the direction of popular expenditure averaged over a considerable period of time, and would be less subject to rapid fluctuations such as characterise boom and depression.

By inverting this condition, we can conceive of an entrepreneur system which would be as prone to excessive demand and over-employment, as our actual system is to deficient demand and under-employment; namely, if the means of remuneration would 'keep' *less* readily than the output. In this case there might be a tendency for workers to find themselves, irrespective of what wage bargains they had been able to make with their employers, working from time to time for a real wage which was less than the marginal disutility of the work by which they had earned it.

A draft of chapter 3 from the last 1933 draft table of contents (vol. XIII, p. 421).

3 THE CHARACTERISTICS OF AN ENTREPRENEUR ECONOMY

I

So as to bring home the essential features to the reader's intuition, let us construct a simplified model of an entrepreneur economy.

Production, let us suppose, is organised by a number of firms which do nothing but exercise entrepreneur functions. I mean by this that they rent their fixed capital equipment from capitalists, in return for an annual rent, payable over the prospective life of the equipment, which the capitalists expect to recoup them for the sum which they have laid out in originally purchasing it from the firm which produced it; and they hire labour, whenever they decide to use this capital equipment to produce output, for the period of production of that output. On the other hand, it is convenient, though not essential, to assume that the firms own their working capital, which means that they find the cash required to rent the capital equipment and to meet the variable costs incurred between starting up their capital equipment (or some part of it) to produce output and the sale of this output for cash. As soon as their output is 'finished', they must sell it for cash; but there is no impediment to partly finished goods changing hands for cash between firms.

The distinction which is here implicit between fixed and working capital is the same as the usual distinction between finished and unfinished goods. This distinction applies just as much to capital goods as to consumption goods. Consumption goods are 'finished' when they are ready for sale either to a consumer, or to a capitalist for the purpose of holding them in stock as a speculation. Capital goods are 'finished' when they are ready for use by consumers as consumption-capital (e.g. houses) or by producers as instrumental capital. The line of division is, I think, at least as clear and precise as such lines usually are in the construction of economic models. The alternative of considering all capital goods as being in a sense 'unfinished' goods seems to me to be inconvenient and does not fit in with an analysis which is endeavouring to keep as close as it can to the actual facts of business calculation.* I shall mean, therefore, by *production period* the time which elapses between the decision to employ labour in conjunction with capital equipment to produce output and the output being 'finished'† in the above sense of the word.

---

* The question is purely one of convenience. No fundamental point of theory is involved in drawing the lines between consumption goods and investment goods, between 'finished' goods and 'unfinished', and between working capital and fixed capital. This will be made clear in Chapter   below.

† I shall ignore in this simplified model conundrums arising out of the classification of repairs to capital equipment and out of surplus semi-finished goods held in stock. They raise no fundamental issue.

An entrepreneur firm has, therefore, two sets of decisions to make, the first when it decides to rent capital equipment, the second when it decides to hire labour to work the capital equipment to produce output. The first relates to a period covering the life of the capital, and depends on the firm's expectations as to how much cash it will be able to earn out of the difference between its sale proceeds and its variable costs (i.e. the costs which it will incur in working the capital equipment exclusive of its rent) in the successive production periods during the life of the capital equipment. After the first decisions have been taken, the second set of decisions will be necessary from time to time during the life of the equipment, each of these covering a shorter period, namely a production period; and it will be the object of a firm, after it has taken the decisions which have determined the amount of its capital equipment, to provide during each production period the amount of employment with which it expects to maximise the excess of its sale proceeds over its variable costs incurred during that period.

The firm is dealing throughout in terms of sums of money. It has no object in the world except to end up with more money than it started with. That is the essential characteristic of an entrepreneur economy.

Now each entrepreneur firm is pitting its wits against the others' to make good bargains with the capitalists and the workers and to anticipate correctly the strength of demand for different classes of finished goods. The classical theory of the individual firm is concerned with the analysis of its behaviour under these influences. By good fortune or good management some firms will be more successful than others and will make profits over and above the rents and variable costs which they have incurred; whilst others will make losses. The former will tend to expand its capital equipment, the latter to contract. By this means there will be a tendency for the survival of the most efficient.

But there is another element in the situation, an element peculiar to an entrepreneur economy, which affects all firms alike, and is not one of the incidents of the competitive struggle between firms. The firms are incurring certain costs of production, partly rents to capitalists and partly variable costs mainly wages. Against this they are getting back the sale proceeds of their output. The firms *compete* to attract to their own output as large a share as possible of this current expenditure. But there is not only the question as to how this expenditure will be divided between different outputs and how far this division will correspond to the costs incurred in producing each. There is also the question as to how its *aggregate compares* with the aggregate of the costs.

If over any period the aggregate expenditure is approximately equal to the costs which have been incurred on output which has been finished during that period, the firms will have made in the aggregate neither gain nor loss, the losses of individual firms being exactly balanced by the gains of other firms. Thus assuming the firms to be similar in their response to a given expectation of gain or loss (a simplification which we shall remove in later chapters), there will be no tendency, apart from time lags in changing over from one job to another, for the aggregate of employment to change. For when one firm is reducing employment because of its poor prospects, some other firm will be increasing employment to an equal extent because of its good prospects due to its success in attracting to itself the expenditure which the first firm is failing to attract.*

But if the aggregate expenditure varies in a different manner from aggregate costs, then the diminished incentive

* I am assuming that a change in demand will affect output and profits in the same direction. In the case of perfect competition, this is easily shown, since individual firms will be operating during each production period, i.e. given thei[r] capital equipment, under conditions of diminishing returns. It is also generally true in less restrictive conditions, though 'fancy' cases can be devised in which it does not hold good. For my main argument it is sufficient to assume that those 'fancy' cases are not frequent enough to dominate the result.

to employment in one direction will not be exactly balanced by an increased incentive to employment in another direction. If aggregate expenditure increases relatively to aggregate costs, there will be, on balance, a greater incentive to employment than before; and if aggregate expenditure decreases relatively to aggregate costs, there will be a diminished incentive to employment. Thus fluctuations in employment will primarily depend on fluctuations in aggregate expenditure relatively to aggregate costs. This is the essential feature of an entrepreneur economy in which it differs from a co-operative economy. It means that the aggregate of employment can fluctuate for reasons quite independent of a change in the relation between the marginal utility of a quantity of output and the marginal disutility of the employment required to produce that quantity.

If, however, some mechanism is introduced into an entrepreneur economy so as to insure (1) that aggregate expenditure and aggregate costs always keep step and change by equal amounts and (2) that chance causes operating to keep employment below full employment are counteracted, then our entrepreneur economy will behave in the same way as a co-operative economy, and will therefore satisfy the conditions laid down by our definition for a neutral economy. The second of the above conditions is required because the effect of the first condition by itself is, as we shall see subsequently, to establish a state of neutral equilibrium so that the system is in equilibrium for *any* level of employment. Hence a touch may be required to insure that the actual level will be one of full employment as it would be in a co-operative economy, i.e. a state in which the marginal utility of the quantity of output produced is equal to the marginal disutility of the effort required to produce it. In my *Treatise on Money* the equality of savings and investment, as there defined, was a condition equivalent to the equality of aggregate expenditure and aggregate costs, but I failed to point out that this by itself provided only for neutral equilibrium and not for, what one might call, optimum equilibrium.

II

If the conditions for a neutral economy are *not* satisfied, in what ways will the inequality between costs and expenditure have come about? To answer that question precisely is the task of the ensuing chapters. But in pursuance of the object of giving the reader a general outline of the present method. I will endeavour to explain the answer briefly in general terms.

Let us suppose that in the current unit of time the firms increase their working capital, i.e. the cost of the unfinished goods on hand, by X_1', and receive X_2 from sale-proceeds of output which has cost them X_1, which means that their current costs of production are $X_1 + X_1'$. The question is—what can cause inequality between X_2 and X_1. In a model constructed as our present model is constructed, it is easily seen that such inequality can only develop in one or other of two ways; and if the reader understands them, he will, I think, find it easy to apply the same way of thinking to other more complicated models:—

(1) The first cause of inequality between X_1 and X_2 is a change in the amount of working capital. For if working capital is changing, i.e. if X_1' is not zero, the current income of the public, namely $X_1 + X_1'$, is different from the cost of the current supply of finished goods, namely X_1. Hence if the public are exactly spending their current incomes either on consumption goods or on finished capital goods, at a time when working capital is changing, there will necessarily be an inequality between X_1 and X_2. Indeed, on the hypothesis that the public are exactly spending their current incomes either on consumption goods or on finished capital goods, at a time when working capital is changing, there will necessarily be an

inequality between X_1 and X_2, and on this hypothesis a change in working capital is the only possible cause of such inequality.

(2) If, however, the public are not exactly spending their incomes in these two ways, what can they do with the difference? Buying capital goods or promises or anything else from other members of the public, i.e. what we may call *swaps*, gets us no further as an explanation. It merely pushes the problem on a stage from the individual who has bought to the individual who has sold. In the aggregate there are only three things that the public can do with their incomes. They can use them to purchase the current output of the firms' finished goods (X_1); they can hoard part of their incomes in cash (H); they can lend the money to the firms either to finance an increase in the latter's working capital or to make good their losses (L). This is on the assumption that there is no third body besides firms and individuals. If we introduce a third class in the shape of banks, there is a fourth thing which the public can do with their incomes,—they can purchase an asset from a bank or pay off a debt to a bank. Let the net amount of purchases of assets by the public from the banks and paying off of debts to the banks be $-M_1$.*

(3) Bringing (1) and (2) together we have

$$X_1 + X_1' = X_2 + H + L - M_1,$$

so that X_1 and X_2 are unequal, if

$$H + L \text{ and } X_1' + M_1 \text{ are unequal;}$$

in other words, if the sum of the public's hoarding and loans to the firms differs from the sum of any increase in the assets and promises purchased by the banks from the public and in the working capital of the firms.

The equality is satisfied, for example,—to take a simple

* M_1 is not equal to the change in the quantity of money, since we have not precluded the firms also from having transactions with the banks.

case—if the two conditions are satisfied, (1) that any increased hoarding by the public is balanced by increased purchases of assets and promises by the banks, and (2) that the loans of the public to the firms are exactly equal to the increase in the firms' working capital; which conditions, namely that the public never hoard out of their incomes and never lend to the firms to finance the latter's losses, are, of course, not usually fulfilled in practice. It is obvious, however, that the equality of $H+L$ and $X_1'+M_1$, or alternatively of $H-M_1$ and $X_1'-L$, is a much more complicated idea than that of *hoarding* as ordinarily understood. Nor can the idea of hoarding be stretched so as to mean $H+L-M_1-X_1'$, except by an extension so artificial as to result in a misleading, rather than a helpful, use of words. For a change in expenditure relatively to costs does not disclose itself in the banking or monetary statistics, since these are not capable of earmarking the particular transactions in which we are interested in this context; so that our conclusions cannot be expressed in terms of hoarding or of the velocity of the circulation of money.

The reader will find that he can easily adapt the above condition to any model as complicated as he likes to make it and as close to actual conditions, and that in all cases the substance of it comes to substantially the same thing. In particular, the condition that the firms own their own working capital but not their fixed capital is not in the least essential to the argument; nor is the precise degree assumed above in the integration or non-integration of productive functions. The substance of the condition elucidated above is of absolutely general application. But when the problem is handled in a more general form, its relation to more familiar ideas is not so easily grasped. My simplifications are for the purpose of facilitating, not the proof, but the exposition.

III

It is interesting to consider what sort of means could be adopted to keep an entrepreneur economy in a neutral condition. They fall, I think, into four main types*, of which the first three are practical and the fourth, perhaps, Utopian.

(1) Loan expenditure by the government†, whether on current or capital account, might be brought in as a balancing factor, being increased when private expenditure was falling off relatively to costs and decreased when private expenditure was increasing, becoming if necessary negative, i.e. previous loans being repaid.

(2) Expenditure might be stimulated or retarded by changes in the rate of interest, because, as we shall see subsequently, a lowering of the rate of interest is calculated to stimulate expenditure both on consumption and on investment.

(3) Income might be redistributed so as to fall, increasingly or decreasingly, into the hands of individuals more likely to expend it.

(4) Provision might be made for preventing, on the one hand, the available means for expenditure from exceeding the current costs of production, and, on the other hand, for causing unspent income to go stale and valueless in the hands of the holder.

The first three, which are the practical methods of control, I have discussed in many places. The fourth may be worth elaborating a little, because it is well suited for illustrating the sort of steps which would be necessary if the use of income otherwise than for expenditure, either on finished goods or on working capital, were to be, so to speak, forbidden.

Let us suppose that instead of money, we have dated

---

* In a closed system. In an unclosed system further expedients are possible for keeping a *part* of the system nearer to equilibrium, e.g. tariffs, quotas, foreign-exchange management.

† I.e. not balanced by a corresponding change in taxation.

counters which have to be reissued each time they become income, and let us begin by assuming that the amount of working capital is constant. Firms would then pay the factors of production in counters inscribed with the date by which the output which they were helping to produce would be finished, and these counters would be used in due course to purchase the current output of finished goods. They would not be available except for this purpose and any counters not so used by the date stamped on them would be cancelled. The firms, however, receiving the dated counters for finished goods would be entitled to receive new counters available for their next period of production; and in the event of any counters being wasted by the public (by inadvertence or for any other reason) the firms would be given a proportionately greater number of new counters for the old counters handed in; e.g. if one-tenth of the counters were cancelled through not having been used, firms would receive in new counters ten-ninths of the number of the old counters which they were handing in.

If, however, aggregate working capital was being increased, some authority (the government or the banking system) would have to induce the public to surrender to them (either compulsorily by taxation or voluntarily by offering a rate of interest) an amount in counters falling due equal to the increase in working capital; and if working capital was being decreased, corresponding steps would have to be taken to augment the current purchasing power of the public.

IV

With such or similar safeguards and if we assume that we start initially in a state of full employment, the assumptions of the classical theory would be perfectly fulfilled. For the firms as a whole could not over a period of time, make either a profit or a loss above or below what they have paid out to the factors of production they employ, the losses made by certain firms being exactly equal to the profits made by others. There could be no general boom or general slump. Nor could there be any obstacle to an optimum level of output except as a result of miscalculation, or insufficient time to make the proper arrangements, or a stupid obstinacy about terms on the part either of the firms or of the factors of production. In fact unemployment could only be due to one of those aberrations of a temporary or otherwise non-fundamental character such as the classical theory has always envisaged as a possibility.

But if we conceive of a system in which no steps are taken to synchronise the aggregate sale proceeds up to any given date with the aggregate cost of the output finished at or before that date, the receipts of the firms *as a whole* may either exceed or fall short of their costs of production. In so far as they foresee or anticipate such a situation, their aggregate willingness to employ the factors of production will be affected—in a degree which depends on their conditions of short-period supply, as we shall show in detail subsequently. This possibility introduces a new cause affecting the volume of employment of which the classical theory has taken no account; and the situation is characterised by the following features.

I. The firms, taken as a whole, cannot protect themselves from loss by the expedient of producing more of this and less of that, which is appropriate when effective demand is changing in direction but not in amount. It may, therefore, be to their advantage to reduce employment in the aggregate.

II. The firms, taken as a whole, cannot protect themselves from loss by making revised (i.e. more favourable) money bargains with the factors of production. This is the point which those nurtured in the classical theory find it most difficult to understand. They suppose that, if the factors of production are prepared to accept a sufficiently low money wage, this will be reflected in lower real wages and will, therefore, serve to redress the balance in favour of the entrepreneur firms. But, in arguing thus, they forget that it is the earnings paid out to the factors of production which constitute the demand for the output of production. So long as their outgoings (after adjustment for changes in aggregate working capital) are not returning to the firms in full, there is no conceivable money bargain between the firms and their factors of production which will protect them, taken as a whole, from loss. Moreover an individual producer is not interested in the smallest degree in the level of real wages. He does not, in his business capacity, even enquire what it is. He is solely concerned with the prospective selling price of his own product relatively to his variable costs.*

III. The process of calculation which decides the volume of employment is as follows.

Each firm calculates the prospective selling price of its output and its variable cost in respect of output on various possible scales of production. Its variable cost per unit is not, as a rule, constant for all volumes of output but increases as output increases. Output is then pushed to the point at which the prospective selling price no longer exceeds the marginal variable cost. In this way the volume of output, and hence the volume of employment, is determined.

The *aggregate* volume of employment is determined in a similar way, provided that we allow for the fact that the decisions of each firm are influenced by the expected results of the decisions of other firms, so that a set of simultaneous equations has to be satisfied.

* It is only in equilibrium when the price of the marginal product attributable to one additional unit of employment is the same in every industry that real wages come into the picture at all, and they come in then simply because they are equal to the marginal product of the wage-good industries. Any other marginal product would do just as well; for when the prices of the marginal products of every industry (corresponding to one unit of employment) can be assumed to be equal, any one of them can be adopted as our measure of value in substitution for money without its making any difference.

If aggregate expenditure is kept constant relatively to aggregate variable cost, aggregate employment will also be constant, except in so far as expenditure is shifted from firms having one type of supply function to firms subject to more or less elastic conditions of supply; though we must, until we have introduced a further condition, allow for the possibility of the volume of aggregate employment being in neutral equilibrium.

If money wages rise, this will do no injury to non-wage-earners in the aggregate, (i.e. to entrepreneurs and rentier-capitalists taken together), provided that aggregate expenditure rises equally, i.e. if the conditions for neutrality hold good. The money cost, and therefore the price, of the marginal product will, however, rise, with the result that there will be a re-distribution of purchasing power favourable to entrepreneurs and unfavourable to rentiers. Real wages will only be affected if this redistribution of purchasing power between non-wage-earners leads to a re-distribution of their consumption as between wage goods (i.e. the commodities on which wages are predominantly spent) and non-wage-goods. If in a neutral system we discover a tendency for real wages to rise, this necessarily indicates either that there has been an increase in the efficiency of industries producing wage-goods or that these industries are becoming relatively less profitable owing to there being a diversion of demand, in which case real wages will fall again after there has been time to increase equipment in the non-wage goods industries which have become by hypothesis more profitable. The normal level of real wages will be determined by the other forces of the system. Until a state of full employment is reached, they are a result, and not themselves one of the determining forces. Altering money wages will not, in general, affect them. Only when there is full employment, i.e. when no more labour is available except at a wage worth more in terms of wage goods than the current wages, does the supply schedule of labour in terms of wage goods become an operative factor. When there is full employment, it is true that the volume of employment will only change in response to changes in the supply schedule and real efficiency of labour, unless it be for reasons of time lag in response to the changing character of demand and in particular owing to the diversion of demand to firms having differently shaped supply functions. But when the conditions for full employment are not fulfilled and unemployment (in the strict sense) comes into the picture, the volume of employment no longer depends on these factors.

In an entrepreneur system which is free to depart from neutrality, we may well discover empirically a correlation between employment and real wages. But this will occur, not because the one causes the other, but because they are both consequences of the same cause. We shall find, for example, that *cet. par.* increased investment will increase employment; and we shall also find that increased investment will *cet. par.* diminish real wages. If the other factors are assumed to be unchanged, it is impossible to alter employment by altering real wages, not because *if* real wages were altered, employment would not change also, but because, so long as other factors are constant, it is impossible to change real wages. If, for example, the working classes were persuaded to put more of their earnings into the savings bank, real wages would rise and employment would diminish; but it would be misleading to call the rise in real wages the cause of the unemployment – for *both* would be consequences of the increased propensity to save.

Or again, if employers choose to consume more wage goods themselves or to employ more labour on producing non-wage goods, such action may be expected to reduce real wages; whilst if they consume less wage goods themselves or employ less labour on producing non-wage goods, that will raise real wages. And these results will follow absolutely irrespective of what bargains about money wages may have been made between employers and the employed.

Addendum to chapter 3: the section removed in re-drafting (above p. 92)

II

The classical theory makes the fundamental assumptions, (1) that the value of the marginal unit of output is equal to the variable cost of producing it (value and cost being measured in the same unit), and (2) that the marginal utility of output is equal to the marginal disutility of effort.

The first of these assumptions is (subject to the usual qualifications not essentially relevant to the present context) of general validity and is the starting point of what I here call the General Theory of Employment, just as it is of the classical theory. If we substitute 'expected value' and 'expected variable cost' for value and cost, it is as true over short periods and in positions of disequilibrium as it is in the long period and in equilibrium. But the second assumption is not generally valid—not necessarily, as we shall see subsequently, even in a state of equilibrium. In a co-operative economy or in a neutral entrepreneur economy it will be true. But in an entrepreneur economy, even in one which satisfies the first of the two conditions for neutrality given above but not the second, it is not true. Thus the classical theory is, in effect, assuming either a co-operative or a neutral economy.

That the second assumption is not always fulfilled *in fact* will be obvious to the reader when he reflects that it is virtually equivalent to the condition for full employment. A state of unemployment can, I think, only be defined as a situation in which the marginal utility of output is greater than the marginal disutility of effort, i.e. a failure of organisation which prevents a man from producing something, the equivalent of which he would value more highly than the effort it had cost him. Thus in so far as the classical theory depends on the second of the above assumptions, it is from the outset ruling out altogether the possibility of chronic unemployment as distinct from temporary unemployment due to time-lags. It is not surprising, therefore, that it should have proved a blunt instrument wherewith to construct the theory of chronic unemployment. The existence of chronic unemployment is, in itself, a proof that the classical theory is insufficiently general in its postulates.

Fourth we have two fragments which are harder to date than the above sequence of drafts. The first handwritten fragment comes from a chapter on meanings of saving which, with its explicit multiplier, seems clearly to date from 1933. The second is a typed and handwritten chapter entitled Quasi-Rent and the Marginal Efficiency of Capital, which we cannot tie to a particular table of contents but would seem to date from this period.

Fragment from a draft chapter on meanings of saving, 1933

...[savings,] being equal to the excess of the volume of current output over the volume of current consumption, must be equal to the value of the increment of aggregate wealth, i.e. must be exactly equal to current investment. Thus an individual act of saving cannot lead to an increase in aggregate saving unless investment is being increased *pari passu*. It is, in fact, implicitly assumed that an increase in individual saving does lead automatically to an equal increase in aggregate investment. The maxims of 'sound' public finance are largely based on this supposition. The conclusion that every individual act of saving enriches, not only the individual responsible for it, but the community as a whole, has been deeply inculcated into all of us as an indisputable truth.

Yet it should not need much reflection to perceive that an increase in individual saving may effect, not an increase, but merely a redistribution, of aggregate wealth. The act of individual saving is entirely distinct from the act of individual investment. The two acts are generally performed, as I pointed out in my *Treatise on Money*, by different persons, and there exists no mechanism to establish a necessary or automatic link between them. What is indubitable, namely the equality between the aggregate of individual acts of saving and of individual acts of investment can be satisfied, not only by an individual act of increased saving being balanced by an individual act of increased investment, but also if it is balanced by another individual act of *decreased* saving. And unless something occurs to increase investment *pari passu*, this is primarily what must of necessity result. For the *direct* consequence of an individual act of increased saving is to decrease someone's income and, therefore, that someone's saving unless his consumption is diminished; and if his consumption is diminished, the loss of income is passed on to another; and so on. It is true that there would be no resting place, and consequently no position of equilibrium, if everyone, when his income falls, were to reduce his consumption by an equal amount, keeping his individual saving constant. Thus, it is a necessary condition of equilibrium that, when aggregate income falls, the aggregate expenditure on consumption should fall by a lesser amount than the fall of income. That this condition is fulfilled in practice is, however, in accordance with what our knowledge of popular psychology leads us to expect; and the fact that a point of equilibrium is reached in experience when incomes fall is confirmation of the validity of this expectation.

The actual causal chain by which an individual act of increased saving, unaccompanied by simultaneous individual acts of increased investment, leads to decreased saving in other quarters, operates through the effect of the initial act in diminishing incomes down to a level at which the aggregate propensity to save (as we shall call it in the next chapter) leads to the same actual aggregate saving as existed before the individual initiating the disturbance decided to save more.

The first approximation to the view that increased saving will not necessarily 'find its way' into increased investing, has been to admit no more than that increased investment will not ensue if the increased saving takes the form of actually hoarding money. If the increased individual savings are not hoarded in money but are used to purchase some asset, then it has been supposed that they will lead to increased investment as a result of their having raised the price of investment goods.

But even this is not correct. There is no reason to expect an increased demand for investment goods merely because one man's savings have increased, if we happen to know that other men's savings have been diminished by an equal amount. The first man's increased savings will be required merely to make good the deficiency of demand for investment goods due to the decrease of savings in other quarters. An act of increased individual saving cannot *cause* an increase of investment by raising the price of investment goods, because it is only an increase of aggregate savings which would have this effect; yet it is impossible that there can be an increase of aggregate savings until investment has increased; and moreover, if and when investment has increased, even so there will exist no reason why the price of investment goods should rise, since the supply of investment goods will have increased in value as a result of the new investment by exactly the same amount as the demand for them has increased as represented by the increased aggregate saving. Indeed increased or decreased saving can, in itself and apart from its possible indirect results in re-distributing incomes, have no effect whatever, as we shall see subsequently in more detail, on the price of investment goods, in as much as the increased demand from new saving will always be exactly balanced by the increased supply of new investment. The price of investment goods must be governed, as we shall show, by some other factor.

There is, however, another version of the argument just considered which should be mentioned at this point. If instead of spending my income on consuming bread, I decide to use the money to buy a machine (or a house) instead, what possible reason is there why the value of output as a whole, and hence the level of incomes, should decline? It is admitted, of course, that the price of bread will fall, but why will not the price of machines rise? My argument seems to say—indeed it does say—that if a man eats less bread and more butter, this will leave incomes unchanged, butter prices rising as much as bread prices fall; whereas if he eats less bread and buys more machines, it will cause incomes to fall. What is the peculiarity of consumption goods compared with investment goods which leads to this paradoxical result? I believe that I showed in my *Treatise on Money that* this must be so; but I cannot claim to have shown clearly to the reader's intuition *how* and *why* it must be so. Mr D. H. Robertson, as well as other critics, has raised this objection in various forms; and it is one which has to be met. I cannot, however, embellish satisfactorily my negative proposition that a transfer of an individual's expenditure from bread to machines will not tend of itself to raise the price of machines (although it will have the effect of lowering the price of bread), until I have reached the stage of my argument at which I deal positively with the factors which do determine the price of investment goods. I must, therefore, ask the reader to wait a little (until p.   ) for the demonstration how and why it is that a transfer of income–expenditure from consumption to the purchase of investment goods has no tendency in itself to increase the price of the latter.

The conclusion is, therefore, that *any* act of saving will increase my own wealth by the amount of my saving, but it will reduce the incomes of others down to a level at which their savings decline by an equal amount. Its direct effect, therefore, will be a re-distribution of saving without any increase in its aggregate, and at the same time a decrease in aggregate income. The indirect effect will vary according to the attendant circumstances. But it may often not even be so innocent as to leave the position unchanged, and may actually diminish aggregate saving. For the act of individual saving will in itself diminish quasi-rent, so that, if it has been anticipated or if it is expected to continue, it will, unless it is offset by a fall in the rate of interest or in some other relevant factor, diminish the motive towards increasing capital equipment, so that new investment, and consequently aggregate new saving, will be diminished.

Thus an increase in aggregate saving is brought about (for example) by building a house. If we build a house, we can be certain *cet. par.* that this will result in an increased excess of aggregate income over aggregate spending exactly equal to the value of the house. Aggregate incomes will rise as a result of the house having been built up to a level at which the public choose to save the proportion of their increased incomes equal to the value of the house. It is, indeed, the act of investing which 'finds its way' into saving, rather than the other way round. On the other hand, individual acts of saving not only do not necessarily 'find their way' into investment, but are liable to have precisely the opposite effect. This is the explanation of why the conventional opinions on this matter have had so disastrous an influence on human prosperity.

II

It should now be evident that, if we are to mean by aggregate saving the aggregate excess of income over consumption, we must associate with it a different set of ideas from those commonly associated with it. For the ordinary man certainly does not appreciate that the mere act of investment leads automatically to a corresponding increase of saving, and that there can, consequently, be no object in adjuring the community to increase its saving so as to provide for current investment (or the cost of the war or whatever the enterprise afoot may be). Nevertheless when we adjure individuals to save, it seems unlikely that we are recommending a course of action which will be futile in all circumstances; and the significance of such action requires further examination.

That there is here a problem for elucidation has been admitted in much recent writing on this matter by attempts to distinguish what is called forced saving (or some similar expression) from what is called voluntary saving. But none of those attempts (in my opinion) give a clear explanation of the distinction, because they are made to depend on some change on the side of money, e.g. in the effective quantity of money or in the disposition to hoard money. Changes in the propensity to hold money, which I shall discuss later under the name of *liquidity preference*, are certainly not without importance in this connection, but their effect on the relation between a change in individual saving and a change in aggregate saving is complicated and indirect, so that it is impossible to establish a precise and invariable relationship between the former and the latter except in highly simplified and artificial cases, which lack interest because they lack generality and fail, therefore, to get to the real bottom of the matter.

If, however, we are to make a distinction between two kinds of 'saving', I know of no useful or significant distinction except that between S and S', i.e. between the traditional sense of the term and the definition which I gave in my *Treatise on Money*. If 'voluntary saving' is to be given any clear sense, it must, I think, correspond to S'; and an 'increase of voluntary saving' (which is the preferable concept to use) to $\Delta S'$, i.e. to *economising*. This can be shown as follows: wherever $\Delta I = \Delta S$, we have $\Delta I = \Delta Q + \Delta S'$, which tells us that a change in the rate of investment is made up of two parts, namely the change in quasi-rent and the amount of current economising. Now if we identify an increase of 'voluntary' saving with economising, an increase in voluntary saving will cause a given volume of investment to be associated with a smaller increase in quasi-rent than would be the case otherwise. Now quasi-rent is the excess of the sale proceeds of output over its variable cost. Thus, in general a decision on the part of individuals to economise will cause any given volume of investment to be associated with a lower price level for output than would rule otherwise. Hence 'forced' saving represents that part of the volume of increased investment which is provided for out of the benefit accruing to entrepreneurs from the resulting rise of prices,—the part provided (to use a vulgar expression) out of 'inflation'.

We can also arrive at the same result as follows. We have $P.O = Q + E$ where P is the price of output, so that $P\Delta O + O\Delta P = \Delta Q + \Delta E$. But $P\Delta O = \Delta E$, since the price of the marginal product will (subject to certain assumptions) be equal, in general, to the increase of variable cost. Therefore $O\Delta P = \Delta Q$, so that $\Delta I = O.\Delta P + \Delta S'$, which shows directly that a given increment in investment involves a smaller increment in price if $\Delta S'$ is increased.

Whilst, however, the distinction between 'forced' and 'voluntary' saving has an important significance if we identify it with the distinction between $S - S'$ and S', nevertheless I do not favour this use of terms. For in so far as it suggests that an increase of 'voluntary' saving is always juster and better for the earners as against the entrepreneurs than 'forced' saving, it may be seriously misleading.* Moreover the relationship between economising and social well-being is different and more complicated than this schematism indicates;—as, at the expense of partially anticipating a later stage of the argument, I will try to illustrate.

Since saving and investment are necessarily equal in amount, an increment of investment means that the community as a whole has somehow been induced to save a correspondingly increased sum. There are two ways, however, in which the necessary increment of saving can be brought about:—

(1) The public can be urged to economise to an amount equal to the desired increment of investment, with the result that investment can be increased without any increase in aggregate income, both the price and the quantity of aggregate output being unchanged; from which it appears that economising permits a corresponding increment of investment without any disturbance to the *status quo*.

(2) If, however, the public do not economise, the effect of increased investment will be both to raise prices and to increase output. Thus both money incomes and real incomes will increase, whilst at the same time the former real income will be re-distributed in favour of entrepreneurs as against earners, until the public's pre-existing propensity to save leads them, at the new level and distribution of income, to choose to save the necessary extra sum.

The extent to which output will rise as a concomitant of a given increase of investment, will depend on what proportion of an increment of real income the public's propensity to save (after allowing for the effect of any redistribution of

---

* Those who speak of 'forced saving' have not, I think, invented a corresponding term for the *excess* of 'voluntary saving' (in the above sense) over investment. Perhaps we might call it 'predatory saving' or 'exploitatory saving' to indicate that it is made wholly at the expense of other people and without benefit to the aggregate wealth of the community.

incomes) leads them to choose not to consume. The extent to which prices will rise, given the extent to which output will rise, will depend on the shape of the supply function. (The mentions of the propensity to save and the supply function anticipate later chapters, but their names and the context probably suggest to the reader a sufficient idea of what they mean).

Except in the limiting case, in which the public is disposed to save the whole of any increment in their real income, the increase in output will be greater than the increase in investment; and except in the limiting case, where the supply function is perfectly elastic, there will be some rise in prices.

Thus the normal concomitants of an increase of real investment will be

(1) an increase of real consumption;

(2) an increase of Q due to higher prices;

(3) an increase of economising.

If the increase of real investment is ΔO_2, the increase of real consumption will be $(k-1)\Delta O_2$ where k is the multiplier (see p.   ) and depends on the propensity to consume. Further, $\Delta I = \Delta Q + \Delta S'$ where ΔQ is the 'forced' saving and $\Delta S'$ 'voluntary' saving.

Now the greater $\Delta S'$ is, the smaller will ΔQ be and the less will prices rise. So far, so good. But it also follows that the greater $\Delta S'$ is, the smaller will be the increment $(k-1)\Delta O$ of real consumption. In other words the greater $\Delta S'$ is, the less efficacious will be a given ΔI in increasing employment. Moreover we must not blame too much the existence of ΔQ. For ΔQ is merely the unavoidable concomitant of an increase in output $k\Delta O$, as determined by the nature of the supply function. Given the supply function, there is no method of increasing employment in a degree corresponding to an increase $k\Delta O$ in output, without bringing about an increment ΔQ of quasi-rent. ΔQ is merely a reflection of the fact that industry is operating in the short period subject to diminishing returns, so that employment can only improve with an increase in profits.

Thus 'voluntary' saving is detrimental (and 'forced' saving beneficial) whenever employment is sub-optimal, and in such circumstances there is indeed no possibility of employment improving except to the accompaniment of an increase of 'forced' saving. An increment of 'voluntary' saving, i.e. economising, is only to be welcomed as socially beneficial when employment is supra-optimal and earners are finding themselves tricked by the industrial machine into exerting themselves on a scale, the marginal disutility of which is not adequately rewarded by their marginal product,—a state of affairs which actually in the modern world is very infrequent.

Draft chapter 5, presumably written in 1933–4, although there is no supporting table of contents.[17]

5 QUASI-RENT AND THE MARGINAL EFFICIENCY OF CAPITAL

I

The quasi-rent of an asset in any period is the money value of the services it renders, or money income derived from it, in that period. The prospective quasi-rent is the anticipated series of such annuities during the life of the asset.

Upon what will the amount of the quasi-rent depend? Upon four factors—(i) the scarcity or abundance of the asset, i.e. the supply of assets capable of rendering similar or equivalent service, (ii) the demand for its services relatively to the

[17] Throughout the first two sections of the manuscript of this draft, except in paragraph four, Keynes crossed out the word 'productivity' and replaced it with the word 'efficiency' after he originally wrote out the chapter. Where these changes occurred the word 'efficiency' is underlined. The same occurs when m.e.c. replaced m.p.c. as a short form.

demand for other things, (iii) the state of profits and (iv) the value of money. If, as in our present context, we are concerned with the quasi-rents of assets generally rather than with the quasi-rents of particular assets, we can substitute for (ii) the demand for goods and services, in the production of which the services of assets play a large part, relatively to the demand for goods and services, in the production of which the services of assets play a smaller, or a negligible, part. Similarly we can substitute for (i) the scarcity or abundance of assets in general, i.e. of capital, relatively to output as a whole.

If this is the meaning of *Quasi-rent*, what is the significance of the *Marginal Productivity* (or *Efficiency* or *Utility*) *of Capital*?* These are familiar terms which we have all frequently used. But what exactly do they mean? I have not been able to discover any attempt at precise definition.

We intend by them, I think essentially an equilibrium concept. On the one hand, we do not say in a year in which business is being run at a loss that the marginal productivity of capital is zero or negative. Nor, on the other hand, when during a financial crisis the rate of interest rises to a high level, do we say that the marginal productivity of capital is unusually high.

It is an equilibrium concept, changing indeed year by year by degrees, but only for reasons arising out of the gradual growth of capital relatively to output as a whole and out of the elasticity of demand for goods requiring more capital to produce compared with the elasticity for goods requiring little capital to produce.

---

* With such terms as these, there always arises the ambiguity over meaning the increment of physical product due to the employment of one more physical unit of capital, or the increment of value of product due to the employment of one more value unit of capital. The former involves considerable difficulties as to the definition of the unit. At any rate, I am concerned here with the latter. Perhaps we might use the term *marginal productivity of capital* [when] we mean an increment of product, and *marginal efficiency* or *utility* when we mean an increment of value.

If this is a correct account of the matter, marginal efficiency of capital (or m.e.c.) is the equilibrium concept about which quasi-rent oscillates, quasi-rent being, so to speak, the short-period version of m.e.c. I think it possible that Marshall would have been more consistent if he had always spoken of marginal efficiency of capital where in fact he speaks of the rate of interest.*

The fluctuations of the annual quasi-rents around the equilibrium m.e.c. appropriate to the same year will depend on the fluctuations of profit, and on changes in the value of money measured in terms of cost of production. There will also, of course be the fluctuations of estimated risk arising out of uncertainty, default and moral risk. In short, the marginal efficiency of capital sums up factors (i) and (ii) above, whilst quasi-rent takes account of factors (iii) and (iv) as well.

Thus, apart from allowance for risk, the money value of capital assets at any time, which we have analysed above as depending on prospective quasi-rent in conjunction with the

* The phrase which Marshall himself uses is 'marginal efficiency' of a factor of production. The following is a summary of the most relevant passage which I can find in Marshall's *Principles* (3rd edn pp. 580–586. I have run together a number of non-consecutive sentences to convey the gist of what he says [)]:— 'The margins of the applications of each agent of production are determined by the general conditions of demand and supply. In the very act of governing the marginal uses of each agent, those general conditions govern also its marginal net efficiency in each use; and therefore its exchange value in each use. Every businessman estimates as best he can how much *net* addition to the value of his total product will be caused by a certain extra use of any one agent. The result is the net product of that agent, and he endeavours to employ each up to that margin at which its net product would no longer exceed the price he would have to pay for it...In a certain factory an extra £100 worth of machinery can be applied so as not to involve any other extra expense, and so to add annually £3 worth to the net output of the factory, after allowing for its own wear and tear. If the investors of capital push it into every occupation in which it seems likely to gain a higher reward; and if, after this has been done and equilibrium has been found, it still pays and only just pays to employ this machinery, we can infer from this fact that the yearly rate of interest is three per cent. But illustrations of this kind merely indicate part of the action of the great causes which govern value. They cannot be made into a theory of wages, without reasoning in a circle... Suppose that the rate of interest is 3 per cent per annum on perfectly good security; and that the hat-making trade absorbs a capital of one million pounds. When they have this amount, the marginal utility of the machinery, i.e. the utility of that machinery which it is only just worth their while to employ is measured by 3 per cent.'

rate of interest, can be further analysed as depending on four factors,—(1) prospective m.e.c., (2) prospective windfall profit and loss, (3) prospective value of money in terms of cost of production, and (4) the complex of current rates of interest.

Let p_r be the cost of production at time r

k_r m.e.c.   ,,

q_r profit   ,,

d_r present value of £1 deferred r years.

Then $\Sigma(p_r k_r + q_r) d_r$ is the present value of an equity assuming all the relevant quantities are known. In the case of a gilt-edged debt, expressed in terms of money $k_r = 1/p_r$ and $q_2 = 0$, so that its value is Σd_r.

The volume of development at any time will depend on the relation between the money-value of each category of capital goods arrived at in this way and its current cost of production.

II

I said above that quasi-rent is *so to speak* the short-period version of the marginal efficiency of capital, because there are also two other respects in which it differs. In the first place it is usual to include in quasi-rent the total current delivery from an asset, including such part of the current delivery as is required to provide for amortisation, whereas the m.e.c. is the net yield after providing for amortisation. In the second place, quasi-rent is an absolute sum, whereas m.e.c. is a ratio, namely the ratio of the net yield of an asset to its cost of production. To this extent m.e.c. is a concept more nearly analogous to the rate of interest. But even if we allow for this and abstract from the fluctuations in profits and in the value of money which complicate the concept of quasi-rent, there still remains a vital respect, generally overlooked, which separates, even in fullest equilibrium, the marginal efficiency of capital from the rate of interest.

For the marginal efficiency of capital at any time clearly depends on the demand and supply of capital *at that time*, whereas the tendency in full equilibrium is for equality between the rate of interest on a debt, the amortisation of which will be spread over the same period as the life of the asset, and the prospective marginal efficiency of the asset year by year during its life. For example if current capital consists of houses having a life of 50 years in front of them, the marginal efficiency of capital (excluding short-period factors) is measured by the present rent of such a house relatively to its cost of production. But (still excluding short-period factors and risks arising out of uncertain knowledge of the future) the rate of interest, which will make the ownership of the house and the ownership of a debt due for repayment over 50 years equally attractive, will depend not on the present marginal efficiency of capital but on the prospective marginal efficiencies year by year over the life of the capital. And this, in turn, will depend on the prospective supply of capital and the prospective demand for it.

This conclusion serves to bring out even more the essential independence of the rate of interest as a factor in the economic situation, and the hopelessness in a non-stationary system of attempting to derive it, even in conditions of fullest monetary equilibrium, from the marginal efficiency of capital. For we have seen that, at best, the rate of interest tends to equality with the mean prospective marginal efficiency of capital, and that the mean prospective m.e.c. depends on the prospective supply of capital relatively to the demand for it. But the prospective supply of capital depends on the prospective rate of interest. Thus unless we already know the prospective rate of interest, we cannot determine the prospective marginal efficiency of capital, and consequently we cannot discover the quantity towards equality with which the current rate of interest tends in conditions of fullest equilibrium.

III[18]

I much prefer to speak of capital as having a quasi-rent to speaking of it as being *productive*. The reason why an asset yields up during its life services having an aggregate value greater than its cost of production, is solely because it is *scarce*. I sympathise, therefore, with the classical doctrine that everything is *produced* by labour together, if you like, with what used to be called *art* and is now called *technique*, aided by natural resources which are free or costing a rent according to their scarcity or abundance, and by the results of past labour, embodied in assets, which can command a price equal to or exceeding the cost of the labour embodied in them according to their scarcity or abundance.

It is true that some lengthy or roundabout processes are efficient. But so are short processes. Lengthy processes are not efficient because they are lengthy, any more than short processes are efficient because they are short. Some lengthy processes would be very inefficient, for there are such things as spoiling or wasting with time. With a given labour force there is a definite limit to the quantity of labour embodied in roundabout processes which can be used to advantage. Apart from many other considerations, there must be a due proportion between the amount of labour employed in making machines and the amount employed in using them. The ultimate quantity of value will not increase indefinitely, relatively to the quantity of labour employed, as the processes adopted become more and more roundabout.

Moreover there are all sorts of reasons why various kinds of services and facilities are scarce and therefore expensive relatively to the quantity of labour involved (measured, let us say, in time effort). For example, smelly processes command a high reward, because people will not undertake them unless they do. So do risky processes. But we do not go about saying

[18] Portions of this section survived to Ch. 16 (II) of the *General Theory*.

that smelly or risky processes are efficient as such, or that the smellier or riskier we make them the more efficient they will be. Indeed, quite the contrary. Other things being equal, a process is inefficient by reason of its being smelly or risky. And so with a lengthy process. An invention is efficient if it is able to shorten the process by which a given amount of labour produces a given amount of product. Not all labour is accomplished in equally agreeable attendant circumstances; and conditions of equilibrium require that articles produced in less agreeable attendant circumstances (characterised by smelliness, risk or the lapse of time) must be kept sufficiently scarce to command a higher price.

In considering, therefore, why capital assets normally produce in the course of their life aggregate quasi-rents greater than their cost of production, the essential question for enquiry is why such assets are so scarce that the demand for them, at a price spread over their life equal to their cost of production, is greater than their supply.

The answer usually given is to the effect that the aggregate quantity of assets (or capital) must in equilibrium be kept down to a sufficiently low figure to prevent its marginal efficiency falling below the marginal disutility of 'waiting' on a scale equal to the aggregate quantity of assets. I shall analyse further in the next chapter the concept of 'waiting', and I shall prefer at this stage to substitute 'the rate of interest' for 'the marginal disutility of waiting'. It will beg fewer questions and at the same time raise controversy with no-one to say that the quantity of capital at any time depends on the past, present and prospective rate of interest. It is the rate of interest which keeps the quantity of capital in check. If the rate of interest, actual and prospective, could be kept sufficiently low for a sufficient length of time, the quantity of capital would increase up to a point where its marginal efficiency was tending to zero; i.e. assets would cease to be scarce. The question why assets are scarce is, therefore, the same question as to why the rate of interest exceeds zero. We cannot, however, make further progress towards answering it until we have analysed the concepts dealt with in a later chapter.

IV

The nearest we can get to an equilibrium relationship between the rate of interest and the marginal efficiency of capital seems to be the following: 'The rate of interest is in equilibrium with prospective quasi-rent if their relative values are such that the amount of current gross investment approximates to the amount of current gross saving.'

This corresponds to what in my *Treatise on Money* I called 'the natural rate of interest'. It does not correspond precisely because, when I wrote the *Treatise on Money*, I had not arrived at any clear conception of the significance of the rate of interest; so that it is more accurate to say that this is the definition of the natural rate of interest which I ought to have given.

The reader will notice that the natural rate of interest is no longer defined by reference to a price level, but by reference to the equality of two lump sums of money;—which is, I think an improvement.

We have now reached, I believe, the answer to the question, what tacit assumption is required to make sense of the traditional theory of the rate of interest. This theory assumes, I suggest, that the actual rate of interest is always equal to the natural rate of interest, in the sense in which we have just defined the latter. If the traditional theory is thus interpreted, I see nothing in it to which to take exception. The references to the rate of interest in Marshall's *Principles of Economics*, in particular, then become straightforward and intelligible.

If this is correct, the theory of neutral economics assumes

that the banking authority maintains the market rate of interest in a state of continuous equality with the natural rate of interest thus defined; and it investigates what laws will govern the distribution and rewards of the community's productive resources subject to this assumption. With this limitation in force, the volume of output depends solely on the volume of productive resources, including the current equipment of techniques. But without this limitation, the volume of output also depends on the relationship of the market rate of interest to the natural rate. The theory of fluctuations in output corresponding to fluctuations in the relationship of the market rate of interest to the natural rate will be the topic of our Book II.

Note (to Chap. 5) on Böhm-Bawerk's Rate of Interest

The distinction of fact lying behind the distinction between the rate of interest and quasi-rent is, obviously the same as that with which Böhm-Bawerk attempted to deal by his distinction between what he called the loan-rate of interest and the natural rate* of interest. But he sows the seeds of a further confusion---which Marshall's *quasi-rent* avoids, since it is an absolute sum not a rate—by speaking of the natural *rate* of interest, as being in some sense the yield of real capital assets, without making it clear what the other term of the relationship is—on what capital value the natural rate is calculated. For if, as Marshall rightly does, we calculate the value of a capital asset by capitalising its quasi-rent on terms supplied by the loan rate of interest, then, by virtue of the circularity of the procedure, the quasi-rent of an asset reckoned as a percentage of its capital value is necessarily the same thing as the loan-rate of interest, and the natural rate of interest does not exist as an independent entity.

* *Prima facie* Böhm-Bawerk's natural rate of interest has, at first sight little in common with Wicksell's. But the foregoing discussion has shown that they are in fact closely akin. Wicksell's natural rate appears to be the loan rate which prevails when the loan rate is equal to Böhm-Bawerk's natural rate.

If, on the other hand, we take what seems to be the only alternative course of reckoning the natural rate of interest yielded by an asset by taking prospective quasi-rent in relation to its cost of production, then we shall be led along much the same lines as that of my own argument.

For the period after 1933, less new material has come to light. During the Lent term of 1934, work on the manuscript appears to have gone on quite well. On 19 February, Keynes reported to Lydia that 'Alexander has proved to me that "my important discovery" last week is all a mistake.' After the term, as recorded in Volume XIII (p. 422) Keynes had a series of fruitful discussions with Richard Kahn, who came down to Tilton. From these discussions, two notes from Kahn survive in addition to the note by Keynes printed in Volume XIII (pp. 422–3).

From R. F. KAHN,[19] *20 March 1934*

My dear Maynard,

I have got held up over your fundamental definitions. I daresay I am being stupid, but at least I suspect that your exposition might be well modified. I am enclosing three different versions. *B* is, I think, what you *are* saying, *A* what one is inclined to think you are saying, *C* what you may feel inclined to say.

It is surely clear that so long as you define the difference between income and investment as the *actual* value of consumption, they cannot *both* be independent of *actual* prices at which consumption takes place.

In any case, so far as physical amounts (as contrasted with prices) are concerned, your definitions are, I think, completely *post-mortem*. The element of expectation refers only to prices.

Yours ever

R. F. K.

A

X_1 actual value of initial capital
X_2 actual value of eventual capital
X_2' value of eventual capital at forward prices ruling at commencement of period
C actual value of consumption

[19] A P.S. to this letter, purely concerned with personal matters, has been omitted.

Define investment I as $X_2'-X_1$

Then define income Y as $I+C = (X_2'+C)-X_1$
$$= Z-X_1, \text{ where } Z = X_2'+C$$

Define capital appreciation A as $X_2-X_2'-$ so that $I = (X_2-X_1)-A$

If this is correct, then it is true that *investment* depends only on *expected* prices, but this is not true of *income* (and *quasi-rent*), which depend on the *actual* prices at which consumption goods are sold.

B

X_1 actual value of initial capital
X_2 actual value of eventual capital
X_2' value of eventual capital at forward prices ruling at commencement of period
C actual value of consumption
C' value of consumption at forward prices ruling at commencement of period.

Define investment I as $(X_2'-X_1)-(C-C')$

Then define income Y as $I+C = (X_2'+C')-X_1$
$$= Z-X_1 \text{ where } Z = X_2'+C'$$

Define capital appreciation A as $(X_2-X_2')+(C-C')$, so that $I = (X_2-X_1)-A$

If this is correct, then it is true that *income* (and *quasi-rent*) depend only on *expected* prices, but this is not true of *investment*, which depends on the deviation between *actual* and *expected* prices at which consumption goods are sold.

So far as any part of consumption happens to be sold at a price higher than that expected, this *by itself* causes a decline in *investment* (offset by an equal '*capital*' *appreciation*).

C

X_1 actual value of initial capital
X_2 actual value of eventual capital
X_2' value of eventual capital at forward prices ruling at commencement of period
C' value of consumption at forward prices ruling at commencement of period

Define investment I as $X_2'-X'$

Then define Y as $I+C' = (X_2'+C')-X_1$
$$= Z-X_1, \text{ where } Z = X_2'+C'$$

Define capital appreciation A as X_2-X_2', so that $I = (X_2-X_1)-A$

Then both *investment* and *income* (and *quasi-rent*) depend only on expected prices.

From R. F. KAHN, *21 March 1934*

I shall arrive at Lewes Friday at 5.21. I am afraid my operations on your book have been badly held up by after-term *malaise*. But I am now fully recovered. It is clear that I shall worry you with trivialities. I really do feel that you have got home. If anything, I feel you make it all appear *too simple*.

I am so much looking forward to seeing you both.

Yours

R. F. K.

For the rest of the period prior to publication, no new material has emerged. However there are two exchanges of letters from Keynes' other papers and five fragments kept by Keynes in the bundles of papers relating to the composition of the *General Theory* which, although difficult to date with any precision, are of some interest.

The first exchange of letters occurred with Erik Lindahl, who had stayed in Cambridge in January 1934.

From E. LINDAHL, *7 November 1934*

Dear Mr Keynes,

In case it should be of some interest for you, I send here a little draft,[20] containing some ideas concerning the relation between saving and investment and some other questions and I hope to elaborate a little more in the English edition of my book on the monetary problem.[21]

The main difference from your construction lies therein that I have replaced your concepts 'cost and value of investment' with 'planned and realized investment'. The 'value of investment' is the same thing as the 'realized investment', but the 'cost of investment' differs from the 'planned investment', as the former partly refers to the producers' and the latter only to the buyers' conception of the investment goods.

At first I tried to keep your concept of 'cost of (net) investment'. I wrote namely the equation system (1) on page 2 in the following way (my J is the same quantity as your I'):

[20] See below, pp. 123–31.
[21] *Studies in the Theory of Money and Capital* (London, 1939).

$$PaTa = E - J$$
$$PbTb = Da + Ja$$
$$\dotsb$$
$$PnTn = Dm + Jm$$
$$O = Dn + Jn$$

$$PT = E + D$$

In that case

$$PaTa' - PaTa = (E - S) - (E - J) = J - S,$$

that is, the difference between Investment and Saving is equal to the unexpected increase of the selling value of the consumption goods, or, as you express it, to the windfall gains for the producers of such goods. But this is a very difficult construction, as J is the sum of $Ja, Jb\ldots$, and Ja must be defined as the difference between $PbTb$ and Da, that is between the selling value of the capital goods, calculated by the *producers* of these goods, and the depreciation of the existing capital goods, calculated by the *users* of these goods.

In either case, I think it is of interest to note that the difference between the planned investment and the planned saving, that is in my notation $(I - S)$, is equal to the total profit, that is your Q, while in your construction the difference between cost of investment and planned saving is equal to your Q_1.

May I seize the occasion to thank you very heartily for your kindness to me during my short stay in Cambridge in January this year. I hope to see you again next time I am going to England.

Yours very sincerely,

ERIC LINDAHL

A NOTE ON THE DYNAMIC PRICING PROBLEM
The Setting of the Problem

If we start at an arbitrary point of time, t, the then prevailing *plans* for production and consumption which regulate the actions of the individuals for some period of time forward can be regarded as given. In these plans the exterior economic factors are included as psychic conceptions. In conformity to the plans, there are also given certain *supply prices*, that is, the offers of the producers to deliver goods or services, immediately or at some future date. (In certain cases, the demand prices must instead be regarded as given, but as these cases can be treated analogously, they are not considered here.)

After the elapse of a certain period of time, say at the point $t+1$, the producers and the consumers find that they have to modify their plans of action which have hitherto regulated the carrying on of production and consumption and the transactions between the sellers and the buyers. As no individual has a perfect knowledge of the plans of the other individuals, for each individual the realization of the plans of the other individuals has given a new light to his own problems. A producer finds, for example, that the demand for his products has been greater or smaller than he expected when he previously announced his supply price. He can also ascertain that other exterior events have implied certain surprises to him. As in the real world such events, more or less unforseen, are continuously occurring, the period of time between t and $t+1$, under which the plans of actions are assumed to be substantially unaltered, must be fairly short, for example a day.

The problem referring to this process is to analyze what happens during the said period, that is, to determine the situation at the point $t+1$ as a *result* of the situation at the point t. When this problem is solved, the situation at the point $t+2$ can in the same manner be explained as a result of the situation at the point $t+1$, and so on. In this lies, therefore, in point of principle, the solution of the whole dynamic problem.

Definitions and Notations

Economic quantities which are based on subjective estimations, in general alter their values more or less with the point of time when the estimation is made. In the present case, however, we can restrict the points of time for the estimation to the beginning and the end of the period to which the quantities in question refer, that is, to the points t and $t+1$. Quantities which are based on estimations at the point t, are denoted with letters without index, quantities referring to estimations at the point $t+1$ with letters with the index '.

For indicating the different stages of the productive process, we use the indices $a, b, c, \ldots n$. The stage a contains the production of services and non durable goods which are sold to the consumers, the stage b the production of capital goods which are sold to the producers in stage a, the stage c the production of capital goods which are sold to the producers in stage b, etc. In the last stage n, no capital goods are received from producers in other stages.—Letters without such indices indicate either the *sum* or the *average*, as the case may be, of all the quantities marked with such indices. (For example, E signifies the total income and is therefore the sum of the terms

Ea, Eb,... En, but *P* is the average price level and therefore the average of the terms *Pa, Pb,... Pn.*)

Our system of notation, then, is as follows:

P: the average price of all goods and consumers' services that have been sold during previous periods for delivery during the present period, or that the producers expect to sell during the present period. Thus *P* is not quite identical with the supply prices prevailing in the present period, as the previously contracted prices can differ more or less from these prices.

T: the corresponding quantity of products, calculated in a unit that is in accord with the notation *P. PT* denotes the total value of what the producers at the beginning of the period expect to deliver during that period, *PT'* denotes the value of the transactions actually performed.

E: the sum of all net incomes that the owners of the factors expect to receive. Profit expectations are included, but, in other respects, it is for the present problem of no greater importance how the concept of income is defined. *E'* signifies the same income, calculated at the end of the period in question.

D: the expected depreciation of the capital stock, occasioned by the delivery of products during the period, *minus* the appreciation of the same stock that is expected to take place, f.ex. on the ground that the output will exceed the delivery of products. The term is based on the estimations of the entrepreneurs at the beginning of the period. *D'* refers to the corresponding estimations at the end of the period.—The definition of this term must be in accordance with the definition of the income, as the sum of the two terms must have a definite meaning. (How this sum is to be apportioned to the two terms can, on the other hand, be solved in different ways.)

I: the investment, defined as such increase of the capital employed by a firm, that is planned by the entrepreneurs at the beginning of the period, and that shall be realized through either the purchase of capital goods produced by other firms, or the augmentation of the stocks of the firm, in so far as the sum of these two items is in excess of the depreciation of the previous capital stock of respective firms. *I'* is the same investment calculated at the end of the period.

S: the total saving planned by the consumers at the beginning of the period. The definition of the concept must be in accordance with the definition of income, so that *E−S* is equal to the sum of what the consumers intend to pay for goods and services during the period, and *E'−S'* equal to the actual value of the consumption, calculated at the end of the period.

The Relation between these Quantities, referring to a certain Period of Time

The situation at an arbitrary point of time, taken as the beginning of such a period as discussed above, can be characterized by the quantities, entering in the following system of equations:

$$
\begin{aligned}
Pa\,Ta &= Ea + Da \\
Pb\,Tb &= Eb + Db \\
&\cdots\cdots\cdots\cdots\cdots \\
Pn\,Tn &= En + Dn
\end{aligned}
$$

$$\overline{\quad PT = E + D \quad}$$

(1)

These equations are based on the assumption that that part of E that is contractual income is known by the entrepreneurs; the income expectations of the wage-earners are thus, for the period in question, equal to the sum that the entrepreneurs expect to pay as wages for this period. In such a case, the equations are only a method of stating the definitions given above.

The same equations can be based on estimations performed at the end of the period. Then they denote that the actual selling value of each stage during the period is equal to the sum of the net income plus the depreciation of the capital. But in that case, it is possible to add some further equations. The value of goods and services, actually delivered to the consumers, must be equal to the actual consumption. And the value of capital goods, delivered by producers in a certain stage, must be equal to the net investment of the producers that have bought these goods *plus* the net depreciation of their other capital. The investment of the producers in the stage n who do not receive capital from other stages can only consist in an increase of the stock, that is, an excess of output over the selling value. If the term In' is positive, the term Dn' must thus denote the corresponding negative value. The now discussed equations can be stated as follows:

$$
\begin{aligned}
Pa\,Ta' &= Ea' + Da' = E' - S' \\
Pb\,Tb' &= Eb' + Db' = Da' + Ia' \\
&\cdots\cdots\cdots\cdots\cdots\cdots\cdots\cdots\cdots \\
Pn\,Tn' &= En' + Dn' = Dm' + Im' \\
O &= Dn' + Dn'
\end{aligned}
$$

(2)

$$\overline{\quad PT' = E' + D' = E' + D' + I' - S' \quad}$$

The quantities in this system which are marked by the index ', are unknown, and, as before said, the problem is to determine them with help of the quantities given at the beginning of the period. For this purpose, we must utilize the further assumptions made above, namely that the plans for production and consumption, existing at the beginning of the period, have been actually realized during the period, in so far as regards the amounts that the comers have granted to their consumption and the producers to the providement of new capital goods to be delivered during the period.

Thus we have
$$E - S = PaTa' \tag{3}$$

and
$$Ia + Da = PbTb'$$
$$Ib + Db = PcTc'$$
$$\dots\dots\dots\dots \tag{4}$$
$$In + Dn = O$$

$$\overline{}$$

$$I + D = PT' - PaTa'$$

The sum of the terms in (3) and (4) is

$$E + D + I - S = PT'$$

The Significance of the Relation between Saving and Investment

On the basis of the equations (1)–(4), the relations between the *ex ante* and the *ex post* concepts of saving and investment can be stated in the following way:

$$I' = S'$$
$$I' - S = E' - E$$
$$I' - I = D - D'$$
$$I - S = E' + D' - (E + D) = P(T' - T)$$

If savings and investment both are calculated at the end of the period, they are thus identical. Savings in this sense means only the excess of the income, calculated ex post, over the actual consumption. In so far as this excess is greater than the saving planned at the beginning of the period, it represents also, as is seen from the second equation, a sort of income gain for the individual. This can also be expressed so that what, at the end of the period, appears as income gains, corresponds to a sort of 'unconscious' (not 'forced') saving performed during the period. The individual doesn't know his real income, and therefore he is a saver.

The difference between the actual and the planned investment has its ground in the fact that the value of the producer's capital stock has increased through unforseen events during the period. The producer has, for example, been more successful in his production than he originally expected, and through this he has increased his stock. But the stock can also have increased through an unforeseen event of less favourable character, that is, through a reduction of sales. The term $(I'-I)$ has, therefore, no definite meaning as regards the behaviour of the entrepreneurs.

Whereas these now characterized differences are a *result* of what has happened during the period, the difference between the planned investment and the planned saving which quantities both are given at the beginning of the period, has a *causal* significance as regards this process. The relation between these terms is therefore of importance for the analysis at its present stage.

The last equation makes it evident that $(I-S)$ is equal to the difference between the value of the goods that actually have been delivered during the period and the value of the goods that the producers at the beginning of the period expected to deliver. The actual events have, in other words, surpassed the expectations of the entrepreneurs in this respect. The result of this will be income gains for the producers, that is, a positive value of the expression $(E'-E)$, if that is not prevented by an increase of the depreciation term D'. In that latter case, the only immediate effect of the excess of planned investment over planned saving will be a diminishing of the stocks of the producers.

It is instructive to study a little more in detail how the situation of producers in different stages is affected by a difference between I and S. From the equations (1)–(4) we can extract the following:

$$Ea'-Ea+Da'-Da = E-S-PaTa$$
$$Eb'-Eb+Db'-Db = Ia+Da-PbTb$$
$$\dots\dots\dots\dots\dots\dots\dots\dots\dots\dots\dots\dots\dots\dots$$
$$En'-En+Dn'-Dn = Im+Dm-PnTn$$
$$O = In+Dn$$

$$\overline{E'-E+D'-D = E+D-PT+I-S = I-S}$$

We see here that the amount of planned saving is of direct importance only for the producers of consumption goods and services and that the investments terms only affect the producers of capital goods. If a positive value of $(I-S)$ is ceteris paribus caused only by a diminished value of S, that is, an increase of $(E-S)$ in relation to the expectations of the producers of the a stage expressed by the term $PaTa$, then the whole gain will go to these producers of consumption goods, if we for the moment neglect the reactions of the other terms. On the other hand, if only some

I-terms are increased but S is unchanged, then the producers in the nearest higher stages who sell the capital goods to the investors in question, will reap the whole benefit.

When the conditions for an *economic equilibrium* are discussed in the terms of savings and investment, it seems most appropriate to define these terms as S and I above. That implies that $(E-S)$ and $(D+I)$ signify the actual demand for consumption respecting capital goods, to be delivered during the period at prices previously offered by the respective producers.

Regarding this discussion, we here restrict ourselves to the following remarks. If the future were perfectly foreseen by all individuals, then of course I must be equal to S. In other more realistic cases, the equality between these quantities is neither a necessary nor a sufficient condition for an economic equilibrium, supposed that the equilibrium is not *defined* in such a way that the expectations of the producers should be realized.

It is, for example, possible to imagine a fairly stationary state where the production and consumption are carried on after similar lines year by year, but where the expectations of the producers are never realized to the full extent, and where, therefore, S permanently is greater than I. Being of an optimistic nature, the entrepreneurs during every period *hope* that the result in the future will be better than in the past, in spite of the fact that these hopes in times past always were disappointed. As such a situation, from a certain point of view, can be called an equilibrium, it follows, that $I = S$ is not a *necessary* condition for such an equilibrium.

Nor is it a *sufficient* condition. $I = S$ implies only that the *sum* of all expected delivery should be equal to the *total* value of the transactions actually brought about during the period. But even if that is the case, there can be on the one side positive and on the other side negative differences between the realized and the expected selling values that can be characterized as disturbances not compatible with the equilibrium concept. If in the stationary case just considered, where S was permanently greater than I, an equality between these terms is brought about for a certain period, for example through a lowering of the interest rate, than there would probably be a movement of factors from consumption to capital industries, breaking the former stationary conditions.

A more full discussion of this question should necessitate a definition of the term 'economic equilibrium' which seems, even from a pure monetary point of view, to be very difficult regarding a society of non-stationary character and with imperfect foresight of the future.

The Relation between Quantities, referring to
different Periods of Time

So far our reasoning has only led to the conclusion that, if certain quantities, referring to a fairly short period, are given at the beginning of that period, it is possible to determine other quantities referring to the same period but based on calculations made at the end of the period. Of course this does not represent the whole solution of the dynamic problem as it has been stated above. On the basis of the situation at the point t, the situation at the point $t+1$ has been determined only with reference to certain calculations for the period running from t to $t+1$. Thus the task remains to determine the calculations at the point $t+1$ that refer to the next period, running from $t+1$ to $t+2$.

For solving this problem, it is necessary to know more than the ex post quantities for the first period that have been determined above, that is, the terms T', $(E'+D')$, $(I'+D')$, and $(E'-S')$. When the individuals at the point $t+1$ alter the plans for production and consumption that have been valid from the point t, they are influenced by a more exhaustive knowledge of what has happened during the past period than is expressed by the terms just stated. First, then, more data are requisite regarding the past period. Secondly, one should also know how the individuals in their planning react on the basis of these data.

By a theoretical treatment of the problem, various *assumptions* may be made regarding both the further data requisite for the past period and the individual reactions, expressed in the modification of their plans for production and consumption. Which assumptions are necessary regarding the former data, depends on the character of the assumptions made regarding the reactions. For example, if in the latter respect it is assumed that, if the output is not altered through exterior events, the new terms P, $E-S$ and $D+I$ that are a result of the plans of action valid for the second period, can be expressed as mathematical functions of the same terms referring to the first period, then the only assumption regarding the data that is necessary for the solution of the problem, is unaltered technical conditions for the production.

By proceeding from the second to the third period, and from the third to the fourth and so on, new assumptions must be made in the same respects. If these are stated in the same manner for all periods, then the whole dynamic process can be deduced from the data, given at the beginning of the first period. It should, however, be remarked that, even in that oversimplified case, the dynamic process as a whole is not a continuous one, but that, from a theoretical point of view, it consists of *two* types of movements: first the events during certain *periods* of time, and, secondly, the events at the transition *points* between these periods. The determining of these latter *discontinuous* changes, that is, the alterations of the plans of production and consumption, especially as regards the supply prices and the producers' and the consumers' demand for goods and services, may be regarded as the central part of the dynamic theory.

23 October 1934   ERIK LINDAHL

To E. LINDAHL, *8 December 1934*

Dear Professor Lindahl,

Many thanks for sending me your note on the dynamic pricing problem. As you may suppose, there is much in this which I find sympathetic. Indeed, I have been using recently a notation not very different from yours, except that I take the capital letter unqualified to mean the actually realised price and add a dash to indicate the expected price; whereas yours is the other way round.

I am inclined to think, however, that your way of dealing with time leads to undue complications and will be very difficult either to apply or to generalise about.

Yours sincerely,
[Copy initialled] J. M. K.

The second exchange of letters occurred with R. B. Bryce, who was then a research student in Cambridge.

From R. B. BRYCE, *3 July 1935*

Dear Mr Keynes,

I am sending you herewith a copy of a paper I prepared for Dr Hayek's seminar at the London School of Economics and which I discussed there at four of their meetings. I might add their chief difficulties were with the definitions of income and investment, with the concept of the propensity to spend, and with the way in which equilibrium would establish itself again after, say, an increase in the quantity of money. On the whole, however, they seemed able to understand it and were quite interested.

There is probably nothing new in this paper to you, but I thought it might interest you to see how your ideas are taken up and then put down in slightly different form by research students here.

Before leaving the country for a couple of years,[22] I should like to thank you for the considerable interest and pleasure which I have derived from being a member of your Political Economy Club, and also for your kindness in other ways.

Yours sincerely,

R. B. BRYCE

AN INTRODUCTION TO A MONETARY THEORY
OF EMPLOYMENT

This paper is an attempt to give an example of the type of monetary theory held by Research Students in Cambridge. It represents only my own views on the matter. These have been very largely influenced by Mr Keynes['s] lectures and subsequent discussion in Cambridge, but they cannot be taken in any way as a statement of even what I believe Mr Keynes['s] views to be. I have not seen nor heard any part of his forthcoming book on the subject, except what may have been in his lectures or other publications. The present paper does not attempt to go deeply into all the points involved, nor can it in so short a compass clear up all the difficulties, but it aims at setting forth the general principles as clearly and concisely as possible.

I

The general purpose of the theory is to explain the determination of, and thereby changes in, total employment and production, and to trace its relation to the amount of investment (capital formation), the rate of interest and the quantity of money. In doing so a new theory of the determination of interest rates is involved, and a new approach to price level problems is opened up—though not explored. The method is such as to be of some use in analysing the process of change as well as the requirements of equilibrium.

The basic divergence of this theory from orthodox equilibrium theory is that while it retains the primary postulate that the self-interest of entrepreneurs maintains the marginal productivity of labour in all its uses equal to the wage rate (or to marginal labour cost), nevertheless it rejects the assumption that the action of labour maintains the marginal disutility

[22] Bryce was about to go to Harvard.

132

of labour equal to the wage (or, to the marginal income). For the theory is interested in a world where unemployment may be present, and unemployment we understand to mean the existence of labour not employed but willing to work for a money wage worth in real goods as much as or less than the present money wage. When such unemployment is present the marginal disutility of labour in all uses cannot be equal to the wage. The present theory assumes usually, though it can deal with all cases, that unemployment can exist without causing money wages to fall; and it denies that a general fall in money wages leads to a fall in real wages except indirectly through its effects on investment and the distribution of income.

That unemployment as above defined often exists in the real world without causing significant reductions in money wages let alone real wages, is only too obvious. It includes of course those unemployed because their Trade Union holds out for a given money wage but not for a given real wage. Incidentally it is worth noting the fundamental difficulty involved in trying to use orthodox equilibrium theory to explain the amount and causation of unemployment when one of its fundamental postulates denies the possibility of unemployment.

The present theory holds that money is of considerable significance in determining employment. On reflection I think it only has this importance because labour so often sets its supply price in money rather than real terms—or else custom or policy prevents reductions in money wage rates.

In this paper I shall assume until section (V) that the general level of money wages remains unchanged and that the supply of labour at this wage is elastic up to the point where it is all employed. Differences in value of labour will be considered rather as differences in amount, e.g., a skilled workman getting £6 a week is considered as twice as much labour as an unskilled man at £3. Because the best men to be had for the going wages are likely to be in employment and in the most productive situations, an increase in employment will reduce the efficiency and therefore the marginal productivity of labour, and the real wage—but not the money wage—that will be offered and accepted. I shall also assume a closed system for simplicity of exposition, until section (VI) is reached.

The definitions now used in Cambridge are much more in accord with the ordinary usage of terms than formerly but a clear understanding of them is essential to the argument. So far as possible only those terms have been used whose quantitative character is clearly observable, though the actual delimitations may have to be somewhat arbitrary.

Employment we have defined above, as the number of men working multiplied by their time and made commensurable one with another by considering one man to be providing more labour per unit time than another if he gets a greater wage per unit of time. Thus if W be the rate of money wages for a given kind of labour (e.g., common road labour) chosen as standard then the total employment is equal to total wage bill divided by W. N is used as the symbol for total employment.

Income is defined as the money receipts of all individuals in the community in the given period of time (or as a rate at a point of time) accruing to them for their productive services or rights *used* during that period (or at that point of time). These receipts are considered to include those not actually paid over—for example wages earned but not paid till the end of the week, or profits earned but not paid till the end of the year and so forth. Some difficulty may be found in the exact delimitation of income, especially the residual income of the entrepreneurs but as long as any reasonable limit is taken and used consistently it will not affect the validity of the argument. Changes in the value of existing assets due to changes in expectations of future value, to changes in the rate of interest, or to events not caused by the process of production should be excluded from income in any case.

It is perhaps worth while to notice that income has two aspects. First it is received by individuals, either in money, in kind or in equities for their services, and they must dispose of it between saving and expenditure on consumption. Secondly it is paid out by entrepreneurs (including of course their own profits which may be in a real form) in the production of goods and services for present consumption and future use. What the entrepreneurs 'pay out' including profits must be exactly equal to what they 'receive' from the sale of what has been produced or the retention of assets at their market value, losses being of course negative income 'paid' to themselves.

The next essential term is expenditure. This is defined as the amount spent by individuals from their income for consumption goods, i.e., for goods which they intend to use themselves, during the given period (or as a rate at the given point of time). As in the case of income the exact boundaries of what is to be considered expenditure must be arbitrary, but only a consistent usage is required for this argument.

Both investment and savings are defined as the difference between income and expenditure, when both relate to the same period or point of time. Strange as this may appear at first sight it is quite in accord with common sense. From the point of view of individuals as receivers of income their savings at any time are what they receive as income less what they spend on consumption. From the point of view of production that amount of money is being invested which is being paid out in production (including any profits being drawn, normal or abnormal, positive or negative) but which is not balanced by current receipts from the sale of consumption goods. We should recall in this connection that the net income earned and paid out in producing consumption goods in any period is no more and no less than the receipts from the sale of consumption goods in that period, i.e., expenditure. Consumption goods produced in excess of current sales are part of investment. And of course in real terms a society can only save what it is creating over and above consumption, and must be 'investing' (whether voluntarily or accidentally) those of its efforts which are not being used to satisfy present consumption.

Of course by these definitions, savings and investment, being just different aspects of the same thing must be equal at all times and under any conditions. Their equality is 'guaranteed' so to speak by the definition of income and effectuated by the variation in income. For example, if part of the community is 'saving' more than total investment, the other part must be 'dissaving' to the extent of the difference, selling assets to the first part to finance their own expenditure, so that net saving remains equal to investment and total income is still the sum of investment and expenditure.*

The next and very important term is the propensity to spend (or its converse the propensity to save). This refers to the desire of the community to divide its income between saving and expenditure on consumption goods. It is defined as the function relating the amount that the community will spend to the amount of their income, i.e. if Y is income and C expenditure, $C = F(Y)$ where F is the propensity to spend. The propensity to save can be deduced from this—since savings must always equal income minus expenditure.

The propensity to spend will depend upon the preferences of individuals as between saving and spending, i.e. their time preference; on the amount of real income represented by the money income, i.e. the level of prices; particularly upon the distribution of income as between individuals and classes with different preferences; on expectations of future conditions, and on the rate of interest. In turn, as we shall see the propensity to spend itself influences these other factors.

It is necessary to make one fundamental assumption about the propensity to spend but it seems very likely to be true of the real world. This is, that if incomes increase, savings must also increase, not necessarily as a proportion of income but absolutely. Therefore if incomes increase

---

* Investment as here used is essentially the same as used in the *Treatise on Money* but Saving is different—being equal to the sum of 'Savings' and 'Profits' as there defined.

expenditure on consumption may increase but it cannot increase by as much as incomes, as long as the propensity to spend remains the same.

It will be convenient too, to have a term which we shall call the supply curve, or supply function of consumption goods, although it actually will only represent an aggregation of many supply curves for individual firms. This function will relate the quantity of labour which will be employed in making consumption goods, N_1, to the expenditure on consumption goods C. It is possible of course that actual employment and expenditure may diverge from those associated values given by this curve in so far as entrepreneurs make mistakes in estimating the future expenditure. However we will assume that the curve is the short-period equilibrium curve so that any deviation of expenditure off this curve will lead to an adjustment of employment to that amount required by this equilibrium condition. The curve will be determined by all the technical and cost conditions, and demand conditions for each firm as well. A similar curve may be conceived for employment on investment goods—relating the number employed there, N_2, to the money volume of investment. These two curves will be interrelated, and the distinction between what labour belongs on one and what on the other is one of type only and the dividing line arbitrary. We shall assume in each case—and it seems quite reasonable —that higher quantities of employment are associated with higher expenditure or investment (i.e. that the 'elasticity of supply' is not less than 1).

II

We come now with a fairly complete set of terms to the first step in the analysis of how employment is determined. Now in truth all our quantities,—employment, income, investment, expenditure and our functions—the propensity to spend and the supply curves of consumption and investment as well as others that will be later introduced, are interrelated and hence the actual determination of the quantities must come as the working out these interrelationships. We *could* only find what they would be by solving a number of simultaneous equations, and could only observe the effect of a change by noting how it worked through or changes these equations. In this respect the problem is like that of the general equilibrium theory of value. But just as the general theory of value can be broken up to observe the working of, and conditions of equilibrium within, one part of it, so this general theory of employment can be taken apart to see how it works, and the conditions of equilibrium found within certain regions of analysis. It is only by doing so that we shall ever be able to know what happens in the whole.

Therefore let us begin by assuming that the amount of investment, the supply functions of consumption and investment goods, and the propensity to spend are given. Then we can show that income, expenditure and employment are determined by these data. For the amount of investment being given, income must be such as to yield that amount of saving, with the given propensity to save and spend. Any other income would be incompatible with one or other of the two conditions, and as we shall show in a moment, any attempt to change this income—as by mistakes on the part of the entrepreneurs—will produce forces that will lead back to this equilibrium value. Income and the propensity to spend being then determined and given, expenditure must be determined. Expenditure being determined and the supply function of consumable goods, the employment in producing consumable goods is determined. Because investment and the supply function of investment goods are known, employment in investment is easily determined. Therefore total employment is determined.

None but this unique value of employment will satisfy all the conditions. If employment in consumption industry were different while the propensity to spend remained the same, income from producing consumption goods would be no larger—the reduction in income of the entrepreneurs off-setting the increase in wage income, in the case where employment was greater than the equilibrium level. Expenditure would not be greater than the equilibrium value, and therefore entrepreneurs would reduce employment toward the equilibrium value. Similarly if employment were less than the determined value, income and net savings would be the same—the reduced income of others being balanced by increased entre-preneurial income. Expenditure would be no less than before, so that competition between entrepreneurs would expand employment toward the equilibrium level. It can now be seen why our fundamental assumption about the propensity to spend (on p. 3 [p. 135]) is necessary—for if when income increased expenditure increased equally then the output of consumption goods would be in neutral equilibrium, for an increase in employment could generate sufficient expenditure to maintain itself. It is because this is not the case that unemployment can persist in a state of at least short period equilibrium, and that the actual amount of employment is a function of investment.

While it is true that employment cannot increase without a change in some one of these five things, a change in any one of them will cause a change in employment. Thus an increase in the propensity to spend will increase expenditure, incomes and employment in consumption. There-fore anything which increases the propensity to spend may increase employment, and similarly for a decrease. Therefore in so far as chance variations, mistakes perhaps of entrepreneurs, increase employment beyond equilibrium and in doing so change the distribution of income, they may change the propensity to spend and thus total incomes, while saving remains the same. Hence for a stable equilibrium we need to stipulate that temporary variations in employment shall not permanently increase the propensity to spend and particularly that an increase in employment beyond the equilibrium value shall not cause enough redistribution of income to increase the propensity to spend sufficiently to increase expenditure to that value which will hold employment at its new level. It seems hardly likely that a change in employment will produce such a change in the distribution of income if it is a movement to another point on the supply curve of output; but if it is a movement off the supply curve—so that entrepreneurs are making unexpected profits or losses, the distribution itself will only be temporary so that the change in the propensity to spend will also be temporary, and equilibrium will be stable.

The supply functions of consumption and investment goods are determined largely by technical conditions and relative demands. When labour is in elastic supply changes in wage rates will not be arising to influence it—although the varying efficiency of the labour available will do so. The propensity to spend, though dependent to some extent on expectations and the rate of interest will be largely determined by personal and technical considerations and customs, and will be affected by the supply functions through their influence on the distribution of incomes. All these factors, though subject to change from time to time are relatively stable, except perhaps in so far as the propensity to spend is upset by changes in expectations and 'mass psychology'. It is investment, the remaining determinant of employment, whose changes are more important in real life and it is to the determination of investment we now turn.

III

There is probably less new in the present theory regarding the determination of investment than on other matters, so it will be dealt with more briefly. However it must be stressed that up to the state of full employment of labour and other productive resources, an increase in investment, as was shown in the last section need not be accompanied by a reduction of consumption—as orthodox theory assumes—but rather it will usually be accompanied by an increase in consumption.

Now, some of the excess of income over expenditure, that is investment, may be created by entrepreneurs unwillingly—as for example when unsold stocks accumulate. But in general investment is only undertaken when the demand for the investment goods or services (investment can be made in such intangible things as 'goodwill' by means of advertising) is sufficient to induce their voluntary production. This demand is derived from the expected future yield of these investment goods—whether they be stocks of wheat, machinery or houses. And this applies not only to that investment which is new capital—if such can be separated from the total— but to any replacement or maintenance expenditure which is only made because it is expected to yield a future return.*

Because investment goods are demanded only for their future return, the demand price will depend not only upon the more or less uncertain expectation of this future return but also on the rate of interest at which this return must be discounted in order to arrive at its present value, which will be the demand price. This rate of interest used in discounting must be equal to the market rate of interest for loans for the same period of time. Otherwise there will be either a clear profit to be made simply in borrowing to create the investment and repaying the loan from the anticipated future return,† or, if the rate of interest is higher it would pay to lend money rather than use it in the purchase of the investment.

Thus the demand for investment goods depends upon two things,—their expected future returns, or as Mr Keynes has called it, the expectation of quasi rents, and the rate of interest. Given then the supply function of investment goods (discussed in section I) their output is determined by the supply and demand. They will be produced up to the margin where the cost of production of the good in question is equal to the sum of the future incomes it yields discounted at the market rates of interest for the appropriate periods. Keynes has summed it up by defining that rate of interest which equates the present value of the expected quasi-rents of a possible bit of investment to its cost of production as the efficiency of capital in that use, and then states that investment will be pushed to the point where the marginal efficiency of capital equals the rate of interest. Because the most profitable investments will be made rather than others, the marginal efficiency of capital must decline as the amount of investment in a given period increases, e.g. if 400 million £ a year can be profitably

* The exact line drawn between consumption production and investment production must of course be arbitrary and is a practical and statistical rather than theoretical problem. It is related of course to the distinction between expenditure and saving.
† Due allowance must be made here both for risk, i.e. the mathematical expectation of the return must be used, and also for uncertainty and the cost of bearing it.

invested at 4%, then in order that 600 million £ can be invested the rate will have to fall—perhaps to 3 or 2½%.

Thus investment on a given period is determined by the estimated marginal efficiency of capital and the rate of interest. Other things will influence it only through their influence on one of these—as in the case of the ordinary determination of price by demand and supply. The actual amount of present incomes—as well as the state of business confidence may of course influence the expectation of quasi-rents and hence the amount of investment by way of the marginal efficiency of capital. Changes in working capital are of course part of investment and they depend very largely on present and immediate future incomes. The volume of employment in producing consumption goods will also affect investment through affecting the cost of production of capital and thus its marginal efficiency. Of course in a condition of full employment, or when wage rates are not assumed fixed but can vary with employment, this latter consideration is most important.

The fact that much investment is made in the expectation of returns in the distant future, of which our knowledge must be very small, means that the amount of investment will be quite sensitive to changes in 'business confidence' and uncertainty in regard to the general economic outlook. Therefore, and because of the importance of investment in determining employment and income, the whole employment situation is quite sensitive to all the caprices of 'market psychology' and the political and other factors influencing it.

IV

We come now to the determination of the interest rate and here we may pause to examine the inadequacy of the orthodox interest rate theory (as presented, say, by Fisher) in an economy where unemployment is present. This classical theory says, in brief, that the interest rate is determined by the supply and demand for new savings or 'free capital'. The amounts the public and corporations would save at various interest rates are said to give one a supply curve (its actual shape need not detain us here) while the amount of investment, which forms the demand for savings in terms of the interest rate it will yield, is so to give the demand curve. Assuming a perfect market the interest rate will settle at that figure which equates the supply and demand.

However we have seen that savings and investment must always be equal at any rate of interest simply because both of them are the surplus of income over consumption expenditure, and that any tendency for them to diverge is checked by changes in income or its distribution. Now it is true that both the time preference of the consumer and the marginal productivity (or efficiency) of capital must always equal the rate of interest. But this is not enough to determine it, though as we shall see it sets a lower limit to the rate that can be maintained without serious inflation. What does happen is that the time preference adjusts itself to the rate of interest by a variation in income and the proportion of it saved, while the marginal productivity (or efficiency) of capital adjusts itself to the rate of interest by variations in the amount of investment.* It is only because the orthodox theory always assumes a condition of full employment that it can explain the rate of interest in this simple manner. But as we have observed these assumptions are not only unreal but absurd since they rule out the very things that are of most interest.

Searching then for the actual determinants of the interest rate it is not surprising to find them much closer to the money market in the supply of and demand for money stocks. Interest is not the reward for all saving or 'not-spending' but rather and more directly important, it is the reward for 'investing' or not hoarding savings. Hence it is the price paid by an individual (or corporation) for holding his wealth in the form of money rather than as income bearing assets. An individual, either consumer or entrepreneur, derives utility of some kind from holding money, the nature of which we will examine in a moment. In order that he should be in equilibrium the marginal utility of holding money must be equal to the marginal return he can get by investing it, which is the market rate of interest. Therefore we can draw up a schedule or demand curve showing the amount of money that any individual or market will hold at various rates of interest, under given conditions including of course the whole complex of present and expected future prices. If now there is a given supply of money, or supply curve of money in terms of the rate of interest, then the equilibrium rate is determined by the intersection of these two curves.

Should the rate of interest be greater than this equilibrium level people will attempt to buy income-yielding assets, bonds and equities, in order to get the rate of interest. But if their demand curve for money remains fixed the money and capital market will only be in equilibrium when the price of bonds and shares (and short term bills etc.) has been driven up by this competition to buy them to the point where the yield on them is equal to this marginal utility of the given quantity of money. In so far as the fall

* These adjustments will very likely affect liquidity preference and hence the rate of interest as well.

in the interest rate through its effects on investment, employment and incomes increases the marginal utility of the given quantity of money, it reduces the distance the interest rate must fall. Similarly if the rate of interest were less than the marginal utility of holding money stocks the market will attempt to sell income-yielding assets until their yield has increased to equal this marginal utility, which now may be reduced by the effects of the rising interest rate. Thus the rate of interest is not the price balancing saving and investment but rather that balancing the supply and demand for money stocks; it must be such as to bring equilibrium between the desire to hold wealth in the form of money and in the form of income-yielding assets. The speed of business on the capital market enables this equilibrium to be quickly adapted to rapidly changing circumstances.

This demand for money stocks in terms of the rate of interest has been called by Mr Keynes 'Liquidity Preference'.* This follows from the fact that the utility yielded by these money stocks is what is rather vaguely known as 'liquidity'. This consists of the convenience and certainty of having a store of value in the form of means of payment to make purchases or to meet debts. The desire for this liquidity, in conjunction with many objective conditions and estimates of the future, gives rise to the demand for money stocks. These other factors conditioning the demand include expectations and uncertainty in regard to interest rates, prices and obligations in the future, the present levels of wages prices and employment, the methods and costs of making payments and capital transacting and other factors influencing 'market psychology'.

It is through its effect on the rate of interest that the quantity of money actually affects investment, incomes, employment and prices. The relationship of the quantity of money to any of these latter elements is rather complex so that it is no wonder that the simple directness of the quantity theory of money could shed little light on what actually happens.

Changes in the quantity of money, in so far as they affect expectations and 'market psychology' may in themselves alter liquidity preference and the demand for money, so that actually the rate of interest may be

---

* I prefer to use the term 'demand for money', as the actual demand may be regarded as the result of the subjective preferences of individuals together with all the objective conditions such as income, prices, costs of transactions, uncertainties etc. On the other hand must be set the fact that the interest rate must under all these conditions be equal to the amount of preference.

† Expectations of changes in prices will be rather complex in their effects, in so far as they do not directly influence the relative desiredness of holding stocks of money and money-credits. They do influence the profitability of holding any form of fixed money asset, but only in so far as the present prices of future goods are not altered in accordance with the changed expectation of future prices.

unchanged, or even perversely changed; but the cases where this would happen seem likely to be rare, even if perhaps important in times of crises. We will show later that the marginal efficiency of capital and the consumers time-preference as expressed through the propensity to save, set a lower limit to the rate of interest if inflation is to be avoided. We may note too that changes in time preference and the marginal efficiency of capital will affect incomes and prices and thereby the demand for money and the rate of interest. If the marginal efficiency of capital increases and people prepare to increase the amount of investment there will be an increased demand for funds through the sale of new investment securities. This will usually mean an increase in the demand for money stocks of the group carrying on new investment before the increased incomes are actually created from which the increased saving equal to the new investment will come. This will tend to depress the price level of securities and increase the rate of interest, perhaps even above the level that will be in equilibrium when the demand for money returns to what is normal at the higher level of investment and incomes. In other words, the demand for money stocks is apt to be unusually high while investment is increasing.

If we relax our simplifying assumption of an unchanging level of money wages, we may observe that the demand for money will be a function of the level of money wages; both directly in so far as much money is held against wage payments, and also because the price level is a function of the wage level. A general fall in money wage rates in a depression will likely lead to less requirements for money and hence a fall in the rate of interest if the money supply is not decreased, and hence more investment and employment. It may be checked by other factors, such as for example, an expectation of further wage reductions which would tend to deter investment. But we should note that this beneficial effect of the wage reduction could be had simply by increasing the quantity of money with none of the great difficulties of wage deflation.

v

We have now covered the main essentials of the theory and can pause to review it a little by tracing the effects of changes, before we go on to consider some special cases and to remove the assumptions made to simplify the argument. For our first example consider the probable effects of an increase in the quantity of money, other things remaining the same except as they are affected by the changed money supply. The banks will increase the quantity of money through the extension of their advances

143

and the purchase of securities. Both of these tend to decrease the rate of interest directly. But more important, the receivers of money in the community will find their money stocks increasing and will try to buy securities and to some extent consumption goods as well, thus decreasing the rate of interest and perhaps increasing the propensity to spend. The fall in the rate of interest will increase investment, which with given, or possibly increased, propensity to spend will increase incomes and expenditure and therefore the employment in producing consumption goods as well as in investment goods. In so far as the fall in the rate of interest also affects the propensity to spend it may either add to or detract from the increase in expenditure and employment. The fall in the interest rate will finally be checked by an increasing demand for money with increasing incomes and employment so that a new position of equilibrium will be established with greater employment and real income than the first.

As another example suppose that the propensity to spend should increase. This will increase expenditure and incomes investment being still the same. The increased expenditure will increase the output of consumption goods, and employment. In addition the greater present demand for consumption will likely increase the expectation of future quasi-rents and therefore increase investment. However the rise in incomes will increase the demand for money and thereby tend to increase the rate of interest and tend to check, or even reduce investment. Again the new equilibrium will be established with more employment.

Finally take the case where there is a fall in expectations of quasi-rents, and therefore in the marginal efficiency of capital, other things again being supposed to remain the same except as they are influenced by this change. The fall in the marginal efficiency of capital will reduce investment and therefore incomes and expenditure. The first effect of this will be a fall in profits and then a contraction of output and employment will follow both in consumption and investment production. This fall will be checked by a fall in the demand for money and a consequent reduction in the rate of interest which in turn will check the decrease in investment and bring equilibrium at a lower level of investment, employment and incomes.

We should notice that the accumulation of capital in modern economies tends to reduce the opportunities for profitable new investment and therefore reduce the marginal efficiency of capital, except in so far as this is offset by invention. At the same time the increase in real income tends to increase the amount saved at any given level of employment. Consequently we should expect a chronic tendency to under-employment except in so far as the rate of interest falls to offset these two tendencies. If money wages are not reduced this fall in the interest rate will require a steady increase in the quantity of money since the demand for money is likely to increase with real income, though we cannot say in what proportion.

VI

Relaxing now our simplifying assumption of a closed system we look to see how foreign trade and foreign investment fit into this theory. It becomes evident that the excess of exports over imports (including 'invisible' items) is equivalent to investment in its effect on incomes and employment. For the production and sale of exports creates incomes available for spending and saving in our country while the buying of imports reduces the amount of income available for investment or expenditure on home-produced goods. Now this surplus of exports over imports, which we shall call the foreign balance, must be balanced on the exchange market by an equivalent amount of foreign lending (long or short term) or imports of gold.* Both the foreign lending and the imports of gold appear as saving to the home country, which saving is exactly equal to the investment comprised in the foreign balance. Therefore not only is total saving necessarily equal to total investment but 'foreign' saving is always equal to 'foreign' investment, and 'home' saving equal to 'home' investment.

The foreign balance is determined in a different way to the rest of investment and one must analyse it separately. It depends on all the multitude of factors which determine foreign trade, foreign lending and gold movements. It will require the willingness of people to lend abroad (or import gold) in order to exist at all, and its magnitude will depend on their readiness to do so, since that will affect the exchange rate. It will depend upon the level of costs and prices at home and abroad and the rates of exchange. More important in these days it will depend upon tariffs, quotas and exchange restrictions. The rate of interest will influence [it] through affecting peoples' willingness to lend abroad, and also by affecting home investment and thereby incomes and costs, which in turn will influence the demand for imports and the supply conditions of exports. Finally it depends on conditions and events abroad, in fact it is hard to think of anything which does not influence it.

Because the foreign balance is equivalent to investment it is important in its influence on total income and is the principal means by which depression or prosperity is passed from country to country. To some

* Gifts and reparations may be treated as invisible imports if they are made from what would otherwise be expenditure, or as part of foreign lending if they are financed from savings.

145

countries its changes are more important than those in home investment in their effects on incomes and employment. And in such countries even when the foreign balance does not alter a considerable change in exports and imports may have serious effects on the supply conditions of investment and consumption goods and on the propensity to spend, and for both reasons on employment and production.

The foreign balance is not so closely related to change in the amount of money and the rate of interest as is home investment. Interest rates will affect (and be affected by) international capital movements, i.e. foreign lending, and thereby the exchange rate or gold movements. Thus, for example, an attempt to increase home investment by increasing the quantity of money and the rate of interest will increase the readiness of owners of wealth to lend abroad. This will reduce the exchange rate, increasing exports and diminishing imports therefore increasing the foreign balance. In so far as the country attempts to maintain the parity of its foreign exchanges it will have to export (or reduce its imports of) gold or reduce its other foreign lending (or borrow from abroad). In this case the foreign balance will have no tendency to increase, and the rise in costs and incomes at home will probably decrease it.

It may be noted that the technique of managing the foreign balance has been greatly developed in recent years and far more attention has been paid to it than to maintaining home investment. A positive foreign balance for one country must of course be equalised somewhere else by negative foreign balances. Therefore a gain in employment in one country due to it increasing its foreign balance is apt to be offset in part at least by a reduction somewhere else where the opposite change occurs in the balance. Differences in the propensity to spend, as well as in more indirect effects will mean differences in the size of the changes at home and abroad following from equal but opposite changes in the foreign balance so that changes in foreign trade can bring about net increases or decreases in world employment.

When the foreign balance is considered, changes in the general level of money wages may have considerable influence on investment and income when exchanges are stable. Thus reduction in money wages will reduce the cost of exporting and reduce the ability to buy imports and hence increase the foreign balance and employment. But just as no more advantage in employment could be obtained in a closed system by cutting wages than by increasing the quantity of money, little more is to be gained in an open economy by cutting money wages than by depreciating the exchange rate. We may notice also that both actions are likely to lead to similar action abroad.

VII

A few remarks about what happens when there is no unemployment will show how this monetary theory fits in with the classical theory. Under this condition of full employment the wage is equal both to the marginal productivity of labour and its marginal disutility, in all employments.* The supply of labour will now be somewhat elastic in terms of real wages but not in terms of money wages alone. However an increase in output by increasing employment could only yield a smaller real wage, so that it is not possible.

Even in this condition all we have said holds good about income depending upon investment and the propensity to spend—but we must remember that they are defined in money terms, and that real income cannot now be increased. However a decrease in investment will still lead to a reduction of income and, therefore, of expenditure on consumption goods, and as a consequence a decrease of output and employment in both investment and consumption goods. Thus to a movement in this direction the general remarks apply.

However it is the effects of a possible increase in investment that are now interesting. Suppose that a new discovery enables capital to be made more productive and this increases its marginal efficiency, and therefore investment begins to increase. This will increase incomes, expenditure and savings in terms of money. But now the money demand for both investment and consumption goods has increased while employment cannot increase. Entrepreneurs faced with this increased demand, and probably getting abnormally high profits, will compete for the available labour supply by bidding up money wage rates; but while these wage rates rise, prices rise as well and real wages are unchanged.† The increase in wages and prices will increase the demand for money and hence the rate of interest unless the quantity of money is increased to offset the increased demand.

In so far as employment has now increased in the production of investment goods it must have decreased in producing consumption goods. This means people must be saving a larger fraction of their unchanged real income. To some extent the rise in the rate of interest may induce them to do this and increased real investment will be possible with equilibrium.

---

* Due allowance of course being made for rent elements in wages, for imperfection in the labour market, for the divergence of long and short period productivity and transfer costs, and for uneconomic behaviour.

† The new invention will probably enable some increase in real wages to be paid, but this can be neglected, especially if we suppose the invention to be one increasing the future productivity of capital.

147

But if investment is greater than this possible equilibrium level then the increase in the amount saved will be due to unexpected changes or to an unstable distribution of incomes; for it seems unreasonable that an increase in the money value of the same real income should induce people permanently to save more of it. Therefore because real investment is more than people will save in equilibrium, people will be attempting to spend more on consumption than is necessary to maintain its output, and hence the consumption industries will be attempting to expand and bidding up the level of wages in trying to draw labour from investment industries. Prices and wages will be driven higher, increasing further the demand for money.

If now the supply of money is limited the rate of interest will rise until investment is checked and reduced to the amount that will be in equilibrium with the stable propensity to save, which in turn may be greater at the higher rate of interest. Equilibrium will now be possible at a higher level of wages and prices and a higher rate of interest. The increase in the marginal efficiency of capital will have increased the equilibrium level of the rate of interest and probably the amount of real income going into savings and investment.

If however the supply of money is not limited but increases so rapidly that the rate of interest remains below the new equilibrium level, then investment will continue to exceed the amount that would be in equilibrium with a stable propensity to save, and expenditure will always remain in excess of that needed to keep consumption industries in equilibrium. Hence wages and prices will increase rapidly and without limit and we will have a cumulative inflation which can only be stopped by limiting the supply of money.

Hence it can be said that the marginal efficiency of capital and the propensity to spend determine the lowest limit of the rate of interest at which equilibrium is possible. If the rate should fall below this, prices and wage rates rise until it returns, while if the rate is held below this prices and wages keep rising, at a rate dependent, in part at least, upon the divergence between the market rate and this lowest limit of the equilibrium rate. This limit we can see to be just a special case of the generalisation that the marginal efficiency of capital and the propensity to spend (that is, capital productivity and time preference) determine that rate of interest which will give any particular volume of employment up to full employment.

VIII

We may return now to clear up a few minor points ruled out by our assumption that the supply of labour was perfectly elastic. We assumed that employment could increase without an increase in the general level of money efficiency wages,—that the unemployed would come back to work at a money wage per unit of product no higher than the prevailing money wages. But obviously this may be quite untrue of the real world, and either convention or the action of labourers individually or collectively may require that the general rate of wages rises if employment increases, i.e. that the money wage supply curve of labour is rising. In this case whatever increased employment by our former argument will increase it now but in addition will increase wage rates, and similarly for decreases. The changing money wages will show themselves on steeper supply curves of employment in terms of money investment and expenditure. That is, investment and expenditure will have to increase more in order to increase employment a given amount, while the increase in wage rates and therefore prices will make the demand for money increase more rapidly with increasing employment than otherwise. However employment and output will still be determined in the same way as under our assumption of a perfectly elastic labour supply.

One further point remains. When the amount of unemployment is small in a modern progressive economy, those unemployed (in our technical sense) will consist largely of those who have been fairly recently thrown out of work by shifts in demand or changes in technique. In order to find new employment these people will probably have to accept a lower real wage for some time—as their relative efficiency will be less in the new than the old job. However it seems reasonable to expect that they will resist this for a while and spend some time in looking for work paying a money wage equal to what they used to get, and that they will gradually reduce the money wage which they would be willing to accept until they find a job. Now it will be seen that if money wage rates generally are rising those techno- logically unemployed will find work at a satisfying money wage sooner than if wage rates were stable and therefore they will spend less time unemployed and hence total employment will be greater with rising than with constant wage rates. The more rapidly wages are rising under these conditions the less time men will spend looking for work and therefore the greater will be total employment, until we approach completely full employment as a theoretical limit attainable only with rapidly rising wages.

In order that wage rates should be permanently rising in this manner and the economy be in equilibrium the money value of investment, income and expenditure must be also rising, and the rate of interest somewhat lower than that rate which would give maximum employment with constant money wages. The amount of money would have to increase steadily. Price levels might be either falling or rising, depending on whether or not technical advances and the accumulation of capital were lowering marginal real labour costs more rapidly than the wage rates were increasing. Indeed it would appear that the stabilisation of a representative price level of consumption goods with fairly full employment in modern times would require this steady rise in money wages. However I can see no reason to believe that such a condition of employment with slowly but steadily rising wage rates is any more unstable than any other condition, providing only that the amount of money is being increased at the appropriate rate. It can form a consistent and desirable structure of expectations in which the need to reduce money wage rates, the notoriously sticky elements in modern economies, is reduced as near to the minimum as is practicable.

R. B. BRYCE

To R. B. BRYCE, *10 July 1935*

My dear Bryce,

Many thanks for sending me a copy of your essay. I think it is excellently done, and I am astonished that you have been able to give so comparatively complete a story within so short a space. I am not surprised that your hearers found it a bit difficult. For a theory which is unfamiliar anyhow does not become easier through compression. All the same, you have got into it the main elements in my theory.

I am interested to hear that some of their chief difficulties were with definitions. I am not at all surprised, though it is extraordinarily tiresome and boring that it should be so. In my book I have deemed it necessary to go into these matters at disproportionate length, whilst feeling that this was in a sense a great pity and might divert the readers' minds from the real issues. It is, I think, a further illustration of the appalling state of scholasticism into which the minds of so many economists have got which allow them to take leave of their intuitions altogether. Yet in writing economics one is not writing either a mathematical proof or a legal document. One is trying to arouse and appeal to the reader's intuitions; and, if he has worked himself into a state when he has none, one is helpless!

Yours sincerely,

J. M. KEYNES

Four fragments in papers relating to the composition of the *General Theory* which did not survive to publication

C = Capital goods at any time measured by their replacement cost of production, obsolete goods being appropriately written down

r = rate of interest

$C.r$ = charge of total product for interest

In a stationary society interest cannot be more than marginal productivity of capital but it may be less—it might be zero.

In a stationary communist society only charge on output necessary is for obsolescence.

In a stationary capital society there is also a charge arising out of the part bargained away to a particular section for war debts or goodwill.

In a *progressive* society there is also a charge to provide new capital. This may be done by raising rate of interest nearer to productivity or by credit cycles. Where time-preferences are such that rate of interest equals net productivity of capital, there can be no progress except by credit cycles. What determines whether a society is progressive?

It depends on the level of wages.

Social productivity of capital/productivity to entrepreneurs

n Number of workers fixed or determined by non-economic causes

x Capital not fixed but dependent on rate of interest

Units of work and capital not interchangeable in the aggregate.

Product of $n+x=y$

$$n+x+dx=y+dy$$

Marginal productivity of capital $=\dfrac{dy}{dx}$

Product of $n+dn+x=y+dy$

Marginal productivity of labour $=\dfrac{dy}{dn}$

Let rate of wages $=w$ and rate of interest $=r;$ $v=$ volume of product. Then

$$w.n+x.r=y.v$$

$$r=\frac{y-w.n}{x}$$

$$n-\frac{dy}{dr}+x-\frac{dy}{dx}=y.v$$

Suppose wages are fixed by decree at a proportion f of y so that $w.n=f.y.$ Then

$$x.r=(1-f)y$$

$$r=(1-f)\frac{y}{x}$$

NOTES ON THE RATE OF INTEREST

In order to exhibit the idea running through these notes, it is not necessary to consider the most general case. It will be assumed that the population is determined by non-economic causes in the sense that it is not a function of the rate of wages. Further it will be assumed as a first approximation that the population is stationary.

I. Consider, first, a communist society in which all the capital is owned and the saving and investment performed socially. There are a workers and b units of capital cooperating to produce c units of product. Let us suppose that the subsistence wage for the workers is q and the rate of deterioration and loss of capital is r. Then in order to maintain a stationary position, the amount of the product assigned to the workers must not be less than $q.a$ and the amount of production of new capital per annum must not be less than $r.b$. Then $c-q.a-r.b$ ($=s$) is the community's assumed surplus. They are free to choose what proportion of this they will consume in the year and what proportion they will add to capital. How will they decide? The richer they get per head, the less sacrifice but also the less advantage in further investment. Does an increment x of consumption a year hence outweigh in advantage a decrement of y of consumption now? If the society has a time-preference t, in the sense that it values well-being today at t times an equal well-being a year hence, its decision will be governed by the value of y which makes

$$f(s+y+z)+tf(s-y)-(1+t)f(s)$$

a maximum, where $f(z)$ is the social well-being derived from the consumption of a surplus z, and $y+r$ is the additional product available a year hence by saving y now. i.e. y is given by the equation

$$f'(s+y+z) = tf'(s-y).$$

On the assumption of the diminishing marginal utility of increased consumption we have

$$\frac{f(s+y+z)-f(s)}{f(s)-f(s-y)} > \frac{y+z}{y}$$

$$= \text{(say)} \; \frac{1}{k(y)}\left(\frac{y+r}{y}\right) \quad \text{where } k(y) > 1;$$

So that if $r = Q(y)$ i.e. if, additional saving y yields an additional product $Q(y)$, the decision as to the amount of saving y is given by the quotient

$$\frac{y+Q(y)}{y} = k(y).t$$

where $k(y)$ and t are not greater than 1.

This equation indicates what rate of progress it is reasonable to aim at, having regard to the productivity of saving, the rate of decrease of utility per unit of consumption, and the society's rate of time preference. It will be noticed that the *average* productivity of the aggregate of saving, and not the *marginal* productivity of saving, is the relevant factor.

The value of y given by the above equation may be the 'social rate of saving'.

II. Take now an individualistic society of the present type. $k(y)$ and t may be different for the individuals who save than for the community as a whole, owing to inequality of wealth, etc. Let us assume that this cause of divergence between the behaviour of the two societies is absent, so that all individuals are assumed to have the same $k(y)$ and t functions.

There is, however, another cause of divergence. The rate of interest paid to those who save will not be $(y+Q(y))/y$ i.e. the *average* productivity of saving y, but $(y+Q'(y))/y$ where this is the *marginal* productivity of saving y,—the difference between the average productivity of saving and its marginal productivity going as increased wages to individuals *qua* workers and not as interest to them *qua* savers.

This means that what we may term the individual rate of saving will be less than the social rate of saving. In practice this conclusion will be mitigated or aggravated according as $k(y)t$ is less or greater for those who save than for the community at large. $k(y)$ may well be less, but t, on the other hand, may easily be greater for mortal individuals than for an immortal society. It is, however, very hard to say what the relationship is between the rate of interest and the rate of saving for a present-day community with wide differences of wealth, etc.

III. The main conclusion, however, to be drawn from the above is a simple one, namely that there is no reason to suppose that the offer of a rate of interest equal to the marginal productivity of capital has any tendency whatever to stimulate the rate of saving which is socially most desirable.

NOTES ON THE MEASURE OF 'ROUNDABOUTNESS'

There are possible sources of confusion or ambiguity in the conception of 'roundaboutness' or 'length of the production period', as to which I seek instruction.

I

To begin with, let us deal with a stationary community in equilibrium; and let us assume that we know what we mean by the aggregate volume of output and the aggregate volume of capital,* as distinct from the money value of output and capital.

Let O stand for current gross output of goods and services, A for the aggregate of capital, B for the part of gross output necessary to make good the current wastage of capital if the aggregate is to remain unimpaired and O' for net output (so that $B = O - O'$).

We can then write $A = m.O = m'O' = n.B$.

Now in ordinary language it is n which measures the average life of capital. If buildings are characteristic of capital, then if buildings are made more durable, n increases. In Jevonian language A measures the 'amount of investment

---

* For example, let each be measured, as M^r· Gifford measures them above, in time units. [Presumably, C. H. P. Gifford, 'The Concept of the Length and Period of Production', *Economic Journal*, December 1933.]

of capital invested', i.e. the quantity of capital multiplied by the average length of time during which it remains invested.

When one speaks of 'lengthening the process of production' it is easy to suppose that this is the same thing as increasing n. But this is certainly not what Böhm-Bawerk and the Austrian school mean by this expression.

Let us take as our unit of time the period of production of that part of current output which has the shortest period of production. The average 'length of the production period' would then seem to be given by

$$\frac{O'x_1 + Bxy}{O} = O' + A = \frac{m}{m'}(1 + m')$$

This is, I think, substantially the same as M^r. Gifford's definition, if we suppose that capital has come into existence and is wearing out at a steady rate, so that existing capital is, on the average, half-way through its life.

Now $m' = [(m.n)/(n-m)]$, so that 'roundaboutness' is measured by $1 + m/n[(n-1)]$. Thus anything which increases $m - m/n$ increases roundaboutness. It follows that an increase in the amount of capital relatively to the amount of gross output is compatible with a *shortening* of the production period, if $n-1/n$ is falling faster than m is increasing.

There is, I think, nothing in this inconsistent with M^r. Gifford's conclusions; for he avowedly disclaims the possibility of comparisons between two 'organisations of labour' (in his terminology) with different techniques. But it means that there could be two societies of equal labour power but different techniques of production, of which the first had the greater quantity of capital and the second the longer period of production. This would be relevant if we were to attempt to apply the concept to a non-stationary community.

II

If, however, we are dealing with a community subject to change or one which is not in equilibrium, can any clear meaning be given to 'the length of the production period'? If so, I do not know what it is. Perhaps those who apply this concept to credit cycle problems will instruct us as to what it means in this context.

For example, suppose that 10 per cent of our capital equipment is out of use or that our equipment is only being employed to 90 per cent of its capacity, is the quantity of capital the same as before or different? Is the length of the production period the same as before or different?

A bundle of papers labelled by Keynes 'Discussion with Piero'

From P. SRAFFA [*undated*]

The initial output is *OM*; the final equilibrium output, after wages have been cut ½, is *ON*.

Transition
Suppose entreps. make a small increase *MT*, as a tentative step. They pay out in wages *MCFT*: the addit. income is insufficient to buy the addit. goods at price *BM*; it falls short of that by the excess of the rectangle *BM.MT* (not drawn) over *MCFT*. The price will have to fall to such an extent that the fall in price of old output *OM* is equal to excess of total price of new output *MT* over its cost *MCFT*. The required price will certainly be higher than *EM*; for, if it were *EM* the fall in total price of old goods would be *RQBE* which is = *CED*; while the excess of total price of new goods would be *CEHF < CED*.

The price (somewhere between *BM* and *EM*) will still be in excess of marg. cost *FT*, there will be a further increase in output, etc., etc. Only at *ON* will both conditions (equality of incomes and total price; equality of price and marg. cost) be satisfied.

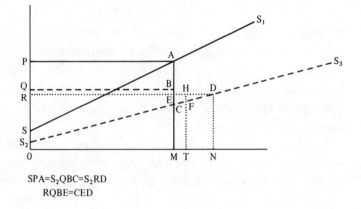

SPA=S₂QBC=S₂RD
RQBE=CED

To P. SRAFFA [*undated*]

If *W* is changed, it is, in general, impossible that there should be a new position of short-period equilibrium (with price = marginal wage cost) with *Q* unchanged.

Therefore we must make *some* hypothesis as to how *Q* will change.

If, whenever each individual entrepreneur's real income is increased, his psychology is such that he increases his real consumption by at least that amount, the position is one, not of neutral, but of unstable equilibrium and any increment of investment however small will cause full employment.

If, however, his real consumption is increased by less than the increment of his real income, then there is only one level of employment which is compatible with equilibrium, unless investment increases; namely the one which existed before the wage cut.

To P. SRAFFA [*undated*]

See p. 19 of the attached definition of 'marginal propensity to consume'.[23]

If this marginal propensity is unity, equilibrium is neutral

[23] This has not survived.

and *any* level of output up to full employment is possible. What the level of output is, is a matter of indifference to entrepreneurs as a whole. The assumption that Q is constant, however, adds an additional condition. It involves a value of unity for the marginal propensity to consume, but also the entirely bizarre condition that the value of entrepreneur's consumption is constant in terms of money.* The result of this second condition is that the level of money wages fixes which of the multiple positions permitted by the first condition will be taken up.

If, on the other hand, we introduce the psychological law that for the community as a whole the marginal propensity to consume is less than unity, then any expansion of output gluts the market and diminishes prices until speculators are induced to take some of the output into stock, or, which is in substance the same thing, consumers anticipate their needs. Competition between producers to sell forward brings the forward price down to the new marginal cost of production; and speculators will not take the goods into stock until prices have fallen sufficiently below this level to provide carrying charges. Thus some subsequent production period starts with prices temporarily reduced *more* than in proportion to the reduction in wages and the new equilibrium is found with prices, and all income reduced exactly in proportion to wages.

If producers are far-sighted, they will avoid spending money on speculators' services, and prices will at once fall in proportion to wages. At any rate this course of action will maximise profits for producers as a whole.

This is an example of the general principle that *any* expansion of output gluts the market unless there is a *pari passu* increase of investment appropriate to the community's marginal propensity to consume; and any contraction leads

* I.e. that they have a club rule which insists on their paying a price for output which has this effect.

to windfall profits to producers unless there is an appropriate *pari passu* contraction of investment.

Thus, given the marginal propensity to consume, the amount of investment determines the equilibrium level of aggregate employment.

I have omitted complications resulting from the shapes of the supply functions which determine what proportion of the value of output accrues to entrepreneurs.

PART II
DEFENCE AND DEVELOPMENT

Chapter 4

AFTER THE *GENERAL THEORY*

The additional post-*General Theory* material falls into three broad classes. The first class, largely consisting of Keynes–Robertson correspondence, is supplementary to that already published in that it fills gaps in the material in Volume XIV. The second relates to the correction Keynes published to the *General Theory* when Simon Kuznets pointed out some errors in Keynes's use of statistics that Kuznets had generated.[1] The third is correspondence relating to various aspects of the *General Theory* which was not previously available.

With the exception of one letter, the additional Robertson material relates to 1937–8. The exceptional letter, written on board the Cunard liner *Georgic* while Robertson was travelling to America, precedes the Keynes letter printed on p. 87 of Volume XIV.

From a letter from D. H. ROBERTSON, *28 September 1936*

(II) I've spent a lot of time this summer on the said book [*The General Theory*]. It's no use pretending I like it much better, or that I don't agree more or less with most of the Prof.'s review, including the first section.[2] I've tried to set down some notes on some parts of the book which may see the light in the *QJE* or elsewhere.[3] I think it would be a mistake to attempt to discuss them before they are published, if they are going to be. Whether afterwards you will feel that the sort of tabu which has arisen between us can profitably be removed, I don't know. Last year I was myself unwilling to discuss further till I had seen the whole thing: but I was also baffled by your attitude that I must either agree with you more *or less*, which I didn't and don't think a reasonable one!

---

[1] The errors occur in *JMK*, vol. VII, pp. 98–104. Keynes's correction appeared as 'Fluctuations in Net Investment in the United States', *Economic Journal*, September 1936 reprinted as Appendix 2 to *JMK*, vol. VII.

[2] 'Mr J. M. Keynes' General Theory of Employment, Interest and Money', *Economica*, May 1936.

[3] They did, as 'Some Notes on Mr. Keynes' General Theory of Employment', *Quarterly Journal of Economics*, November 1936.

Anyway, once we know whether we're going to discuss fundamental economics or not, perhaps we could meet rather oftener than we have done this year,—and talk about drama and foreign policy (in which I find you advocating courses of caution and suspended judgement which I find very seductive!) and even ephemeral economic situations?

The second group of Robertson–Keynes letters began with Robertson's receiving an advance copy of Keynes's 'The "Ex Ante" Theory of the Rate of Interest' (*Economic Journal*, December 1937; *JMK*, vol. XIV, pp. 215–23).

From a letter from D. H. ROBERTSON, *28 November 1937*

I am a little sad to have to stand down as a target in favour of Ohlin, as last time in favour of Viner![4] But to some extent of course, my article and Ohlin's covered the same ground. I do wish, however, that you could depute someone to reply some time to §7 of my article: for I don't think Hawtrey (Sept. *E.J.* p. 438) and I can be alone in being mystified by the turn your thought seems to have been taking on that matter...

I enclose copies (not for return) of 2 papers I have read this term at Liverpool and Manchester. (The latter will appear in due course in more convenient format.)[5]

Keynes replied on 6 December, enclosing the note dated 5 December which appears on pages 223–6 of Volume XIV.

From a letter to D. H. ROBERTSON, *6 December 1937*

If I had attempted to cover, in my *Economic Journal* contribution, what you wrote, I should only have limited myself to trying to taunt you into producing some more constructive account of your own view, in which it could be seen in its entirety and separately, and not merely as a by-product of an attack on something else. But since getting your letter, I have

---

[4] The reference is to Keynes's 'The General Theory of Employment', *Quarterly Journal of Economics*, February 1937 (*JMK*, vol. XIV, pp. 109–23). In this article, a comment on the Leontief, Robertson, Taussig and Viner symposium on *The General Theory* (*Quarterly Journal of Economics*, November 1936), Keynes had called Viner's comment 'the most important (vol. XIV, p. 110).

[5] The Liverpool paper was 'The Future of International Trade', *Economic Journal*, March 1938. The Manchester paper was 'A Survey of Modern Monetary Controversy', *Manchester School*, No. 1, 1938.

written out for you the enclosed note about your paragraph 7...[6]

Many thanks for your two papers. I liked the Liverpool one very much indeed. You do not say whether you have already made plans to print this. If not, I should like to have it for the *Journal*, in spite of its being of a rather elementary character. I am sure it is the sort of thing which a great many of our readers would enjoy and benefit from, and I sometimes feel that we have far too few general, sensible articles of this sort.

I have found the Manchester article extremely interesting. Indeed, it is a brilliant effort, and it strikes me as scrupulously fair. But it is an extreme example of your chivalry towards the under-dog argument and your sentimental attachment to words which have once meant something to you! 'Even the muddiest river winds somewhere safe to sea' would be a good title. I feel, after reading it, that the strictly intellectual differences between us are probably very small indeed at bottom. But I am trying all the time to disentangle myself, whilst you are trying to keep entangled. You are, so to speak, bent on creeping back into your mother's womb; whilst I am shaking myself like a dog on dry land.

Robertson acknowledged Keynes's letter and comments on 19 December.

From a letter from D. H. ROBERTSON, *19 December 1937*

Monetary Theory Many thanks for putting yourself to the trouble of framing a reply to my §7. I have read it, and have been meaning to get back to it, and your Dec. *Journal,* and several other things in the same terrain: but have been diverted by other things. So I will say no more for the present except that I'm very glad you found some things to like in my Manchester paper,—even though in my view you haven't rightly detected *which* is the 'under-dog' argument to which I was trying to be chivalrous!

---

[6] This deletion and the one in the previous letter concern either personal or irrelevant matters.

On 1 January 1938 he followed up his acknowledgement of 19 December with a letter enclosing two notes, reprinted on pages 226–9 of Volume XIV. The covering letter ran as follows.

From D. H. ROBERTSON, *1 January 1938*

My dear Maynard,

Do not bother to read this letter or enclosures till you are at leisure. There is nothing urgent in them. And, though of course I hope you *will* read them in due course, I don't want to ask you to *answer* them. Even when one is in robust health,[7] I think these exchanges take it out of one and yield d.r. after a point (I always have to break off with Hawtrey in the end!): and I don't want to put any further tax on your energies for my private benefit. If you find anything in what I say to influence your next public contributions, *tant mieux*.

But *if* you have kept a copy of your note of Dec. 12 [*sic*], will you return me my copy without comment? (I enclose my copy in case you haven't kept one).

I send a copy of my Sept. *Journal* article[8] for convenience of reference: and a copy, in more convenient format, of my Manchester paper, to substitute for the other.

As regards the whole question of terminology, of course it seems to me to be *you* who are tumbling into pot-holes under the weight of your home-made great-coats! For instance, (i) it is, I think, the barren savings-investment tautology which has now led you into the curious doctrine that some revolving fund is automatically released or replaced by the act of the entrepreneur in *spending* a bank-loan: (ii) while you still reject the notion of a 'supply of loanable funds', its obvious common-sense and convenience are now, as it seems to me, leading you to edge your way back towards it with the aid of your new brood of monstrosities such as 'the supply of finance', 'the supply of liquidity' and what not.

On the broader question of our respective attitudes to the work of our predecessors (and contemporaries of other schools), there *is* of course a difference of temperament, as there was between Marshall and Jevons. By way of varying your picturesque metaphors, may I suggest that I—managing to keep throughout in touch with all the elements of the problem in a dim and fumbling way—have been a sort of glow worm, whose feeble glimmer

---

[7] Keynes was still recovering from his heart attack of 1937.
[8] 'Alternative Theories of the Rate of Interest: II', *Economic Journal*, September 1937.

lands on all the objects in its neighbourhood: while you, with your far more powerful intellect, have been a light-house casting a far more penetrating, but sometimes fatally distorting, beam on one object after another in succession.

I could, I think give several instances, but will confine myself to one, to which I have already alluded in a footnote to my *E.J.* article.[9] At the Macmillan Committee in 1930 you questioned me on the rate of interest. I got very muddled (largely because you were using the word 'investment' in the now commonsense [way] which was then new to me, which I was using in the old-fashioned sense of buying securities): but in the end I seem to have managed to stammer out (though no doubt I did a lot of tidying up in proof afterwards) what seemed to me, I think, to be fairly orthodox stuff about the difficulty of getting the long rate down in a slump. I will quote, since you probably haven't the volume at hand.

Q4834. (JMK) Here are excessive savings. I quite agree it may be that the public cannot be induced to spend any part of them; it may not be possible at 5 percent to find enough borrowers: but if you could then proceed to lower the rate of interest—not merely the short, but the long-term rate—is it at all probable that in present circumstances you would not find adequate borrowers coming forward at a reasonable level?

(DHR) No, I think it is not. But I still think there is a difficulty of lenders coming forward; you may get such a lack of confidence that people may prefer to go on getting 1 per cent on their deposits with the bank rather than invest in bonds which are yielding 3 or 4 or even 5 percent. I do not know whether I am right.

This train of thought woke no response in you whatever: you went on repeating that the reason why Bank rate remained high was that there were 'rows and rows of foreigners who were very willing to pay extremely high rates for the money',—which was the only aspect of the problem that was interesting you at the moment! But later on the 'liquidity' aspect burgeoned in your mind till it swallowed up everything else for a time: and later on again all other things have had to be, or are still having to be, reintroduced one by one, by side-winds and in codicils.

This method of successive over-emphasis is, I expect, very productive of knowledge and enlightenment in the end. Even those of us who react most strongly against the successive manifestations of it learn a lot from them,—more, probably, than it is always easy, under the smart of irritation, to admit. But it's inevitable, I think, that we should feel a little

[9] 'Alternative Theories of the Rate of Interest: II', *Economic Journal*, September 1937, p. 433 fn. 2.

cynical when we see younger teachers being completely carried away by them: and also that our withers shouldn't be very much wrung by friendly taunts about returing to our mother's womb,—an occasional visit to which often reveals objects of surprising beauty and interest (as the world's best biographer is not ignorant!).[10]

Well, enough.

Yours ever

D. H. R.

P.S. I send two copies of each note, in case you care to pass one on to Kahn.* And I am sending a copy of the 'Ex-Ante' note to Ohlin, and one to Hawtrey.

From a letter to D. H. ROBERTSON, *3 January 1938*

I kept a carbon of the enclosed, so return the original. I have not yet absorbed your material. But I will probably act on your suggestion that I should not send anything further in reply. I very much agree with you about the diminishing returns of these controversies after a point.

In the end Robertson did send a comment to the *Economic Journal* entitled 'Mr. Keynes on "Finance"'.[11] On receiving it, Keynes wrote to his assistant editor.

From a letter to AUSTIN ROBINSON, *22 March 1938*

1. I have received the enclosed from Dennis. To my prejudiced eye it seems completely worthless and, what is more, intolerably boring. I also enclose a brief rejoinder which I have written. I am afraid that it is impossible for me to reject it, and perhaps no harm would be done to good causes by printing it. Could you let me have both the enclosures back with your comments, if you have any? or Joan's?

On seeing Keynes's comment and Robertson's note, Joan Robinson wrote to Keynes.

[10] The reference is, of course, to *Essays in Biography* (*JMK*, vol. x). See above p. 17.
* who wrote me a very friendly note about my Manchester paper.
[11] It appeared in the *Economic Journal* for June 1938.

AFTER THE GENERAL THEORY

From JOAN ROBINSON, *23 March 1938*

Dear Maynard,

I am so glad you like my note on Hoarding.[12] D. H. R. seems to grow more and more perverse. I can't make any sense of this at all. He seems to be wandering vaguely about in a featureless wilderness.

I think your reply would be more telling if you put in the working a bit more. Abandon D. H. R. as hopeless and write as tho' for a 2nd year man who is hoping to get a II 2. You want the reader, emerging dazed from D. H. R., to feel that you represent simplicity and commonsense.

e.g. (1) put in a brief account of what happens step by step—the bank loans, the funding the actual investment and saving. You do this in a way, but the 2nd year man couldn't follow as it is.

(2) last 4 lines. Expand and emphasise this point. It is extremely important that you should emphasise (a) that you have always allowed for the increased demand for money which accompanies an increase in income (b) that 'finance' is a point of the same order as the increase in active circulation. I find a lot of confusion on this point in many quarters.

(4) line 10. Say probable, not possible, and repeat/explain why a decline in income releases money. Line 16—surely he means simply an increase in propensity to save. That is obviously what he has in mind. He is looking at it this way—entrepreneurs are wanting to increase investment but are held back by shortage of finance. If in this situation, thriftiness increases, investment will be able to increase. He regards the limitation of finance as working in the same sort of way as the limitation on labour at full employment.

I believe he has now got as far as seeing that you say that an increase in propensity to save does not, in general, raise the demand for securities. Of course he will never grant the point, because the fact that $S = I$ is a truism absolves him from believing that it is true. But it would be something if he saw that you believe it.

I heard that Hicks's appointment is now definite tho' not yet public.[13] My love to Lydia. It was nice to have a glimpse of you both.

Yours,

Joan

Austin says he agrees in general with these remarks.

P.S. Dennis appeals to Lange. Lange's article tho' silly is formally quite correct, and if Dennis really accepts his argument he has given away everything. You might make some use of this in your reply.[14]

[12] 'The Concept of Hoarding', *Economic Journal*, June 1938.
[13] As Jevons Professor of Political Economy in the University of Manchester.
[14] O. Lange, 'The Rate of Interest and the Optimum Propensity to Consume', *Economica*, N.S., February 1938.

To JOAN ROBINSON, *30 March 1938*

My dear Joan,

Thanks for your note on my note to Dennis's note. I could, of course, make it much clearer if I were to write a new article. But that I do not at all want to do, having written a clear one already. My object here is to deal with any specific points as perfunctorily as possible so as not to let them go by. However, I have revised what I wrote in the light of what you say.

Yours,

[Copy initialled] J.M.K.

When Keynes had finished his rejoinder to Robertson, he naturally sent him a copy, which drew comment.

From a letter from D. H. ROBERTSON, *5 May 1938*

'FINANCE'

Thank you for your rejoinder. Of course I don't find it satisfying, and of course I am writing a re-joinder, which of course I think carries the matter further. But I dare say that as Editor you will feel that this correspondence must now cease as far as the *Journal* is concerned. In that case I have been wondering if we could spare the reader some scratching of head over one point. You attribute confusion to my 'thinking of "finance" as consisting in bank loans'. But I think if you look again you will see that all I have done is to follow faithfully, in my main argument, your own model* in this respect. In a footnote (the last) I have considered the case—to my mind very probable—in which 'finance' is provided otherwise than by the banks. So I really do think it will puzzle the careful reader unnecessarily to find me taken to task on this score! However, of course it's as you wish, and perhaps it's anyhow too late.

I will send you my note when completed—and I think, if you decide to close down in the *E.J.*, I should probably like to cyclostyle it round to the 50 or so people who follow these things with unslakeable zest.

...I do quite often read large chunks of the *G.T.E.*!

* 'In a simplified schematism...but one which is in fact sufficiently representative of real life, one could assume that "finance" is wholly supplied during the interregnum by the banks.' *E.J.* December 37, p. 666 [*JMK*, vol. XIV, p. 219].

To D. H. ROBERTSON, *22 May 1938*

Dear Dennis,

FINANCE

I am not quite clear whether you mean that you always understood me rightly to mean that 'finance' meant cash or whether you are accusing me of having myself used 'finance' in the sense of 'bank loans'. If the former, then I have been misled into making a wrong criticism. But I do not think the passage you refer to will bear out the second. To say that under artificial simplified conditions one can assume that finance is wholly supplied by bank loans implies the direct contrary. For if finance consisted in bank loans there would be no necessity to make any reference to simplified conditions. To say that in certain circumstances people supply themselves with cash by borrowing from a bank does not mean that cash and bank loans are interchangeable terms.

I have added to the proof a brief footnote to try to prevent any reader from being confused on this point.

Yours,

[Copy initialled] J.M.K.

Keynes's rejoinder appeared after Robertson's note in the *Economic Journal* for June 1938 (vol. XIV, pp. 229–34). However the controversy continued.

From a letter from D. H. ROBERTSON, *28 May 1938*

(1) Here is my kick-back! I am in your editorial hands on whether it appears in the Sept. *Journal*, or whether I print it for circulation to those likely to be interested.

From a letter to D. H. ROBERTSON, *30 May 1938*

2. As regards your kick-back, I do not want to be in the position of being a judge in my own case. So after the June *Journal* is out I will send it to the Professor for his verdict. The general principle of the *Journal* is that when the author

of an article is criticised he has the right to a rebuttal. Generally speaking the critic has no right to what in [the] old days when I discussed it with him, Edgeworth used to call 'sur-rejoinder'; though if such is allowed the original writer may then proffer a sur-rebuttal. Such rules, however, are not invariably kept. The grounds for breaking them are either a fairly clear case of misrepresentation or that the matter is not merely one of personal controversy, but general public interest.

If your sur-rejoinder were published the only bit on which I should wish to comment further would be the passage near the beginning of paragraph 2 which you underline.[15] You are here putting words in my mouth which I have not only not used myself but which I have expressly repudiated if they are interpreted in the traditional sense. No objection at all to your quoting what I did actually say. But this use of language which is either, in fact, the opposite of what I mean* or, at the best, only gets away with it by means of ambiguity both as to use of language and to what conditions are assumed, only darkens counsel.

From a letter from D. H. ROBERTSON, *1 June 1938*

Good, let the Prof. decide,—if he will, though it will bore him stiff.

On §2 I should be willing to substitute 'For it amounts, in my view, to agreement...' for 'For he agrees...'. I don't think there should be any doubt what 'increase of thrift' means, as I have explained in §1, (ii) the sense I attach to these words: but I could add a reference back in a footnote. I don't really think you can be allowed to collar *all* the ordinary words for the science of the Grand Tautology, leaving us only with the mouth-splitting 'reduction of the propensity to consume' for the other things!

I always use the latter phrase under protest, (a) because a mere change

---

[15] The offending passage ran 'Nevertheless, I must thank Mr Keynes for rightly intuiting what question I was trying, in the penultimate paragraph of my §5, to ask him: nor is his answer unsatisfactory. *For he agrees that normally, and not merely at those rare moments of full employment, an increase of thrift will tend to lower the rate of interest.*

* On the assumption that thrift means saving.

in the propensity doesn't affect anything unless it finds vent in action, (b) because, if I decide to save £100 instead of spending it on gramophone records, I'm not at all sure that it's correct to say that my propensity to acquire gramophone records has changed at all,—it is my will to indulge that propensity that has changed.

If you reply that this is theological hair-splitting, I can only reply that you began it!

To A. C. PIGOU, *3 June 1938*

Dear Pigou,

May I have your assistance in the following matter: You will have seen in the June *Economic Journal* a controversy between Dennis and myself—namely a criticism by him of an article written by me, and a rejoinder by myself. He now wants to carry the controversy further in the enclosed article. I do not want to be a judge in my own case. So I should like to leave it to you to decide whether or not I should print it.

The rule of the *Economic Journal* about controversy, which was settled by Edgeworth many years ago, was that when a criticism of an article is accepted the writer of the original article always has a right to reply. The general rule is that after that nothing more is allowed. This general rule is, however, naturally open to occasional exceptions, the reasons being either that the writer of the original article in his reply has clearly misrepresented his critic or that the matter under discussion is of considerable general interest and the controversy is following lines which seem to take the matter further.

This will give you the usual criteria for judging the enclosed. If it is accepted then the original writer has, on Edgeworth's rule, a right to what Edgeworth called a 'sur-rebuttal'. In this case, however, I should only claim a single sentence—where in an important passage Dennis has put words into my mouth which I have not used and which are likely to be taken to mean the opposite of what I intend.

The whole question of controversy in the *Journal* is proving a frightful worry. We hardly seem to publish an article nowadays on which someone or other does not send a criticism. All the same, some of the controversies have, I think, helped to make things clearer.

Yours ever,

[Copy initialled] J. M. K.

From A. C. PIGOU, *10 June 1938*

Dear Keynes,

I doubt if I am the person for this job especially as I have been so busy finishing some stuff of my own that I have only glanced at the current *Economic Journal*; still as you ask for it, here's my opinion for what it's worth.

I. I think the rule, nothing after the first rejoinder, ought to be kept very rigid; but the rejoinder-man, as he has the last word, is then under a sort of moral obligation to make his paper mainly explanatory and defensive, not to undertake counter attacks and aggressions. I think your rejoinder does contain some aggressions. So far, therefore, Dennis has some claim to a reply if he really wants one. But he spoke to me about this very thing a few days back and would apparently be quite content to have the discussion stopped now, and to send his note privately to the few people likely to be interested. So it doesn't seem necessary to print anything further out of justice to him.

II. On more general grounds I am quite clear that the discussion ought to stop. There seems to me to have been much too much about this sort of topic in the *Economic Journal* recently. In the current number there are no less than six papers more or less about it. This is particularly unfortunate as the topic is one that centres so much round the Editor. I have no doubt myself that the cause of this concentration lies in the character of the articles that are sent to you; but an unfriendly critic might easily attribute it to editorial bias. Moreover, the thing is cumulative. If people get the impression that the *Journal* more or less specialises in this field, everybody who has an article about it will send it to you, and people with articles on other subjects will send them elsewhere. I think it important that the *Journal* should continue to be 'the organ not of one school of economists but of all'.[16]

I hope this is the sort of thing you want.

I was vetted by Cassidy[17] yesterday and he told me that what I wanted

[16] See *Economic Journal*, March 1891, p. 2.
[17] Pigou's physician. Pigou had been suffering from heart illness.

was more exercise and to get into training, which is a very good pre-
scription for the Long [Vacation].

Ever yours,

A. C. PIGOU

To A. C. PIGOU, *17 June 1938* [*Copy in Lydia Keynes's handwriting*]

Dear Pigou,

Thanks for your letter which is helpful.

I am only too conscious of the large spaces given to what
you call 'this sort of topic' and do my utmost to reduce it.
But I am sent nothing else. I have rejected a large number
of marginal contributions on these lines and I have rejected
nothing even plausible on other parts of theory. Indeed in
the last two years, apart from two things on methodology in
the last issue and descriptive articles, I have only received *one*
important article on theory (Kahn on Duopoly)[18] which would
not fall under your ban.

For example, which of the articles published this June
would you have rejected if you were in my place?

As regards the particular controversy on interest, it was all
started by *three* articles attacking, in various degrees, my point
of view. Of the 10 articles and rejoinders arising out of this
published in the last 10 months, 6 were criticising my point
of view and 4 defending it (and of these 4 three were specific
replies to points of criticism). Would you have had me reject
the criticisms? Or refrain from replying to them?

Is it quite fair in the light of the above to call my attention
to the importance of the *Journal* continuing to be 'the organ
not of one school of economists but of all'? Or suggest the
offence of editorial bias?

The truth really is that these and cognate topics are what
everyone is thinking about and working at and where
progress is being made and new things said. Imperfect
competition and associated problems is the only other branch

[18] R. F. Kahn, 'The Problem of Duopoly', *Economic Journal*, March 1937.

of theory which is interesting people at the moment, judging from what reaches me.

Very glad to hear Cassidy's latest advice to you.

Yours ever,

J. M. K.

From A. C. PIGOU, [*June 1938*]

Dear Keynes,

Thanks for your letter. But mine wasn't an 'attack'. Indeed the explanation you give is the very one I suggested, namely that people send you these articles predominantly. I think, though, that they send them to you in much larger proportions partly because they know you're specially interested in them, e.g. in larger proportions than with the Harvard J. or *Economica* and there is the danger of 'cumulation'. The more of the articles appear in the *E.J.*, the more will be sent.

I don't want to criticise particular articles. Indeed I haven't read this *E.J.* properly yet. But personally there's really nothing to say about savings = investment because it's a matter of what is the *most convenient definition*. I now think yours is; and have been using it in what I've been writing recently. But I can't see that there's anything to argue about.

But that is, of course, a matter of opinion. The real point, as I see it, is that it is a damned difficult thing for you as editor to have a situation when so many people are sending articles about you and your stuff. It's like being chairman and at the same time running a policy. (*Please* don't think I'm hinting that you ought not to go on being editor. I don't think anything of the kind.) But it's worth perhaps considering in the special circumstances whether it might be worth putting in an editorial note calling attention to the difficulty and asking for other sorts of articles as well.

I'm becoming much fitter through having a holiday. I hope you're doing the same.

Yrs.,

A. P.

[There followed a P.S. on an unrelated matter.]

From a letter to A. C. PIGOU, *27 June 1938*

Well, I will do my best, though I do not see how to word a paragraph discouraging articles which cover such a very wide range!

Moreover, I think you will find that the other Journals are nearly as bad. For example, the February *Q.J.E.* has two substantial articles on 'Mr. Keynes' Consumption Function and the Time-Preference Postulate' and 'Saving Equals Investment', while the June *American Economic Review*, just received, has no less than six articles on the subject, including replies and rejoinders, which occupy the whole of the space given to theory, apart from some six pages.

From a letter from A. C. PIGOU, *[July 1938]*

...if the prodding [of two other King's economists for articles] is successful, the unfortunate editor will be shifted from the frying-pan of making the *Journal* all about himself to the fire of having it exclusively written by members of his own college!

Seriously, of course, I didn't mean to object to articles dealing with all *subjects* discussed in your book. As you've touched on practically everything, that would hardly work! But I think there's a good enough working distinction between constructive articles on *subjects* and exegetical articles about what a particular person has said on subjects. For example, all the unpublished stuff I've been doing recently is on subjects touched on by you, but the essence is the *subjects* and comparisons with what you say are incidental notes. On the other hand Dennis has been spending years meticulously examining and criticising Mr Keynes on this and that, instead of getting on, as I think would be much better, with constructive work of his own. The sort of articles I should like barred out, (except, of course, in book reviews), are what I call exegetical articles. I should say, if I was in your place, 'I will not print in a journal edited by me, articles that are predominantly discussions, whether favourable or unfavourable, of my own writings.' I'd especially bar out discussions about definitions. If I choose to define savings and investment in your way, obviously they must be equal; if I define them in Dennis' way, obviously they must not be. Again if I choose to define hoarding as adding to my holding of money, obviously, unless new money is created there can't be collective hoarding. If I define it as withdrawing money out of circulation, obviously there can be. For *A* to argue with *B* that there 'ought' to be one definition rather than another seems to me sheer pedantry. Let each use his own definition and see what he can get out of it. Helas, my pen is running away isn't it; no affair of mine anyway. Forgive unwonted loquacity: perhaps it's anticipation of Swiss air!

Yours,

A.C.P.

From a letter to A. C. PIGOU, *5 July 1938*

I entirely agree with you about not wanting what you call exegetical articles. That ought to be dealt with by the reviewer in the first instance and very sparingly afterwards. At any rate, I am only too glad to have your approval if from now on I reject further personal attacks on myself! But as regards definitions, I am not sure that I do agree. Arguments between people who are using terms differently are, of course, absurd. But it is often useful, and indeed essential, to have articles pointing out the different senses in which a common term is used, as for example in Joan's article on Hoarding; and it is also sometimes necessary to call attention to the fact that terms are being used without any clear definition of them having been given, or that the same writer uses them sometimes in one sense and sometimes in another without apparently noticing.

From D. H. ROBERTSON, *25 June 1938*

Dear Maynard,

Pigou told me the reasons for his judgement, which I was entirely prepared to accept. I accordingly re-wrote my §2, embodying and commenting on your statement, and prepared the whole thing for circulation.

But Piero, on reading it, was struck with the hope of obtaining, for readers of the *Journal*, something like a statement of agreement on a definite and important point, and urged me to scrap all the rest and state this one point as briefly and temperately as possible. This I have endeavoured to do; so perhaps it is just worth considering whether the result (enclosed) is of sufficient utility to justify reconsidering the decision to close down.

I have some sympathy with Piero's desire: but I don't want to infringe the spirit of the Pigou award, and if the enclosed still leaves you with a 'propensity' to reply, or to seek further verbal adjustment by correspondence, then I expect we had better give it up. In that case I will feel free to circulate my fuller document (so far sent only to one or two people in type).

Yours,

D. H. R.

To D. H. ROBERTSON, *10 July 1938*

Dear Dennis,

I agree that your brief excerpt from your previous criticism might be useful. It certainly does not occupy too much space. So I have sent it to the printer. When the proof reaches you, you will find that I have added a sentence of my own. But I do not press for this, and if you feel that it re-opens what is better closed and would demand something further from yourself, just cross it out.

I enclose an off-print of my own last *Journal* instalment.[19]

Yours,

[Copy initialled] J. M. K.

Keynes's proposed addition ran as follows:

I am glad that we have been at cross purposes and that there is no difference of opinion between Mr Robertson and myself on the above point. But I hear with surprise that our forebears believed that *cet. par.* an increase in the desire to save would lead to a recession in employment and income and would only result in a fall in the rate of interest in so far as this was the case.

J. M. KEYNES

[19] 'Mr Keynes and "Finance"', *Economic Journal*, June 1938.

From D. H. ROBERTSON, *22 July 1938*

Dear Maynard,

I am afraid your addition *does* leave me with a propensity to further reply. You imply that I have said that your present doctrine on this matter and the 'classical' doctrine are identical. But I have not said that at all: I have said that they possess an extremely important feature in common. (I have discussed the *degree* of importance to be attached to the divergence between them in *QJE* Nov. '36 pp. 187–190: cf. Hawtrey, *Capital and Employment*, pp. 195–7.)

There seem to be several possibilities.

(1) To omit your addition, as you suggest. This doesn't seem very satisfactory.

(2) To leave it unchanged, leaving the impartial reader to see (as I think he will) that what you 'hear with surprise' you have not heard from me! This doesn't seem very satisfactory either.

(3) To leave the forebears out of it, i.e. for me to omit the words 'with each other (and with our forebears)' and for you to omit your second sentence, leaving the first. I am willing to agree to this.

(4) To scrap the whole thing.

Yours,

D. H. R.

I enclose a copy of my full rejoinder for retention (? and for referral some time).

To D. H. ROBERTSON, *25 July 1938*

Dear Dennis,

I think the best way will be to accept your suggestion to leave out the reference to forebears, and to delete my rejoinder completely. I shall be quite satisfied with this.

Our forebears believed that with these particular *ceteris paribus* the rate of interest depends on the supply of saving. My theory is that it depends on the supply of inactive money. There is no possible reconciliation between these views, and it seemed to me to darken counsel to suggest that the theories agreed with one another because in a particular case, for purely accidental reasons, they would be consistent with the same facts.

Yours,
[Copy initialled] J.M.K.

From D. H. ROBERTSON, *27 July 1938*

Dear Maynard,

Your solution is different from any which I proposed, and I am sorry the reader must go without your first sentence, which I think might have cheered him up! However, I agree, and have sent in the proof accordingly.

Yours,
D.H.R.

To D. H. ROBERTSON, *29 July 1938*

Dear Dennis,

I had thought that I was adopting one of your solutions and did not realise that you wanted my first sentence kept. All the same, now I look at it from that point of view, I would rather delete my note altogether. The principal reason is that I would much rather leave the matter as it is, if I can possibly do so, and I have already stated in the sentence you quote from me that I do agree with the conclusion referred to.

Yours,
[Copy initialled] J.M.K.

At this stage a further complication arose.

From JOAN ROBINSON, *30 July 1938*

My dear Maynard,

Alexander has shown me the D.H.R. file, and I enclose a letter about his reference to my baby book[20] (which I consider most dastardly) on a separate sheet, so that if you felt inclined to send it on to D.H.R. you can do so. If I can come in on your Treaty of Versailles I should like best to have D.H.R. cut out his reference to me.

It is obviously futile for me to make a rejoinder if you don't, but perhaps

---

[20] *An Introduction to the Theory of Employment* (London, 1937).

if he does not omit the reference you could put in a sort of Ed. footnote quoting the passage to which I refer under (3) in the enclosed letter. What a lot of nonsense—the worst of D.H.R.'s behaviour is that it forces us all to act as if we thought all this futility important.

Alexander really has started writing his book[21]—we are having so much fine weather we have some to spare.

Hope you are continuing to improve.

Yours,

JOAN

The enclosure ran as follows:

My dear Maynard,

I am pleased you have reached an agreement with D.H.R., which makes it possible for you to omit your rejoinder—but without any rejoinder from you I am left somewhat in a difficulty—[re] D.H.R. footnote 2 Mrs R. 'affirms without qualification that the desire to save does not promote investment'.

I do feel inclined to protest at this. (1) I say in my preface 'rigour is sacrificed to simplicity' and it seems to me, to say the least, ungenerous, to take advantage of that fact to attack me for making a statement, 'without qualification'. (2) It is not the same thing to say that an increase in thriftiness does not promote investment, as that it does not lower the rate of interest. The fall in the rate of interest has to be great enough to overcome the decline in prospective profit due to less spending for consumption (v. Lange). This of course brings up a question of orders of magnitude, where D.H.R. and I can legitimately disagree, in the present state of realistic knowledge, and I don't want to drag it into the argument, but it does mean that the sentence quoted does not in any way commit me to the view that an increase in thriftiness does not lower the rate of interest. (3) In another passage I definitely state (quoting from memory) 'it is true that an increase in thriftiness will lower the rate of interest but it only does so because...' This occurs in the chapter called Aspects of the Rate of Interest, section called The Regulator.

I do not want to go on with this boring controversy and am reluctant to ask for even a two line Rejoinder, but I do not want my case to go by default. Could you advise me what line to take?

Yours,

JOAN

[21] This was on the theory of the firm. It was never finished.

From JOAN ROBINSON, *Postmark 2 August 1938*

Introduction to T of E p. 82 last line and p. 83 top.

It is true indeed that an increase in the desire to save tends to lower the rate of interest, but it only does so because it reduces activity and so brings about a fall in the demand for money.

This is the reference required in my letter of Sat.

We are hoping to ascend the Za[22] tomorrow—see over.

JOAN

To D. H. ROBERTSON, *3 August 1938*

Dear Dennis,

There is one other small deletion in your note which I should like you to consider, namely, the reference to Joan in the second footnote, where you say that she affirms without qualification that the desire to save does not promote investment. I am quite sure that her view is the same as mine on this point, and it may very likely prove the case that she can find some other passage in the book which makes this clear. Moreover the statement that the desire to save does not promote investment is not quite the same as to say that it does not lower the rate of interest.

The point is that I foresee the probability of a rejoinder from her, if we print this unprovoked reference. If so, how could I refuse it? Yet it would have the undesired effect of dragging the controversy on. Besides, what is the object of attributing to her an opinion which I am pretty sure she does not hold, even if you can find textual criticism to support it.

Yours ever,
[Copy initialled] J. M. K.

From D. H. ROBERTSON, *4 August 1938*

Dear Maynard,

I agree that, since it is decided to close the controversy, it is better not to bring in the name of any other party who might feel disposed to reply: and have instructed Austin accordingly.

[22] Aiguille de la Za, a Swiss mountain.

I disagree with the other two reasons which you put forward for deleting the reference: but since it doesn't affect the issue, I will not argue the matter.

Yours,

D. H. R.

To D. H. ROBERTSON, *9 August 1938*

Dear Dennis,

I have now got hold of the following reference from Joan. *Vide* her *Introduction to the Theory of Employment*, pages 82 and 83:—

'It is true, indeed, that an increase in the desire to save tends to lower the rate of interest, but it only does so because it reduces activity and so brings about a fall in the demand for money.'

Yours ever,

[Copy initialled] J. M. K.

From D. H. ROBERTSON, *11 August 1938*

Dear Maynard,

Thank you for the excerpt, which I had overlooked. I agree that it would not have been proper to quote one passage without the other.

Yours,

D. H. R.

Robertson's note appeared in the *Economic Journal* in September 1938 without Keynes's proposed comment or the reference to forebears by Robertson that had provoked it.

Four additional letters, three from Joan Robinson, precede the discussion in Volume XIV (p. 148) of her *Introduction to the Theory of Employment*.

From JOAN ROBINSON, *18 November 1936*

Dear Maynard,

I hardly like to confess that I am embarking on a fresh project while waiting for my page proofs[23] (but this time you don't have to read it).

[23] *Essays in the Theory of Employment* (London, 1937).

What do you feel about a told to the children version of the *General Theory*? There are obvious dangers and difficulties involved, and if you are discouraging I will drop the idea forthwith. But teaching has lead [*sic*] me to feel the want of a book for freshers and tho' I'm not specially keen on the job for its own sake I feel rather called to undertake it.

I should try to make it very simple without resorting to baby language —keeping in mind the man who is going to get a 2nd in Part I. I would be as uncontroversial as possible and treat everything in the straightforward way that one can with an uncontaminated audience. I have drafted one or two chapters, and it seems to go quite well. But I would like to have your views before putting any more work into it.

I really feel very apologetic. I quite intended to knock off writing for a time after my *Essays*, but I don't seem to have managed to do so.

Yours,

JOAN

From JOAN ROBINSON, *25 November 1936*

Dear Maynard,

I wrote to you last week to ask your opinion on a project of mine. I don't want to seem importunate but I am writing again in case something has gone wrong in the post as I have had some letters go astray recently. Would there be any chance of a word with you in the weekend?

Yours,

JOAN

To JOAN ROBINSON, *2 December 1936*

My dear Joan,

Do not let what I said on Monday evening weigh with you unduly. You are altogether free to follow your own judgement in the matter.

But, as you asked me, I had to try and express my own feeling. So far as I myself am concerned, I am trying to prevent my mind from crystallising too much on the precise lines of the *General Theory*. I am attentive to criticisms and to what raises difficulties and catches people's attention—in which there are a good many surprises. I think that the best popular version may have to be approached along lines of its own. I think about it all a good deal, but I do not feel ready.

185

There is a considerable difference between more or less formal theory, which my existing book purports to be, and something which is meant to be applied to current events without too much qualification by people who do not fully comprehend the theory. So I am against hurry and in favour of gestation.

Yours ever,

[Copy initialled] J. M. K.

From JOAN ROBINSON, 3 December 1936

My dear Maynard,

I have a lot of sympathy with your point of view. What I have in mind is teaching freshers—a problem you never come across, the sheltered life you lead. It's quite a different matter from a popular work. But I agree it's hard to know the best way of putting things. I think I will compile a document for use of my own pupils (+ Austin's and Alexander's) and see how it goes. By this means we can get experience without anybody being committed to anything.

Can you get in a footnote about gilt edged and the Bishop of Bradford in your next reprint.[24]

Yours,

JOAN

The Keynes–Kuznets correspondence concerning Keynes's use of Kuznets' material on gross capital formation in the *General Theory* (*JMK*, vol. VII, pp. 98–104) was presaged by a letter to Keynes from George O. May, an accountant who was a major director of the National Bureau of Economic Research.

---

[24] On 1 December 1936, the Bishop of Bradford remarked in public that King Edward VIII was in urgent need of God's grace. The provincial newspapers used this remark as an excuse to break their silence on the King's affair with Mrs Wallis Simpson. The London newspapers followed forthwith. Gilt-edged securities lost up to 1¼ on 2 December, largely as a result of foreign selling, but regained 1 on 3 December. Other security prices were also disturbed.

From G. O. MAY, *25 February 1936*[25]

Dear Mr Keynes,

I have been examining with interest your new book. Your explorations lead into fields in which I can scarcely claim to follow you, much less to criticize, and therefore I am not going to make any general comment except that I gather the impression that you have at times deliberately overdrawn the picture in order to arrest attention. Your discussion of the influences which determine security prices, though acute and admirably presented, seems to me a case in point; but I have welcomed it as a useful corrective to the views of people like Mr Frankfurter, who think that prices are determined mainly, if not solely, by intelligent analysis of the statistical information which is given to potential traders.

At page 103, however, you enter a field where I can feel reasonably at home, and here I will venture, if I may, to criticize. In your table based on Kuznets, the deductions clearly relate only to business capital formation, and there is no corresponding deduction in respect of state and private capital formation. Consequently, your 'net' figure remains a gross figure in respect of these last-mentioned items (which constitute by far the larger part of the aggregate with which you are dealing) and is net only in respect of one part (considerably less than half) of the whole. It follows that comments based on that net figure rest on unsound premises. For instance, your point that Kuznets must have underestimated the rate of depreciation and depletion is surely not well taken, since your percentage is arrived at by comparing the deduction in respect of business capital with the total amount of capital formation of all kinds.

In casting about for an explanation of the apparent statistical error, I noted that your discussion of the Kuznets figures began with the statement that his figures gave results similar to those given by the English figures of Mr Colin Clark. I have been interested to find that, using only the figures for business capital formation for the four years, this statement is fully borne out, the percentage of net to gross capital formation being approximately 30% in one case and 33% in the other, whereas on the figures in your table the percentages are 70 and 33, which cannot be said to be strikingly similar. This has led me to wonder whether at least a part of your text may not have been written originally in relation to a table derived from Kuznets but dealing only with the formation of business capital.

I have found your book stimulating, and recognise the penetrating

[25] Reprinted from G. O. May, *Twenty-five Years of Accounting Responsibility, 1911–1936: Essays and Discussions* (ed. B. C. Hunt), (New York, 1936), pp. 408–10.

character of much of your analysis, though I have a feeling that you fail to distinguish adequately between what is theoretically possible and perhaps ideally desirable in the way of a planned economy and what is actually attainable under modern political conditions.

Yours very truly,

GEORGE O. MAY

May passed his letter on to Simon Kuznets, who then wrote to Keynes.

From S. KUZNETS, *23 March 1936*

Dear Mr Keynes,

I have read with interest Mr George O. May's criticism of the use made of our estimates of capital formation in your volume on *The General Theory of Employment*; and have compared the figures given in your book with those published in *Bulletin* 52 of the National Bureau of Economic Research.[26] My conclusion is that Mr May's criticism is well taken.

Let me begin with an analysis of the figures cited in the table on page 103 of your book. The first line in this table, entitled 'Gross capital formation (after allowing for net changes in business inventories)' is taken from line A7 of Table 5 in the Bulletin (page 6). It is a wide total which includes not only capital investment by business enterprises but also investment by ultimate consumers in such durable goods as houses, automobiles and furniture, and investment by public and semi-public agencies, primarily in various construction undertakings.

The second line in your table*, entitled 'Entrepreneurs' servicing, repairs, maintenance, depreciation and depletion' has been obtained by taking the entries in line 2 of our Table 10 (page 12), i.e. depreciation and depletion by business enterprises, and adding to them estimates of servicing, repairs and maintenance by business enterprises. These latter estimates were apparently obtained as the difference between the entries in line 2a of our Table 8 (total of producers' durable commodities, business construction and net change in business inventories) and the entries in line 1a of our Table 10 (gross capital destined for business use, exclusive of parts, repairs and servicing, and servicing and repairs and maintenance of business construction). Thus, the items in line 2 of your table cover capital

---

[26] S. Kuznets, 'Gross Capital Formation, 1919–1933', 15 November 1934.

* Some errors have crept into the computation of the items in the second line of your table. The entry for 1928 should be 8,479 instead of 8,481; for 1930, 8,500 instead of 8,502; and for 1933, 6,320 instead of 8,240. The error for 1933 is particularly significant. Corresponding corrections should be made in the residuals in line 3 of your table for these three years.

consumption by business enterprises only, while the items in line 1 refer to total gross capital formation, not only that destined for use by business enterprises but also the rather large volume of capital formation by households and by public and semi-public agencies.

As a result, the net capital formation totals given in the bottom line of the table represent a rather hybrid concept, being constituted of net capital investment by business enterprises and gross capital investment by households and by public and semi-public agencies. The entries in this line are a sum of our estimates of net capital formation destined for business use (line 3a, Table 10, page 12) and of the estimates of gross capital formation destined for use by consumers (line 1c, Table 8), by public and semi-public agencies (line 3, Table 8), and the unallocable part of gross capital formation (line 4, Table 8).

You have designated the totals in the last line of your table as 'net capital formation (on Mr Kuznets' definition)'. I am eager to disclaim such an interpretation of my position. The reason why we presented estimates of net capital formation only for the part destined for use by business enterprises, was that no data were available on depreciation and depletion of capital goods in the possession of ultimate consumers or of public and semi-public agencies. And I have added that even with regard to the estimates of net capital formation by business entrepreneurs, some doubt attaches to the adequacy of the depreciation and depletion charges as measures of the actual volume of current consumption of capital goods. Perhaps the brevity of my discussion has led to a misunderstanding of my position. But I certainly did not intend to imply that 'the assumption that the allowance for depreciation and depletion on the books of business firms describes correctly the volume of consumption of already existing finished durable goods used by business firms' permits the identification of these depreciation and depletion charges on the books of business firms with the volume of consumption of already existing finished durable goods *in all hands*, whether they be business firms, ultimate consumers, or public and semi-public agencies.*

* In this connection I would like to call your attention to the statement on pp. 1 and 2 of the *Bulletin*. On p. 1 the text reads: 'In a study guided by such a viewpoint (i.e. analysis of factors in the business cycle), the concept of gross capital formation appears more useful than that of net capital formation, certainly in the first phases of the analysis. This is especially true when such an investigation is followed by a study of the parallel flow of money and credit: there is considerable fluidity between funds set aside to cover the consumption of already existing finished capital goods (for example, reserves for depreciation) and funds for the financing of additional capital goods. Since the study of which the preliminary results are presented in this *Bulletin*, treats capital formation as a process which exhibits significant peculiarities in the business cycle; and since it is expected that

This error in interpretation may be due to an oversight, as Mr May suggests by inference from your statement on page 102 that 'Mr Kuznets has arrived at much the same conclusion' as Mr Clark, obviously in reference to the 'large proportion depreciation, etc. normally bears to the value of investment' (page 102). The same error obviously accounts for your statement on page 104 that 'Mr Kuznets' method must surely lead to too low an estimate of the annual increase in depreciation, etc.; for he puts the latter at less than 1½ per cent per annum of the new net capital formation'. As far as I can figure out the basis of this statement, it rests upon the ratio of the increase from 1925 to 1929 of the entry in your table for entrepreneurs' servicing, repairs, maintenance, depreciation and depletion (9,010–7,685 divided by four, or 331) to the average volume of net capital formation as given in the bottom line of the table (24,434). And I agree that if the comparison were between the increase in depreciation and depletion charges and the properly measured volume of net capital formation, this rate of 1½ per cent would suggest that the charges are too low. But you overlooked the fact that this combined item of depreciation, depletion, repairs, service and maintenance showed a decline after 1929 while net capital formation, as given in line 3 of your table, continued to be positive. Also, the comparison should properly be made between the change in depreciation and depletion charges, exclusive of servicing, repairs, maintenance, etc., and the volume of net capital formation, exclusive of changes in business inventories. Servicing, repairs, maintenance, etc. are a cyclically variable item which is rather loosely connected with the volume of fixed capital; and inventories are a part of capital to which depreciation and depletion charges are not customarily applied.*

All these considerations lead to the conclusion that the use of our estimates in your book was over hasty. A correct interpretation of these estimates, which would deal only with net capital formation destined for business use, would have shown that the ratio of net to gross capital

this study will be followed by a parallel study of the flow of funds, the concept of gross capital formation was adopted as the basic one. This, of course, does not preclude the possibility of measuring net capital formation, and it is hoped that such measures will be given in the final report.' And on p. 2 I state again: '... it was decided... to deal with gross rather than net capital formation at least at first', the footnote at this point adding 'The results of an attempt to estimate net capital formation destined for business enterprises are presented in Table 10'.

* It is of interest that your table on p. 102, based on Mr Clark's figures, shows an average rise in the 'Value of physical wasting of old capital' of 2 million pounds sterling per year, while the average value of 'Net investment' averages for the four years 220 million pounds sterling, suggesting an implicit depreciation rate of less than 1 per cent per annum, surely too low a rate unless a substantial part of the net investment is accounted for by an increase in inventories to which the depreciation rate does not apply.

formation is substantially the same as in Mr Clark's estimates; that the annual increase in the depreciation and depletion charges during the years from 1925 to 1929 formed 6 per cent of net capital formation, when the latter is made to exclude changes in business inventories, and service, repairs and maintenance; that the depreciation and depletion charges began to decline about the same time that net capital formation turned negative; and that the deduction of charges for the consumption of fixed capital brings about a situation during the depression when net capital formation turns negative.

This correct interpretation of the estimates would have strengthened your final conclusion that 'Above all, net capital formation suffered an appalling collapse after 1929' (page 104). For it would suggest that not only did it decline, but that it actually became a negative quantity. In this connection, you may be interested in a partial estimate of the depreciation charge for some items of capital formation destined for use by consumers. According to Mr Solomon Fabricant, who is at present conducting a study of capital consumption at the National Bureau of Economic Research, the depreciation charges on residential property, not held by corporations, amounted in 1929 to 2·3 billion dollars, and the depreciation for the same year on all passenger automobiles in use in this country amounted to 2·5 million dollars. Our estimates of the corresponding gross capital formation items, viz. residential construction and output of passenger cars at cost to consumers, was for 1929, 2·1 billion and 3·4 billion dollars, respectively. Thus for these two items, the net capital formation in 1929 was 0·7 billion dollars, or only 13 per cent of gross capital formation. It is obvious that the tendency of these depreciation charges to hold their level during the years of depression, and the drastic contraction in the volume of gross capital formation, would produce a huge negative item in the net capital formation column. It is probable that if a proper adjustment could be made for depreciation of other durable consumers' goods and of capital held by public and semi-public agencies, net capital formation in 1931 and 1932 would show strikingly large negative totals.

I am looking forward to reading your treatise, and am grateful to you for sending me a copy. The discussion of our estimates in your book is, as you yourself state, 'in the nature of a digression'. But in view of the misleading impression their treatment may convey to the many readers of your treatise, I am rather perturbed about it. If you can find any way of amending your interpretation and correcting the erroneous impression that it is likely to create, I, and, I am sure, my colleagues at the National Bureau, will greatly appreciate your doing so.

Yours very truly,

SIMON KUZNETS

To S. KUZNETS, *6 April 1936*

Dear Mr Kuznets,

Thank you very much indeed for your letter of March 23rd, dealing fully with the passage in my book where I quote certain figures of yours. It is clear that I have made a confusion, arising from my not realising that your deductions to arrive at net capital formation related to only a part of the capital items included in the grand aggregate of gross capital formation.

I will take an early opportunity, probably in the *Economic Journal,* of clearing the matter up and showing just what the facts are on your calculation.

When I originally worked, I did this, as you will have seen, on the basis of the *Bulletin,* as your book was not then available. Can you tell me whether the present text of the book in any way modifies your calculations in the *Bulletin?*

I should, by the way, be very grateful if you would be so kind as to send me another copy of the *Bulletin,* if you have one available.

Yours sincerely,
[Copy initialled] J. M. K.

From S. KUZNETS, *15 April 1936*

Dear Mr Keynes,

Thanks very much for your letter of April 6. I am sending you under separate cover two additional copies of the *Bulletin.*

The book is still in preparation, but we hope that it can go to press early this summer. The revised totals have not been struck yet, and consequently the extent of changes in the calculations cannot be gauged precisely. I doubt very much that the movement of the totals, with their appreciable rise to 1929 and the very drastic contraction that occurred thereafter, is going to be changed very much. The absolute volumes in question may be somewhat higher than the ones given in the *Bulletin* and there may be some modification in the estimated changes of inventories for the early cycle from 1919 to 1921. However, the movements of net capital formation destined for business use for the period beginning 1925 are likely to remain much as shown by the published estimates in the *Bulletin.*

Sincerely yours,

SIMON KUZNETS

To S. KUZNETS, *11 June 1936*

Dear Mr Kuznets,

I have now looked more carefully into the question of your figures so as to be able to correct the false impression which I gave in Chapter 8 of my *General Theory of Employment.* I enclose a first draft[27] of what I have written, my idea being to publish this in the September *Economic Journal.* I should be extremely grateful for any comments you may care to make on it.

1. May I call your particular attention to what I say about your figures for business inventories? I am not sure whether I have here rightly interpreted you. If I have, would the data in your possession make it possible for you to calculate the figure which I require, namely the difference between the aggregate of inventories at the beginning of each year and the aggregate at the end, both aggregates being calculated at the same price level? This is on the assumption that I am right in assuming that you have applied your price correction not to the two aggregates but only to the difference between them.

2. Have you any estimate of net loan expenditure by public and semi-public authorities?

3. Are there any provisional figures yet available for 1934 or 1935? It would add very greatly to the interest of the figures if we had one or two more years on the upward movement to correspond to those which we have on the downward movement.

Mr Colin Clark has been revising and extending his figures with a view to a new edition of his book, and I hope to be able to add a second section to my memorandum dealing with this.

Yours sincerely,

[Copy initialled] J. M. K.

[27] This has not survived.

DEFENCE AND DEVELOPMENT

From S. KUZNETS, *26 June 1936*

Dear Mr Keynes,

I am enclosing some comments on your note on *Fluctuations in Net Investment*. I hope we answered most of the questions you raised in your letter.

To bring these estimates up to date would be at present a laborious and somewhat thankless task. Since we published the estimates in our *Bulletin* of November 1934, we have been working on a revision and check of the statistical work in the whole study. This work will come to completion by the end of the summer, by which time we shall have a completely revised set of figures covering the period from 1919 to 1934 or 1935. In view of the limited human resources at our disposal, we felt that any time spent on bringing the old estimates up to date would not be justified.

I would like very much to see the final draft of your note before it goes to press.

Yours very sincerely,

SIMON KUZNETS

P.S. Mr Fabricant's *Bulletin* has just come in from the printer and I am enclosing a copy with this letter.

Comments on Mr Keynes's Note on *Fluctuations in Net Investment*

1. *Consumers' Durable Commodities*

With reference to this item I have no comments to make, since the choice of classifying this particular group of purchases under investment or under current consumption expenditures depends largely upon the investigator's definitions and his judgment as to the motivation of such purchases by individuals. However, on the basis of the brief discussion of the question in your note, I would be more inclined than you appear to be to include at least a substantial portion of consumers' durable commodities under investment. Thus, there is a widespread custom in this country to purchase a new motorcar in the expectation of using it for one, two or three years only, and then trading it in for a new car. (This is especially true of the cars in the under $1,000 class which account for an overwhelming proportion of total sales.) In such cases, the individual really sets up a perpetually revolving fund, invested in order to subsidize this periodically changing unit of pleasure-equipment; and accordingly the consumer definitely counts depreciation as part of the current cost of the equipment. On the other hand, your statement on p. 2 which suggests that the setting-up of a financial provision for depreciation, apart from actual repairs and

194

renewals, distinguishes investment from current expenditure, would, if strictly taken, exclude from investment a great proportion of producers' durable equipment. While business units do set up depreciation *accounts*, this does not necessarily mean a provision of replacement *funds*. The difference between the practice of such business units and of an individual who, having purchased a new car, realizes quite clearly the extent of annual depreciation on it, even though he may not provide a reserve fund to cover it, does not appear to me significant.

2. *Consumers' Residential Construction*
This item can better be designated as residential construction, since the magnitudes measured include residential units owned not only by their ultimate consumers but also by business units. With reference to this item, depreciation charges have been estimated by Mr Fabricant for each year in the period.* These estimates introduced into your table on p. 4 yield the following results:

	1925	1926	1927	1928	1929	1930	1931	1932	1933
					(millions of dollars)				
Residential construction	3,050	2,965	2,856	3,095	2,127	1,222	900	311	276
Depreciation†	954	1,079	1,187	1,285	1,368	1,414	1,432	1,437	1,433
Net investment	2,096	1,886	1,669	1,810	759	−192	−532	−1,126	−1,157

3. *Business Fixed Capital*
This is the item corresponding to what we designate as producers' durable commodities, and business construction. Under either item of this combined total we may or may not include parts, repairs and servicing. But if we do include these latter in the *gross* total of capital formation, the deductions in arriving at the *net* total of capital formation should cover not

* This and the other estimate of Mr Fabricant quoted below will appear in his *Bulletin* (No. 60) entitled 'Measures of Capital Consumption, 1919–33'. This *Bulletin* will be out by July 1st and will thus be available to you in time for the preparation of your notes.
† These depreciation charges are as they would be if estimated by accountants—in terms of original cost. If we express them in terms of current (reproduction) costs, we have the following depreciation charges:

1925	1,554	1930	1,901
1926	1,676	1931	1,698
1927	1,754	1932	1,460
1928	1,842	1933	1,567
1929	1,911		

only depreciation and depletion charges, but also charges for current repairs and maintenance. Since it may be assumed that the preponderant part of these items, i.e. parts, repairs and servicing, is treated by the business units as non-durable and financed out of the charges for current repairs and maintenance, we have found it preferable not to include it in gross capital formation, destined for business use (Table 10, line 1a).

Hence, it would perhaps avoid confusion not to refer to two deductions on p. 4 but rather say that the extent of deductions depends on what is included in gross capital formation destined for business use. If it includes item (a), it is then best to put item (a) fully under deductions. If it does not include item (a), then the only deduction necessary is the subtraction of item (b).

This may serve to answer the question which you raise on p. 5 when you say, 'I am not clear on what principles (a) and (b) are distinguished from the other current costs of current output.' Item (a), i.e. parts, repairs and servicing and repairs and maintenance of business construction, is measured on the basis of data directly available for it. In the Census of Manufactures, production of parts and the value of servicing and repairs rendered by manufacturing establishments are reported separately; and while the resulting totals are far short of the total volume of servicing and repairs done on existing fixed capital, they do represent the volume of the more sizable repairs and servicing rendered by manufacturing plants to other units that own and utilize the fixed equipment. Repairs and maintenance of business construction are also measured with the help of direct data available largely for public utilities, and again represent only the more substantial repairs and alterations which business structures undergo. Item (b) is estimated from the corporate accounts, reported to the Income Tax Unit by all corporations in the United States, this item being raised to cover depreciation and depletion by unincorporated business establishments.

Line 1 in the table on p. 5 is thus quite correct. For line 2, i.e. item (b) we now have the revised estimates of Mr Fabricant. His estimates are somewhat higher than our old estimates since they include depreciation on business structures owned by individuals, an item erroneously omitted from our original measurement of item (b). Your table on p. 5 may then be revised as follows:

	1925	1926	1927	1928	1929	1930	1931	1932	1933
					(millions of dollars)				
Gross business capital formation	9,070	9,815	9,555	10,019	11,396	9,336	5,933	3,205	2,894
Depreciation and depletion*	5,085	5,723	5,706	6,027	6,466	6,433	6,177	5,738	5,522
Net investment	3,985	4,092	3,849	3,992	4,930	2,903	−244	−2,533	−2,628

4. *Business Inventories*

This item, quoted on your p. 6 from line A5 of Table 5 of the *Bulletin*, represents a change in inventories not affected by any revaluation of inventories to a new price level. Our procedure, set forth on p. 18 of the *Bulletin*, was, first, to obtain inventories in terms of current valuations; second, to construct price indexes which would reflect changes in the valuation of inventories; third, to translate beginning- and end-of-year inventories to a fixed valuation base (in terms of 1929 prices); fourth, to derive the changes in inventories in 1929 prices; and, finally, to revalue these changes in inventories in 1929 prices to a current price base. Since changes in inventories as we measure them, had to represent genuine diversions from current output into stocks or genuine diversions from stocks into current sales, this was the only method that could be followed.

Thus, your statement on p. 6 and in other places as to our method of estimating changes in inventories is misleading. We do not obtain changes in inventories for 1932 in 1929 prices 'by applying a price correction factor to the *difference* between inventories at the end of 1931 at 1931 prices and inventories at the end of 1932 at 1932 prices'. Since the method used in estimating changes in inventories accords with your concept of net investment, you can use the items on p. 6 of your note in your final summary of net investment on p. 8.

* Here also, the depreciation and depletion charges are accountants' figures. In terms of current prices they become:

1925	5,685	1930	6,712
1926	6,269	1931	6,154
1927	6,313	1932	5,092
1928	6,447	1933	4,971
1929	7,039		

5. *Public and Semi-Public Agencies*

With reference to this item, two comments are in order. First, the item as listed on p. 7 can now be provided for the year 1933, on the basis of more recent estimates by the Federal Employment Stabilization Board. The entry for 1933 now becomes 1,691.

Second, with reference to your concept of 'net loan expenditures', my guess would be that the figures on the net change of public debt outstanding would best serve your purpose. Such net changes in outstanding public debt would, except for the minor changes in the government's cash balances, represent the expenditures of the government not covered from taxes and other revenues, i.e. not resulting from a transfer from the individuals or the business system to the government. Of course, we cannot say that all increases in public debt should be treated as means of financing public construction only. But we can at least proceed on the assumption that what public construction there was, must have been financed either out of revenues or out of borrowing; and that any increase in borrowing should be considered as available for financing of public construction.

The data assembled on the next page refer to public debt only. No such information is available for semi-public agencies; and for the purposes of your analysis it is best perhaps to limit the item under discussion to public construction only. This would yield the following table:

	1925	1926	1927	1928	1929	1930	1931	1932	1933
						(millions of dollars)			
Public construction*	2,717	2,612	3,045	3,023	2,776	3,300	2,906	2,097	1,659
Net change in outstanding public debt†	−43	−280	−244	−10	+441	+1,712	+2,822	2,565	+2,796
Net investment or disinvestment	−43	−280	−244	−10	+441	+1,712	+2,822	+2,565	+2,796

* See *Bulletin*, Table 11, line 22, brought up to date on the basis of more recent data.
† See col. 9 of table on p. 7 of this memorandum [p. 199].

Total and Net Outstanding Issues of Public Debt
(millions of dollars)

	Total outstanding issues			Net outstanding issues				
Date[a] (1)	Federal (2)	State, county, city, etc. (3)	Com- bined (4)	Federal (5)	State, county, city, etc. (6)	Com- bined (7)	Net change (8)	Average for calendar year (9)
1924	20,982	11,633	32,615	20,627	9,921	30,548	—	—
1925	20,211	12,830	33,041	19,737	10,975	30,712	+164	−42
1926	19,384	13,664	33,048	18,790	11,672	30,462	−250	−298
1927	18,251	14,735	32,986	17,542	12,610	30,115	−347	−264
1928	17,318	15,699	33,017	16,522	13,452	29,974	−181	−12
1929	16,639	16,760	33,399	15,773	14,358	30,131	+157	+441
1930	15,922	17,985	33,907	14,969	15,887	30,856	+725	+1,612
1931	16,520	19,188	35,708	16,098	17,457	33,555	+2,699	+2,822
1932	19,161	19,635	38,796	18,673	17,828	36,501	+2,946	+2,565
1933	22,158	19,107	41,265	21,613	17,072	38,685	+2,184	+2,796
1934	26,480	18,942	45,422	25,323	16,771	42,094	+3,409	+2,173
1935	27,645	19,277	46,922	26,137	16,895	43,032	+938	—

[a] (On 30 June in every case.)
Source: Report of the Secretary of the Treasury for year ended June 30, 1935, p. 424.
Total outstanding issue excludes a small volume of matured and non-interest bearing obligations (see ibid. p. 379).
Net outstanding issues are equal to total outstanding issues less those held in U.S. Government trust funds, or owned by U.S. Government or by governmental agencies and held in sinking funds.
The table above does not include the contingent debt of the Federal Government, i.e. obligations guaranteed by the United States. These comprising largely debt issues of the Federal Farm Mortgage Corporation, Home Owners Loan Corporation and the Reconstruction Finance Corporation, were as follows:

Date	Millions of dollars
June 30, 1934	691
Dec. 31, 1934	3,079
June 30, 1935	4,151
Dec. 31, 1935	4,525

(See Cost of Government in the United States, by the National Industrial Conference Board, pub. no. 223, New York, 1936, Table 26, p. 68.)

The omission of construction work by semi-public agencies is not of material importance, because of the relatively small volumes involved (see Table 11 of the Bulletin, line 4).

6. Foreign and Miscellaneous

The net change in claims against foreign countries is truly a miscellaneous item and belongs properly in the total of net investment. But the item designated 'unallocable construction' should, in my opinion, be omitted from the latter total. There are two reasons for this suggestion. First, the item is from the statistical viewpoint most precarious, since it is the residual difference between two estimates of the volume of construction. Such residual items are often subject to extravagant fluctuations, resulting from occasional negative correlation of errors in both estimates the difference between which they represent. Second, if the item has any definite meaning, it represents largely repairs and maintenance of existing structures, even though some share of it may be accounted for by small residential construction. Hence, in interpreting it as net investment, we should reduce the gross amount of unallocable construction by a substantial amount for current maintenance and repair charges. Such a deduction is likely to reduce the magnitude of the item materially. It does appear best to me to omit it completely rather than to include the gross amount of unallocable construction in the total of net investment. With this correction the line on the top of p. 8 becomes:

	1925	1926	1927	1928	1929	1930	1931	1932	1933
				(millions of dollars)					
Net change in claims against foreign countries	428	44	606	957	312	371	326	40	293

7. Aggregate Net Investment

In accordance with the suggestions made for the specific items above we obtain a new total of net investment. This total is somewhat short in that it does not include construction by semi-public agencies and some small share of unallocable construction that could properly be included in a total of net investment. But both omissions are quite minor in character, and could affect but slightly the movement of net investment as shown by the total below.

	1925	1926	1927	1928	1929	1930	1931	1932	1933
					(millions of dollars)				
Residential construction	2,096	1,886	1,669	1,810	759	−192	−532	−1,126	−1,157
Business fixed capital	3,985	4,092	3,849	3,992	4,930	2,903	−244	−2,533	−2,628
Business inventories	916	2,664	−176	511	1,374	716	−725	−4,460	2,970
Net loan expenditures on public construction	−43	−280	−244	−10	441	1,712	2,822	2,565	2,796
Foreign item	428	44	606	957	312	371	326	40	293
Aggregate net investment	7,382	8,406	5,704	7,260	7,816	5,510	1,647	−5,514	2,274

To s. kuznets, *3 August 1936*

Dear Mr Kuznets,

It was extraordinarily good of you to deal so fully in your letter of June 26th with the various questions I put to you. As you will see from the enclosed proof, I have made full use of the opportunities you have given me.[28] Since the *Economic Journal* is published on September 1st, my Memorandum will be printed off shortly. There would still, however, be time to correct an important mistake if you could, soon after getting this, send me a night cable at my expense. I hope this will not be necessary, but, if I have made some plain error, I should like to have the opportunity to correct it before it appears.

You will see that there is one question of logic in which I have departed from your Table. That is to say, I have reckoned depreciation at current reproduction costs, and not in terms of original cost. Is not this correct? If the new construction was in fact exactly making good the physical

---

[28] So much so that the connected tables Keynes published in his note had come more or less bodily from Kuznets' 'Comments' of 23 June. Some of the tables in Keynes's papers show the marking Keynes made in preparing them for press.

condition of buildings after allowing for depreciation, the net investment should be zero, and this result is only obtained by taking depreciation in terms of current costs. You will also notice that I have entered a serious caveat as to the accuracy of your figures for business inventories. This is, of course, notoriously a difficult item to compile comprehensively, and I confess that your figures seem to me to be extremely improbable. This is primarily the case in the years 1932 and 1933. You are in effect alleging that output in 1933 would have been $7,430 million in excess of 1932 (leaving out finished durable goods) even if consumption had been unchanged. Since, however, there was an improvement in employment in 1933, it would seem safe to assume that consumption was greater in 1933 than in 1932. In fact, your other items of investment were more or less the same in the two years. But the improvement in the usual output indices in 1933 does not appear to be anything approaching enough to look after such an enormous increase in the net output for stock between one year and another, in addition to increasing consumption. It would make more sense to me if the decline in inventories in 1932 was as much as $2,000 million less than you have given and the improvement in 1933 also $2,000 million less. I have checked the order of magnitude in your figures by the usual sort of rough tests which I always apply myself and which are difficult to explain to others, and, as I say, your figures here make to me no sense.

Where the error, if there is one, comes in you will know better than I. Is it due to the sample used being unrepresentative? Were there large changes in stocks of e.g. agricultural commodities which have escaped reckoning? Do your figures allow for stocks in the hands of government bodies such as the Cotton Pool and the like? I cannot but think that it would be repaying to work through again both the logic and the arithmetic of this item.

One further question. Have you satisfactory material for

applying to the aggregate of net investment a price-correcting factor, so as to reduce the aggregate net investment for different years to a common price unit? This will be particularly important when your figures for income are available, since they would require a different price corrective to reduce them to a uniform standard. If we had the changes in net investment and the changes in income from year to year, each on its own uniform price standard, very interesting conclusions might come to the surface.

Thanking you again for taking so much trouble.

Yours very sincerely,

[copy unsigned]

From S. KUZNETS, *14 August 1936 (Telegram)*

In interpreting changes in inventories note they cover not only manufacturers' stocks but also stocks of farmers, mines, trade, etc. Revised figures 1932 and 1933 different from those in *Bulletin.* 1932 decline half that in *Bulletin.* New 1933 figures show decline only slightly smaller than new figure for 1932. New figures although unchecked probably better than old.

SIMON KUZNETS

From S. KUZNETS, *20 August 1936 (Telegram)*

Revised changes in inventories in millions of dollars beginning with 1929 are plus 1839, plus 81, minus 550, minus 2,249, minus 2,248. Figures not checked and cannot be released until published by Bureau.

SIMON KUZNETS

To S. KUZNETS, *25 August 1936*

Dear Mr Kuznets,

Thank you very much for your cables which came in time and have been most helpful. The revised figures make the results look much more satisfactory and convincing, though the fall of inventories for 1933 now seems, if anything, too much revised in the other direction. In view of your telling me in your second cable that these figures could not be released at the present stage, I was a little perplexed as to what to do. For I could scarcely publish figures so seriously erroneous as those previously given. I have compromised by entering round figures, not too far from your latest report, with the following explanation in the text: 'From 1929 onwards the figures given in Mr Kuznets' Memoranda of 1934 prove to require correction. Those given above are provisional and approximate estimates pending the publication of revised figures by the National Bureau.' I hope this meets the case.

I will let you have a copy of the final version when one is available. I enclose a cheque for $7, and hope this will cover your cost of cabling.

Yours very truly,
[Copy initialled] J.M.K.

From S. KUZNETS, *19 August 1936*

Dear Mr Keynes,

Thanks very much for your letter of August 3rd and for the proof of the memorandum scheduled to appear in the September issue of the *Economic Journal.* I found little to disagree with in your memorandum, but thought that the interpretation of changes in business inventories was too narrowly in terms of manufacturers' stocks of commodities. Our estimates cover changes also in stocks held by farmers, distributive trades and all other business units, and the fluctuations in stocks of farmers or wholesale and retail dealers often account for a major part of the change in total inventories. I also thought that you would like to know promptly the results of our revision of the inventory estimates for recent years; and for all these reasons decided to send you a cable (at a cost of $4.57), a copy of which is enclosed herewith.

Now as to the questions which you raised in your letter:

1. I agree with your point that in reckoning net investment in current prices one should deduct depreciation in terms of current costs. The reason why we did not do this in the *Bulletin* was that we had, at that time, no estimates of depreciation in current costs, while depreciation in original costs was easily available.

2. With your caveat concerning our estimates of changes in business inventories I am also in agreement, although on grounds somewhat different from yours. The figures for 1932 and 1933 were doubtful, because the basic data derived from *Statistics of Income* were not available at the time we prepared the estimates for these years for the *Bulletin* article. The reasons for doubt which you submit in the letter, however, appear to me subject to question. I am not certain that consumption (ultimate) was greater in 1933 than in 1932. The improvement in conditions did not come until well in the second quarter of 1933; and it is especially to be noted that what we call national income paid out (as distinct from national income produced) was lower in 1933 than in 1932. Whatever increase in production took place from 1932 to 1933 was thus largely confined to an increase in inventories; and we should compare the 7·4 billion dollar excess production in 1933 with total volume of all production of movable commodities (finished and unfinished) in these two years. Now, total output of manufactures amounted in 1933 to about 31 billion; of agricultural products, to about 6 billion; of mines to about 2 billion. The increase in volume of production from 1932 to 1933 was thus, according to the figures, about 23 per cent of the 1932 volume—not an unreasonable figure, since it excludes construction and relates primarily to manufacturing.

However, the revised figures on changes in inventories and the volume of output will give us a more accurate picture of the changes in 1932 and 1933 than the estimates in the *Bulletin*.

3. We do attempt to measure the volume of capital formation in prices of a single year (1929); and for this purpose we use price-adjustment factors which, while specific in their application, yield an aggregate of capital formation in terms of a common price unit. The data available for such price adjustment are none too satisfactory, but we attempted to utilize all the relevant price series.

We are now preparing a rather bulky volume of basic tables used in the study of capital formation, and hope to publish it sometime this year. This volume will give all these supporting materials as well as detailed references to sources and methods used in deriving the final estimates. It is also our hope that in this volume we shall be able to give provisional figures for 1934 and 1935.

Sincerely yours,
SIMON KUZNETS

P.S. In response to your radiogram dated August 19th,[29] we sent you a cable giving revised changes in inventories from 1929 through 1933. I enclose

[29] There is not a copy of this in Keynes's papers.

a copy of this cable, which was sent at a cost of $2.90. Please note that these revised figures have not been checked and cannot be released until they are published by the National Bureau.

To s. KUZNETS, *31 August 1936*

Dear Mr Kuznets,

Thank you for your letter of August 19th which has crossed with mine. I must apologise for having sent you a cheque not quite big enough to pay for the cables. I was calculating from the costs over here.

I shall await your complete material with the utmost interest. In the meantime, there are two points which arise in your letter.

I do not follow what you say in (2); if I have understood your cable correctly, the decline in inventories in 1933 was substantially the same as in 1932 and aggregate investment only a little more. Yet you say, on the one hand, that you doubt whether ultimate consumption was greater in 1933 than 1932 and, on the other hand, that total output increased by 23 per cent. What happened to the difference? Is such an increase in production between the two years compatible with the statistics of employment? I should have thought not. Are not the indications that the improvement in 1933 as compared with 1932 was in all directions, though positive, nevertheless small.

(3) Do I rightly infer that you have figures available to measure the volume of capital formation in 1929 prices, but that the figures given in the tables, which I am using, are not in 1929 prices, but in the price in each of the years in question?

When my final text reaches you, you will find that I have explained more clearly the interpretation of what business inventories mean.

Yours sincerely,

[Copy initialled] J.M.K.

The remaining post-*General Theory* material is best divided into two classes: comments received by Keynes on publication or in early reviews, along with Keynes's replies where available, and more general discussions of issues raised in the book.

Many of the comments Keynes received on publication came from those to whom he had sent complimentary copies of the book. In all, the list in the new collection of papers indicates that he sent out some eighty copies. Amongst the economists who received copies were C. Clark, T. E. Gregory, R. F. Harrod, R. G. Hawtrey, F. A. Hayek, H. D. Henderson, J. A. Hobson, R. F. Kahn, H. O. Meredith, A. C. Pigou, L. C. Robbins, D. H. Robertson, Joan Robinson, G. Shove, P. Sraffa and J. Stamp in England; P. Douglas, R. T. Ely, I. Fisher, C. B. Hoover, F. H. Knight, A. F. W. Plumptre, J. Schumpeter, F. W. Taussig and J. Viner in North America; and G. Cassel, R. Frisch, E. Heckscher and B. Ohlin in Scandinavia. Below we reprint the resulting correspondence with T. E. Gregory, F. A. Hayek, J. A. Hobson and H. O. Meredith.

From T. E. GREGORY, *30 January 1936*

My dear Keynes,

Very many thanks for sending me your last book. You've given me the opportunity, for which I am glad, of being able to say once and for all with what admiration and (I hope) impersonal envy I read every successive piece of work of yours. I loathe and detest the world into which we appear to be drifting and of which you are in some sense a prophet—but there is an element of hope in that economists, of different schools, can still avow mutual regard and respect.

Most sincerely yours,

T. E. GREGORY

From F. A. HAYEK, *2 February 1936*

My dear Keynes,

Enclosed are the proofs of my article. Apart from adding one footnote I have made no changes to speak of.[30]

I should like to take this opportunity to thank you for sending me an advance copy of your book. I have immediately started reading it, but as you will expect, have not yet got very far. I fully agree about the importance of the problem which you outline at the beginning, but I cannot agree that it has always been as completely neglected as you suggest.

[30] F. A. Hayek, 'Utility and Interest', *Economic Journal*, March 1936.

I have also glanced at some of the central later sections of whose main argument I had some idea from the expositions of Bryce[31] and Mrs Robinson. I am still puzzled by the treatment of the saving–investment relationship, of liquidity preference and some other points. But probably all that will be cleared up when I have worked through the whole systematically. But if my present doubts remain I shall probably ask for your hospitality for some notes on particular points in the *E.J.*

But the process of assimilation will probably be a very slow one and even if I should ultimately find that I disagree on many points I have no doubt that I shall have learnt a great deal and probably look in an entirely new light on many problems.

Yours very sincerely,

F. A. HAYEK

From J. A. HOBSON, *3 February 1936*

Dear Keynes,

Accept my best thanks for the copy of your new book which I am reading with deep interest. I find a good deal of it difficult because my brain is getting feeble and unable to concentrate effectively.

Perhaps you will allow me to explain the difficulty which emerges on p. 63 when you deal with income and identify saving as to investment. While the real income of any period must = consumption + more capital (i.e. investment in the shape of plant, materials, etc.), it still seems possible that some remaining income should be withheld alike from buying consumables and buying new capital goods. The crudest example is 'putting into a stocking' or other private hoard which still happens in many countries in periods of crisis. Here it means a slowing down or temporary withholding from production or ordering of more capital goods (investment).

I agree, however, with what you say p. 84 that 'Every such attempt to save more by reducing consumption will so affect incomes that the attempt necessarily defeats itself.' But this process of self-defeat or 'natural recovery' involves a period of underproduction and unemployment—a phase of the trade cycle. I should also urge that what occurs here is not an attempt to reduce consumption but to reduce the proportion of consumption to production. It may well occur that, as I look further in your book I may come to a clearer understanding and acceptance of your position.

[31] See above, pp. 131–50.

I am grateful for the handsome recognition which I see you give to the early book by Mummery and myself.[32]

Yours sincerely,

J. A. HOBSON

From J. A. HOBSON, *10 February 1936*

Dear Keynes,

I have now finished reading your great book, and I hope and expect its shattering exposure of the neo-classical theory and policy will have its due effect on those younger economists who are not too deeply committed to the teaching of their text books. Your 'Concluding Notes' are exceedingly impressive indicators of a social economic policy.

As to my own oversaving theory, I gather (p. 374) that you do not agree that general overinvestment, in the sense of an excessive quantity of plant, power and materials, beyond a profitable level can and does take place. I have assumed that in 1929–30 this situation occurred in U.S.A., stopping any further flow of savings into capital investment and engaging them in gambling and speculation. Excessive investment I have assumed to mean not that *every* industry was over-equipped, but that, as also in Britain, the main branches of industries open to ordinary savers and investors were in this condition. If that were the case, further savings could only find profitable investment in opening up new industries which might stimulate and supply new consumption wants. This is the view taken by Prof. Alan Fisher in a thoughtful book just published by Macmillans under the suggestive title *The Clash of Progress and Security* [London, 1935]. Again, I have supposed there was evidence and support of the view that a 'lag' in the investment of savings took place when a depression was recognised as beginning and that during an actual depression the proportion of saving to spending fell below the level allowable for replacement and enlargement of capital. The order of events, as I have seen it, is underconsumption or oversaving, overinvestment, stoppage of new investment, check on saving and upon all production processes with simultaneous and proportionate unemployment of all factors of production.

But aged as I now am, I hope that my mind is not closed to the acceptance of new reasoning such as you have put in a volume which may, I hope, revolutionise economic science.

Yours sincerely,

J. A. HOBSON

[32] See *JMK*, vol. VII, pp. 364–71.

To J. A. HOBSON, *14 February 1936*

My dear Hobson,

I am very grateful for your two letters. In your second one of February 10th you indicate rightly, I think, the points at which my theory diverges from your own, namely, as follows:—

1. What you have described as general overinvestment, I regard as the pushing of investment to a point where capital is so abundant that further investment cannot for the time being compete in its respective returns with the rate of interest. But this is not absolute overinvestment. The capital is still capable of yielding something in conditions of full employment, but not as much as the current rate of interest requires.

2. The apparent failure of consumption in such circumstances is not really due to the consuming power being absent, but to the falling off of incomes. This falling off of incomes is due to the decline in investment occasioned by the insufficiency of the return to new investment compared with the rate of interest. Thus the decline of investment, by reducing incomes below normal, has the appearance of producing a surplus of consumers' goods. But, just as the appearance of overinvestment did not really represent an absolute overinvestment for social requirements, so the apparent surplus of consumers' goods does not represent a true surplus over what consuming power ought to be. If steps are taken to increase investment, the effect of this on incomes will increase demand up to a point where the apparent redundancy disappears.

3. There is, according to my view, no place in which redundant saving, so to speak, can be in suspense. If some individuals are saving in excess of the flow of new investment, this means that there must be corresponding losses and dis-saving by others who have to live on their capital.

4. I should agree that there may often be mistakes of foresight in a boom and an overexpansion of particular industries beyond all reasonable requirements. But these errors of foresight, while accentuating a boom, are not an essential characteristic of it.

5. I should agree with Professor Alan Fisher that the development of new industries and so forth greatly eases the situation, but I cannot agree that investment has ceased to be socially profitable as long as it yields any return at all. The fact that new investment will not yield more than, say, 3 per cent does not mean that it is socially unprofitable. In my view, investment has only reached saturation point when capital is so abundant that it yields no more over a period of time than its cost of production without any surplus.

These, I think, are the main points on which we have diverged at the later stages of the argument. But I am ashamed how blind I was for many years to your essential contention as to the insufficiency of effective demand.

Yours sincerely,
[Copy initialled] J. M. K.

From H. O. MEREDITH, *15 May 1936*

Dear Maynard,

I have delayed writing to thank you for sending me your *General Theory of Employment* until I should have finished going through it with my small 'honours' class. You certainly have an amazing gift for making your discontent with traditional ideas 'get you somewhere' instead of landing you in a maze of general carping and dissatisfaction. I think you are unjust (not perhaps in your thought but in your expression of it) to the *Treatise on Money* and that on some points e.g. the value of the conception of forced saving and natural rate of interest you have swung too far—but those are questions of emphasis.

I don't like your conclusion that interest might (with continuous full employment) approximate to zero. I've always thought that Marshall's countenancing of this view was one of the very few points on which he went seriously wrong. Your own discussion of m. efficiency of investment seems to me inadequate in not formulating the difference between diminishing m.e. of investment in one line (when investment in all other lines is kept constant) and dim. m.e. in all lines when investment in all lines is extending. I see no reason to suppose that in the latter case m.e. (long period) will decline at all steeply. In the short period it obviously does (*hinc illae lacrimae*) as I conjecture through exhaustion of field[s] for profitable investment which have been sufficiently opened up by technological progress on the one hand and by conscious entrepreneur planning on the other, but each of these forces favouring investment is, I incline to think, capable of almost indefinite growth (given time) as the rate of interest falls. Two further points struck me as inadequate in your discussion of this. I incline to agree with you that a fall of interest will not seriously reduce the rate at which new savings are made: indeed I would go further and even entertain the view that it may stimulate that rate. You don't however, I feel, allow sufficiently for its tendency to raise the rate at which past savings are consumed. In so far as individuals save at one period of life to consume at another period decline of interest implies that they *must* use up their accumulation. You have I think one reference to this, but it's kept very much in the background. The other point was your very cavalier treatment of the notion that 'waiting' is productive. 'Lengthy processes are not physically efficient because they are long.'[33] How true! But how equally true that 'laborious processes are not physically efficient because they are laborious'!! Am I quite silly for supposing that the ability to wait extends the number of alternative ways in which a given result can be obtained and that this extension of the number of options increases the probability that *some* option will be found which presents a high ratio of physical return to effort?

Of course this matter is a side matter to the main themes of your book. There I find myself agreeing with nearly everything you say as to the defects of traditional economics when it comes to handling alterations in the national dividend or its determinants and immensely enlightened by your own treatment. Personally I concluded that Pigou was cracked (on these topics) when I read his *Industrial Fluctuations* years ago and I haven't looked at his [*Theory of*] *Unemployment*. You have probably forgotten asking me even earlier what I thought P. might most advantageously work at and my replying 'the foundations of theory' or words to that effect. I have always been worried by the difficulty (with the old theory) of knowing what happens to the secondary and trifling results of changes if in fact they don't so cancel one another out as to enable the equilibrium to continue. Unfortunately my powers of constructive thought have all along been too

[33] *JMK*, vol. VII, p. 214.

feeble to enable me to 'make anything out' of the difficulties my mind raises. I just get lost in the mists. And (as I began by saying) what I so much admire in you is your gift for 'getting somewhere'.

I'm not quite sure that you have finally finished off 'liquidity premium'. I had a feeling in reading that section that you were constructing an independent or quasi autonomous *cause* of interest out of a *consequence* or reflex of changes in putative marginal efficiency. As I see it (and partly from your own hints in other places) l.p. wanes and waxes as and because entrepreneurs *grow* less or more doubtful of the advantage of investment. *Their* confident inclination (or the reverse) reflects itself in the minds of potential lenders, or on the other side of their own minds since many entrepreneurs operate partly with their own capital and many lenders partly enterprise themselves. Is not a high l.p. in a sense the *same thing* as a judgement that at the margin investment will have a negative net return? It is so that I explain the inability of monetary increase to stimulate investment. However much money there is people won't lend or borrow it if they judge that its investment will be attended by a capital loss.

I'm sorry. The book you see is very much in my mind as I have been lecturing on it in some detail. You on the other hand are probably sick of it by now and off on further adventure. *Bonne fortune!*

H.O.M.

To H. O. MEREDITH, *20 May 1936*

My dear Hom,

Many thanks for your letter about my book. You are certainly not one of the classical economists, and I had some hopes that you would be in sympathy with it. I have not made very good progress amongst the seniors of the subject, but, apart from that, the book is, I am told, making great and rapid progress in London and Oxford as well as Cambridge.

I agree that I must develop more realistically the point I threw out that we might without excessive difficulty reach saturation point in the supply of capital. As expressed in the book it is not much better than an *obiter dictum*. I may very easily be wrong, but I should like to make an attempt to justify more adequately the way in which I feel about the matter.

You are quite right that the chapters on liquidity premium

213

do not carry matters to their final destination. That is a point about which I have been thinking a good deal since the book was out, and I am already conscious of some important improvements which could be made. But I do still feel that the idea itself provides the clue.

Yours ever,

[Copy initialled] J. M. K.

Of the early review articles to provoke comment, two additional ones have turned up, the first that of A. P. Lerner, entitled 'Mr Keynes' General Theory of Employment, Interest and Money' in the *International Labour Review* for October 1936. Lerner sent Keynes a draft, which has not survived.

From A. P. LERNER, *15 June 1936*

Dear Mr Keynes,

Some time ago I mentioned to you an article I had written which was a short account of the main lines of your book. This article was written for the *International Labour Review* after detailed discussions with many economists who violently disagreed with vital parts of your book. By choosing acceptable terminology I have been able to meet many of their objections—which seemed to me to be misunderstandings—so that Haberler, for instance, says that he is in agreement with your theory as I interpret it, but he is doubtful whether you really mean what I say you mean.

I do not think I have departed in any significant manner from your theory, but I would be glad if you would read the article and tell me if I have been led by my discussions into a corruption of your theory or whether I have really been successful in getting it across.

Yours sincerely,

A. P. LERNER

To A. P. LERNER, *16 June 1936*

My dear Lerner,

I think your article is splendid. You have succeeded in getting a most accurate and convincing story into a small space. But you have more experience than I have, I think, of what modes of expression are most effective with the recalcitrant! My only comments are the following:—

1. There are two points which played a considerable part in my own mental development, which you scarcely touch on. The first of these concerns the breaking away from the assumption in some shape or form of Say's Law. This could be described as the re-discovery of there being a problem of the equilibrium of the supply and demand of output as a whole, in short, of effective demand. It was an important moment in the development of my own thought when I realised that the classical theory had given no attention at all to the problem at what point the supply of output as a whole and the demand for it would be in equilibrium. When one is trying to discover the volume of output and employment, it must be this point of equilibrium for which one is searching. I attach importance to this point because whereas the earlier classical economists were quite consciously believing in something of the nature of Say's Law, more recently the whole matter has slipped out of sight. The result is that they have conducted a line of argument which requires Say's Law or something of the kind for its support, without ever giving the matter the slightest discussion.

2. The second point which was important to my own thought was the discovery that, as income increases, the gap between income and consumption may be expected to widen. It seems to me that one can use this conception to express in a very simple and convincing way the essential inter-dependence of the amount of income and the amount of investment. A higher level of income will only be possible without loss to the entrepreneur, if the widening gap between income and consumption can be filled. This can only be filled by investment. Yet it is evident that the requisite volume of investment is not necessarily there. I more and more prefer expounding all this without using the term 'saving' at all. Apart from one's formal argumentation such

215

as that which leads up to the equality of saving and investment, one has to introduce a psychological law from the real world. The widening of the gap between income and consumption as income increases is this psychological law; and it ought perhaps to have more prominence than you give it.

3. On page 5, the complete paragraph strikes me as not quite clear. In any case, it might be better to give less space to this in order to preserve the proportion. Could not your point be put more simply, since it amounts, I think, to saying that a remedy for unemployment which can only come into operation, at the best, *after* the unemployment has developed, must be a second-rate remedy?

4. At the bottom of page 7 you are implicitly using the argument that when income increases, the gap between income and consumption widens. But you are introducing this tacitly, without having yet introduced to the reader the psychological assumption upon which this depends.

The second paragraph on page 13 might be clearer. I have usually distinguished sharply the creation of money by the banking system from the rise and fall of income and have dealt with it by regarding, e.g. the purchase of securities by the banks as involving an equal disinvestment by the individuals who sell them. If you do it your way, the distinction needs to be made clear between the individual who finds himself with more money because his income has exceeded his expenditure and the case of the individual who has more money because he has borrowed from the bank and not used it. I feel that this paragraph is capable of being misunderstood.

I am extremely grateful to you for having been at so much pains to explain matters. From the news which reaches me, I am sure you have been remarkably successful.

Ever yours sincerely,
[Copy initialled] J. M. K.

The second review was by F. H. Knight, which appeared as 'Unemployment and Mr Keynes's Revolution in Economic Theory', *Canadian Journal of Economics and Political Science*, February 1937. After it appeared the journal's editor approached Keynes.

From V. W. BLADEN, *1 March 1937*

Dear Mr Keynes,

I sent you a few days ago a copy of the February number of our Journal in which Professor Knight reviewed your *General Theory of Employment, Interest and Money*, at length. When reading it I could not resist a comparison with Marshall's review of Jevons' *Theory of Political Economy*—or rather Marshall's second thoughts about his review of Jevons, published in the *Memorials*. We feel that we achieved something in persuading Professor Knight to devote a good deal of time to monetary theory and business cycle literature which he had neglected. We wonder what the after effects of this will be.

I can scarcely hope that you will feel ready to reply to any of Knight's criticism, or to undo the damage to Canadian ideas which you will probably feel he has done. But I need hardly say that if you, or Kahn, would care to write a counter-blast we should put as much space at your disposal as we gave Professor Knight.

Yours sincerely,

V. W. BLADEN

To V. W. BLADEN, *13 March 1937*

Dear Professor Bladen,

I am grateful for your letter of March 1st about Professor Knight's review of my book. I read his passionate expiring cries, but, controversial-minded though I am, I could not discover any concrete criticism to reply to. In fact, I really felt that there was nothing at all to be said.

Indeed with Professor Knight's two main conclusions, namely, that my book had caused him intense irritation, and that he had had great difficulty in understanding it, I am in agreement. So perhaps you will excuse me if I leave the article alone.

In a sense I should, I suppose, feel relieved that so able a critic should find so little definite to say. But I cannot really

217

comfort myself in that way, for the truth is, I feel sure, that our minds have not met, and that there is scarcely a single particular in which he has seen what I was driving at. So if I were to write, I could do no more than ask him forgiveness for having been so obscure and so irritating.

Yours sincerely,
[Copy initialled] J. M. K.

On 2 May 1936 at the invitation of the Marshall Society, the under-graduate economics society in Cambridge, Hubert Henderson discussed the *General Theory* which he had reviewed in *The Spectator*.[34] Keynes reported the result to Lydia the next day.

From a letter to LYDIA KEYNES, *3 May 1936*

Hubert came to the Marshall Society yesterday, with Dennis in the chair, to read his paper against my book. I was astonished at the violence of his emotion against it: he thinks it a poisonous book; yet when it came to the debate there was very little of the argument which he was really prepared to oppose. He came off badly in the debate with Joan and Alexander and myself barking round him. The undergraduates enjoyed the cockfight outrageously. One got the impression that he was not really much interested in pure economic theory, but much disliked for emotional or political reasons some of the practical conclusions to which my arguments seemed to point. As a theoretical attack there was almost nothing to answer.

Henderson's paper to the Marshall Society was subsequently published, under the title 'Mr Keynes's Theories' in *The Inter-War Years and Other Papers* (ed. Henry Clay) (Oxford, 1955). After the meeting, the discussion continued.

[34] 'Mr Keynes's Attack on Economics', *The Spectator*, 14 February 1936, p. 263.

AFTER THE GENERAL THEORY

From H. D. HENDERSON, *6 May 1936*

My dear Maynard,

I enclose a copy of some notes which I have sent to Dennis as being my summary of the position as left by last Saturday's discussion.

Yours ever,

H. D. H.

RATE OF INTEREST

(a) Long Term

Maynard admits that the quantity of money has no enduring effect on the rate of interest. Therefore he gives us no long-term theory of the rate of interest at all. He admits that the conditions of supply and demand for savings do affect the rate of interest, though his book conveys throughout the opposite impression. Therefore he cannot deny that the orthodox theory does indicate correctly the factors that matter in the long run. As regards long-period theory his position thus virtually amounts to saying that he is not interested in it.

(b) Short Term

There is no dispute as to the essential facts relating to short-term movement, namely that interest rates rise during a boom and fall during a prolonged depression. Nor is there any very important difference as to the channel of causation. The traditional method of describing the latter is to say that the cash required by the public increases during a boom and declines during a depression. Maynard adopts instead a conception of liquidity preference which lumps this phenomenon (which becomes his L_1) together with an entirely different one (his L_2). These phenomena are totally distinct in character. The first is an inevitable response to the fact that prices have risen and implies no change in 'psychological attitude'. It is not suggested to the mind by the phrase 'liquidity preference' and no reader who cut the algebra would gather that the phrase was intended to cover this phenomenon. The general exposition lays all its stress on the other phenomenon, as, for example, in the assimilation of liquidity preference to 'the state of bearishness' and to 'the concept of hoarding' (pp. 173–174). Moreover on p. 207 the post-war inflations of Russia and Central Europe are expressly cited as providing an extreme example of a low state of liquidity preference, notwithstanding the fact that liquidity preference as a whole, i.e. including L_1, must have been abnormally high. Thus to interpret the variations in the public demand for cash in response

219

to movements in the price level as a form of liquidity preference introduces a serious danger of confusion from which Maynard himself obviously does not escape.

(c) General

The essential issue is whether you can make the rate of interest more or less what you like by manipulating the quantity of money, or whether it is governed by the fundamental factors of the demand curve and supply curve of savings. The fact that interest rates invariably do rise in a boom and fall in a depression, coupled with the admission that the propensity to save and opportunities for investment do exercise an influence, is really conclusive in the latter sense. Maynard cites the experience of the Conversion scheme, but the success of that scheme was only possible because the fundamental economic forces were set in the direction of a big fall in interest rates. The demand curve for capital had fallen to a much lower level, not only temporarily as a slump phenomenon, but permanently, as the result of the collapse of international investment. The play of natural forces would have established a 3 per cent. level eventually even if unaided by policy, but they would have taken an altogether excessive time about it because of the psychological and conventional resistances to which Maynard refers. If on the other hand there had been an enormous demand for overseas issues not prohibited by embargoes, the present level of interest rates could not possibly have been established. Thus the Conversion scheme indicates excellently the true relations between deliberate policy, natural economic forces and psychological resistances, namely that the opportunity for policy is greatest when it is a question of establishing an equilibrium position indicated by the relationship of the natural forces, and obstructed by the psychological factors. Or in other words, the orthodox long-term theory is essential to indicate what policy can achieve.

General Deficiency of Effective Demand

Maynard claims that it is enough for him that this exists during periods of trade depression. He had no answer to make to the arguments that a boom during which prices, wage levels and interest rates rise must inevitably lead to a depression, though I don't think he is ready to admit this. If this is true it follows that you cannot reduce unemployment by making effective demand stronger than it is during periods of boom, and we are back in the question of how to even out demand as between depression and boom. The claim that you can stabilise at the top of a boom is thus essential to Maynard's position.

To H. D. HENDERSON, *28 May 1936*[35]

Dear Hubert,

The whole question raised in your notes to Dennis, of which you sent me a copy, is too large for a letter. But they suggest one or two points which can be dealt with briefly.

1. In admitting that the absolute quantity of money has no enduring effect on the rate of interest, I do not admit that the quantity of money measured in wage units has no enduring effect. My admission merely amounts to saying that, when sufficient time has elapsed for all *relative* prices to be the same as they would have been if the initial change in the quantity of money had been different, the absolute quantity of money no longer has any economic relevance. This, of course, is always admitted by all of us in all contexts. But that does not mean that the amount of money measured in wage units when relative values have shaken down does not matter. It is still this, as before, which in combination with liquidity preference determines the rate of interest.

2. Furthermore, the above deals with what happens in the long run, i.e. after the lapse of a considerable period of time rather than in the long period in the technical sense. The rate of interest is, on my theory, essentially an uncertainty phenomenon. In static conditions where the future does not affect the present or where it of necessity always resembles the past, special limiting conditions enter in. I am not sure whether by 'long-term theory' you mean a theory adapted to some situation of this sort or whether you mean the same thing as I mean above by 'in the long run'. If you only mean the latter, I see no particular difficulty. When relative prices are out of equilibrium, particularly the prices of durable goods and the wage unit, extra complications enter into the determination of the rate of interest. But I need no essential modification of my theory of liquidity preference, operating

[35] The carbon copy was dated 13 May, but this was crossed out on the top copy.

on the quantity of money in terms of wage units, when by the lapse of time these complications are supposed to have evaporated. The rate of interest still depends on the inter-action of liquidity preference and the quantity of money in terms of wage units.

3. I should, I think, be prepared to argue that, in a world ruled by uncertainty with an uncertain future linked to an actual present, a final position of equilibrium, such as one deals with in static economics, does not properly exist.

4. It is important that there should be no misunderstand-ing between us as to the feature of the boom and slump about which there is 'no dispute'. According to my theory, interest rates are determined by the demand and supply for money, not by the demand and supply for durable goods. During a boom the demand for money rises, and during a slump it falls off. This may be either aggravated or mitigated by changes in liquidity preference. If there is no great change in the supply of money, experience shows, I should agree, that the change in the demand for money more than offsets the mitigating change, if any, in liquidity preference, so that interest rates are likely to rise during a boom and to fall during a prolonged depression. But this is all on the assumption that the supply of money is constant. If the supply of money is suitably adjusted, then there is no necessary reason why interest rates need rise during a boom or fall during a depression.

Take, for example, the recent recovery either here or in the United States. The demand for capital has risen very greatly. On the other hand, the supply of money has been amply sufficient, with the possible exception that it was not quite sufficient in the latter half of last year in this country. Consequently, so far from there having been a rise in the rate of interest, both here and in the U.S.A. the rate of interest is much lower than it was during the slump. In the U.S.A. the rate of interest has continuously fallen, and is still falling, *pari passu* with the increase in the demand for durable goods. I should claim the facts of experience in support of the view that the rate of interest depended on the supply and demand for money and not on the supply and demand for durable goods.

You must remember that, according to my theory, the *rate of investment* has to be kept at the level which equates the marginal efficiency of durable goods with the rate of interest. As regards prices, I should remind you that, according to my theory, the rise of prices during a boom is due partly to the rise in the wage unit and partly to the non-homogeneity of resources. Apart from wage changes, it is a consequence of decreasing returns and the employment of less efficient factors. So long as wages do not rise and equally efficient factors are available, a fall in the rate of interest will lead to no rise of prices. An increase in the quantity of money reduces *cet. par.* the rate of interest, the reduction in the rate of interest increases, *cet. par.* the quantity of factors employed. As the quantity of factors employed increases, diminishing returns set in, owing to the employment of less efficient factors, and in addition increasing competition for factors tends to raise their price. The rise of prices, if it occurs, is partly a result of an increase of the wage unit and partly a result of the use of less efficient factors.

5. In general, I wish you would tell me in complete detail what you believe the orthodox theory of the rate of interest to be. When I was writing on the subject, I was astonished to find how difficult it was to discover any statement of the matter. By Pigou it is never mentioned. I have quoted practically every passage in Marshall bearing on it. I much doubt in truth whether there exists any even possibly water-tight statement of the Classical Theory of the rate of interest. The subject has been avoided.

I feel that perhaps you do not do full justice to the complexity and completeness of my theory whether right or wrong. You seem to me to be trying to pick holes in it on the surface, but not to have really tackled it as being what it claims to be, namely, a complete theory with far-reaching implications and connections.

Yours ever,

J. M. KEYNES

From H. D. HENDERSON, *4 June 1936*

My dear Maynard,

Many thanks for your letter. I have delayed answering it until I could get my reply typed.

I assure you that my position is not at all that of trying to pick holes in your theory on the surface. On the contrary it is just because I recognise that it claims to be 'a complete theory with far-reaching implications and connections' that I react so strongly against it. It is as a complete theory, that is to say, that it seems to me essentially false and likely to lead to the misunderstanding rather than the illumination of the economic problems that confront us. There are various detailed parts of it, notably for example your development of liquidity preference (if limited to your L_2) which if you were content to weave them into the structure of the orthodox analysis I should readily accept. I have made quite a sustained effort to understand your theory in all its complications, and in my own mind I am satisfied that I have done so, but the complications are so great that I don't suggest that I was able to develop my criticism adequately in my paper, and I cannot of course attempt to do so now. The issues of interest theory, employment theory and price-level theory are so intertwined together that it is almost impossible to discuss one thoroughly without having to hark back repeatedly to the others. All these issues, however, are really embraced in the question as to whether it would be possible by increasing the quantity of money sufficiently to keep interest rates low during a boom. I deny that this is possible: and it was for this reason that in my paper I laid great stress on the fact that interest rates invariably rose during booms even when they were accompanied by tremendous monetary inflations. You reply with a reference to the recent recovery here and in the United States. But we have not as yet got a boom in either country; and I don't suggest that interest rates must rise during the early phases of a recovery. The phase of boom is not reached until demand generally is stronger relatively to existing supply than it is at present. When this phase is reached prices rise, the demand for money increases and a rise in interest rates must follow. By increasing the quantity of money in that phase you could only succeed in converting the rise of prices into an uncontrolled inflation. The only way of averting this chain of consequences is to prevent the development of strongly booming conditions, i.e. to prevent demand from being so strong relatively to existing supply as to cause prices to rise sharply.

This brings us to your price and employment theories. You say that prices only rise during a boom on account of (a) the tendency of wages to rise and (b) the non-homogeneity of resources. Both these factors are extremely important. According to my view what you call the non-homogeneity of resources is the essence of our long-period unemployment problem; and it cannot properly be regarded as a small-scale, trifling thing. Again, the tendency for wages to rise when demand generally is strong is very important, and these two factors together are enough to establish my essential point that boom conditions, entailing sharply rising prices, may develop though the unemployment figures remain very high. But I can't agree that these are the only reasons why prices rise in a boom. The prices of materials may and do rise substantially when demand is abnormally strong, just because there is a shortage of stocks; and this may work round to an increase in the price of finished goods and to a rise in the cost of living before trade unions have made any demands or before employers have engaged dud workpeople. Incidentally, the rise in the prices of materials absorbs more short-term money in carrying stocks at higher prices, and is thereby a contributory factor to the rise in interest rates. I should agree, of course, that if labour were perfectly homogeneous and perfectly mobile, geographically as well as occupationally, and if further labour did not demand higher wages even after the cost of living had risen, the rise of prices would not go very far until your full employment had been reached. But dynamically considered the rise in material prices may be highly important in starting the vicious circle off. I mention this more or less parenthetically to combat a suggestion which seemed to be abroad in the Marshall Society discussion that if only trade unions would be reasonable there would then at least be no reason why prices and interest rates should rise, however strong demand was made. I avoided discussing your price theory, but it seems to me open to the objection of applying to short-term problems complicated propositions relating to marginal costs and prices which only hold true of the long period, an objection, that is to say, of the opposite sort from that to which your interest theory is in my mind exposed.

But the really essential issue to my mind is whether or not the interest level is dependent in the long run on the fundamental forces indicated by the orthodox analysis. There seems to me no doubt whatever that it is. If I were to try to argue the matter I would merely repeat the argument of my paper, so I will conclude by answering your final question, what I believe the orthodox theory of interest to be. I have always envisaged it as being precisely analogous to the theory of value for a commodity, and I should state my idea of it as follows. The rate of interest (like a price) is determined as the point of intersection of a demand curve and a supply curve. Behind each of these curves lies a governing fundamental factor. Behind the demand curve is the productivity of capital for investment: behind the supply curve is the disposition and ability to save, these corresponding to the utility of a commodity and its costs of production respectively. These fundamental factors are what matter in the long run. In the short run other factors enter into the relations of demand and supply. Again this is analogous to the case of a commodity. A reduction of stocks by, say, a natural catastrophe might raise the price of a commodity materially without altering either the costs at which different quantities could be produced or the utilities of different quantities to the consumer; i.e. without altering the long-run supply curve or the long-run demand curve. Similarly in the case of the rate of interest, variations in the quantity of money are of great importance in the short period. But their influence is transient because in the long run changes in the quantity of money will affect the price level and so lead to consequential alterations in the demand for money. In the above you will understand I am trying to state fairly the impression which the orthodox theory as I have always understood it left upon my mind. It neglected the factor of liquidity preference (your L_2) which did not seem important before the slump; and it doubtless assumed that the reactions of the quantity of money upon prices were easier and quicker than they are, though here again the impression left on my mind has always been that an increased quantity of money would raise prices by permitting them to rise further during a boom and to fall less during a slump than would otherwise be the case.

Yours ever,

HUBERT D. HENDERSON

To H. D. HENDERSON, *11 June 1936*

Dear Hubert,

In reply to your letter of the 4th, I would like to try to reduce the points of disagreement as much as possible. For there are at any rate a few of your points where you have, I think, missed something of what I have been saying.

1. At the bottom of your page 1 you emphasise your denial that 'it would be possible by increasing the quantity of money sufficiently to keep interest rates low during a boom'. But you will find that I have given a good deal of space to emphasising the practical difficulties in the way of this in a society organised in the way in which ours is. There are many passages, but the following will be enough:

On page 164 I emphasise my scepticism as to 'the success of a merely monetary policy directed towards influencing the rate of interest'. At the top of page 320 I return to the same theme with special reference to the trade cycle where I express disbelief in the practicability of sufficiently off-setting the fluctuations in the marginal efficiency of capital characteristic of the cycle by corresponding fluctuations in the rate of interest. On page 327 I emphasise the difficulty of dealing with a boom on what would be theoretically the right basis with anything like the existing systems of control.

2. On the other hand, it is evident that you are no longer maintaining, as I thought you did in your previous note, that the rate of interest would tend to rise if there were an increase in the demand for durable goods. You now say that 'you do not suggest that interest rates must rise during the early phases of recovery'. Precisely; it is not the increase in the demand for durable goods that matters; it is the increase in the demand for money, which does not in practice usually become acute in relation to the supply until the later phases.

3. The ultimate emergence of what I call 'true inflation' is a recurrent theme in my book. When all the resources are employed which are sufficiently efficient for the purpose to bring in a return not less than the marginal disutility of labour, a further fall in the rate of interest can do no good and will merely lead to a true inflation of prices. See particularly page 303, and pages 118–119.

4. There is no ground for your suggestion on the latter half of your second page that I regard the non-homogeneity of resources as a small-scale trifling thing. And it is an essential

part of my argument to point out that the tendency for wages to rise when demand generally is strong is, as you say, important. I have picked out these two factors, namely, the tendency of wages to rise and the non-homogeneity of resources, as my sole explanation of rising prices during a boom prior to true inflation. Since prices frequently do rise during a boom, it is a natural inference that I attach importance to what I regard as the sole explanation of such a rise.

5. But in any case the analysis of the boom is an application of my general argument at a very late stage of it to which I do not devote a great deal of space. You obviously do not like all my wise cracks on the subject and you prefer your own. But you will have to go, as I said before, a great deal deeper if you are to deal with my main theme. You cannot dispose of this merely by discussing in terms of practical policy a particular application of it.

6. The only point in your letter which deals with funda-mental theory is at the bottom of page 3, where you say something about your theory of the rate of interest. I do not quarrel with your last sentence beginning 'Behind the demand curve'—but this sentence would be a good opening to an argument leading up to my theory, not to one leading up to the classical theory. For, if you would continue the argument a little further, you will find that the ability to save depends on the amount of investment so that your supply and your demand curves are not independent and you cannot obtain a determinate conclusion without introducing some additional equation or datum. It is precisely because the *ability* to save depends on the amount of investment that it is impossible to reach a conclusion along the lines you are indicating.

7. However, the question between us is not whether you could, by working at it, produce a better theory than mine, but whether it is true that an adequate theory on different

lines from mine already exists in print. You maintain, I understand, that there is a well-known orthodox theory of interest, open to any student who wants to know what it is, reasonably adequate to the case. Won't you tell me where it is to be found? If I could read the existing theory of the rate of interest set forth in print, I should know what I had to answer.

8. But even the theory of the rate of interest comes in at a very late stage of my argument.

Do not really bother to answer the questions in this letter which can be taken rhetorically. The whole problem is obviously much too large a matter to handle by exchange of letters.

Yours ever,

J. M. KEYNES

From H. D. HENDERSON, *18 June 1936*

My dear Maynard,

It is, as you say, extraordinarily difficult to pursue our argument by means of an exchange of letters. I note that you distinguish between your fundamental theory and what you call your wisecracks, implying that I am merely quarrelling with the latter on grounds that are fairly open to legitimate differences of opinion, while having no substantial criticisms to make of the former. I find it hard to draw this distinction, as the theory and the wisecracks are so persistently intermingled in your argument. The chief impression conveyed by your book is that you hold that the main cause of unemployment in modern societies is a chronic deficiency of effective demand, assumed to be non-existent by the classical economists. I reply by analysing unemployment under the three categories of (a) minimum unemployment, (b) transfer unemployment and (c) cyclical unemployment. I suggest that there is no evidence that there is any unemployment which does not fall under one or other of these categories and I argue that an attempt to make effective demand permanently stronger would not in the long run reduce unemployment under any one of the three heads. You appear to reply that this is a matter of wisecracks upon which you don't agree with me but which leaves your general theory untouched. As I see it, your whole theory depends upon this issue. You contend, for example, with complete generality that an increase in the amount of investment will entail an increase in the ability to save; and this contention is surely an integral part of your fundamental theory But as a general proposition I cannot accept it, holding as I do that an increase of investment when conditions are tending towards boom is likely in the long run to reduce income rather than to increase it. Rejecting this contention, I necessarily reject everything that turns on it, the doctrine of the multiplier, the insistence that there is an equation missing in the orthodox theory of interest, etc.

In the above I have used, as you will observe, the phrase 'in the long run', and this raises an issue on which I am frankly baffled by your attitude. Your mood nowadays seems to be that of saying 'I am not interested in the long run: it never happens.' Whereas it seems to me essential to any clearness of economic thought to distinguish between the immediate and the ultimate consequences of any change. You would not think it unreasonable to say, for example, that while a big increase in the demand for a commodity would be likely to raise its price sharply, the long-run effect would be likely to depend upon the costs at which an increased supply could be produced. The transient nature of changes in the quantity of money on interest rates seems to me analogous to this. But this paragraph is by way of parenthesis.

My general point is that what you call wisecracks are inevitably an essential part of any economic theory. And the question whether particular wisecracks assumed or implied in any theory are true is vital to the question of whether the theory is a helpful and illuminating one. Your theory in particular depends, as it seems to me, entirely upon its incidental wisecracks, and if you once concede that in certain circumstances an increase of investment will result in a decline of employment in two or three years' time, almost all your fundamental propositions are deprived as it seems to me of their general validity. (As regards existing statements of the orthodox theory of interest, my reading of text-books is not fresh enough to be of help, but I suggest that Marshall's *Principles* plus his evidence before the Gold and Silver Commission, plus Cassell contain the whole thing. See particularly the reference to Hume's views in Cassell's *Nature and Necessity of Interest*, pages 19 and 20, where the temporary influence of the quantity of money on interest rates is admitted and any enduring influence denied.)

On the more general question, however, of the sense in which it is true that orthodox economic theory assumes the existence of full employment, I would like to refer you to the last chapter or so of my own little book, *Supply and Demand*, dealing with the nature of real costs (I haven't a copy by me so I can't give you the page references). As you will see there I certainly did not assume that there was no such thing as cyclical unemployment in arguing that resources used to produce one thing were likely in the long run to be diverted from another use.

Yours ever,

HUBERT D. HENDERSON

The remaining correspondence relating to the *General Theory* from the years after publication falls into ten groups of letters: three relating to each of 1936 and 1937 and four to 1938.

The first selection of letters from 1936 contains an exchange with E. F. M. Durbin, then on the staff of the London School of Economics and later a Labour M.P.

From a letter from E. F. M. DURBIN, *20 April 1936*

While I am writing may I say how very much I have enjoyed *The General Theory*. I have read almost nothing else since it came out and I have immensely enjoyed my labours. I find myself in profound disagreement with the political notes in the last chapter and I do not understand which monetary policy you are advocating for the cure of the trade cycle—but the main argument of the book has been most stimulating to me.

To E. F. M. DURBIN, *24 April 1936*

My dear Durbin,

Thank you for your note. I had seen your comments on my book in *Labour*.[36] Assuredly my last chapter is not a necessary consequence of the previous parts. It brings in all kinds of non-economic factors about which economists as such are entitled, as well as likely, to differ *à l'outrance* amongst themselves.

But when, as an economist, you are thinking about the earlier sections I hope you will not overlook the inaccuracy of some of your impressions when you are writing as a politician. For example, you represent me as saying that 'in

[36] 'Professor Durbin Quarrels with Professor Keynes', *Labour*, April 1936.

order to cure unemployment it is, therefore, only necessary to force the rate of interest sufficiently low and maintain it there'. Yet there are many passages in the book devoted to proving that attacks on the rate of interest by themselves are likely to prove an inadequate solution except perhaps temporarily. I, therefore, advocate measures designed to increase the propensity to consume, and also public investment independent of the rate of interest. Again you ask me how I explain away 'the lack of foresight and [the] mistakes in investment'. But I do not seek or require to explain it away. I devote the longest chapter in my book precisely to pointing out 'the lack of foresight and the mistakes in investment'. And this is an important part of the basis of my conclusions that investment is a matter which cannot be left solely to private decision.

In fact, I am afraid that the readers of *Labour* will not get a very clear impression of what *I say* or of what I advocate, even in the last chapter of my book.

Yours sincerely,

[Copy initialled] J.M.K.

From E. F. M. DURBIN, *29 April 1936*

Dear Mr Keynes,

Thank you for your letter of April 24th.

I am very sorry that you feel that I have in any way misrepresented your views. You will I am sure appreciate the strict limits set upon any search for precision of statement by the conditions of pure journalism—suitable for *Labour*. But I wished to be and I hope I was accurate in substance. May I therefore defend the two passages on your purely economic views that your criticise.

To take the less important matter first. When I wrote of your failure to defend private enterprise as an institution for securing the right relative productions I was thinking of the passage on pp. 378–379:

if we suppose the volume of output to be given...then there is *no objection* to be raised against the Classical analysis of the manner in which private self interest will determine what in particular will be produced ...when 9 millions are employed...there is no evidence that the labour of these 9 millions is misdirected...

And therefore

...it is not the ownership of the instruments of production which it is important for the state to assume...

These views of yours may be correct or not but I think I am at liberty to criticise them because I think that a case has been made out for rejecting the *laissez faire* analysis on these grounds as well as on others—and of course it is a vital point to make clear to a Labour public because it is the main difference between your views and those of the Socialist Movement—or at least one of them. When you speak of a 'control of investment' I think that in the light of these passages it is obvious that you are chiefly referring to the volume, rather than the detailed direction, of expenditure on capital.

To turn to the more important point—the question of trade cycle policy—you certainly quote an oversimple phrase that can only be justified by limitations of space and yet what you say in your letter emphasises the point of substance that I had in mind. You say that you also advocate 'measures designed to increase the propensity to consume and also public investment independent of the rate of interest'—both measures of further expansion. That is my point. I simply do not see why you think such a course will cure the trade cycle. Let us imagine the trade cycle to be sufficiently strong to reduce general unemployment to zero. In your chapter on the trade cycle you say that at this point the cure is to reduce the rate of interest—and presumably stimulate consumers' expenditure and increase direct government investment. Now you may have good reasons for believing that the trade cycle movement is quite different from the larger inflations that accompanied the war. We know that it is possible for upward movements in monetary expenditure to proceed beyond the level of full employment to a rise in prices—even to infinity. You contemplate this possibility in other parts of your book. As I say, you may have excellent reasons for thinking that the upswing of the cycle is different from a cumulative expansion that would proceed through the condition of full employment to a rise in prices. Unless there are such reasons—and I do not find them in the *General Theory*—you have given no reason for supposing that your 'cure' would not simply lead to an accelerated inflation, an ultimate rise in prices and the continuous dilemma between allowing the movement to gain further impetus or checking it. And if the movement is checked the disappointment of expectations is the crisis and produces the depression.

Your statement that the crisis is due to a fall in the marginal productivity of capital through the exhaustion of the current rate of invention seems to be simply an assumption.

My own view as to the problem is more complicated than this—arising from the disposal of resources in such a way that full employment can only be reached when investment is partly financed by the creation of new money—the consequences of which I have tried to work out in the last chapter of my book.[37] But I fail to see how you propose to stabilise the boom without allowing the expansion of money to go on after full employment has been reached.

Although it is to be expected that economists will disagree about political matters it is difficult for me to understand how the author of the *Economic Consequences of the Peace*—familiar in part with the world of labour and the history of trade union emancipation—can argue that one advantage of a *laissez faire* system lies in the freedom it gives to certain privileged persons to exercise their sadistic impulses in the control of industrial workers. It is as though you argued that it was one advantage of possessing an Empire that we could get rid of our cruellest countrymen in Kenya. Free enterprise with the whip. After all, the sufferers are only black! The petty tyranny of the employer–employee relationship—irresponsible, hidden, without redress—is surely not a lovely thing. As Tawney says the religion of inequality seems to make it possible for even men of generous good will to forget that workmen are also men.

There are many other points in this most stimulating book that I should like to discuss. But I have already written far too much for you to read. Perhaps you will allow me to repeat how very greatly I have enjoyed it. I wish it had come out before I had published my own book. I should have had much to add and some things to alter. Reading parts of your book gave me the kind of aesthetic thrill that I last remember at Oxford when I was reading Berkeley's *Theory of Vision*—deep insight and clear logic expressed with an economy of words and a sense of prose rare indeed in the sloppy literature of our subject.

Yours sincerely,

E. F. M. DURBIN

To E. F. M. DURBIN, *30 April 1936*

Dear Durbin,

Many thanks for your letter. I did not mean to make any complaint about your article in *Labour,* for I am well aware of the exigencies of politics. I only wanted to be sure that, when you were writing more responsibly, you would not

[37] *The Problem of Credit Policy* (London, 1935).

overlook the complexities of the matter, and the actual character of my argument; and your letter shows, I am glad to find, that you do not.

Following your own principle, I will not attempt to enter into a detailed argument. But there is one observation I might make in the hope of diminishing misunderstanding. When a condition approximating to full employment exists, I should not, of course, reduce the rate of interest further or use any other expansionist expedients until I was afraid that the existing rate of interest etc. would be insufficient to maintain the full employment. You seem to argue that because a further dose of expansionist expedients would merely lead to a rise of prices when the existing dose is sufficient to maintain full employment, therefore they would have the same effect when the existing measures were not sufficient to maintain full employment. At least, that is what your arguments seem to amount to.

On the other hand, I agree that our methods of control are unlikely to be sufficiently delicate or sufficiently powerful to maintain continuous full employment. I should be quite content with a reasonable approximation to it, and in practice I should probably relax my expansionist measures a little before technical full employment had actually been reached.

Yours sincerely,
[Copy initialled] J. M. K.

Another discussant was Hugh Townshend (1890–1974), who, after taking a first in mathematics in Cambridge in 1912, had been a pupil of Keynes while preparing for Civil Service examinations in 1914. He had then entered the Post Office.

From H. TOWNSHEND, *6 March 1936*

Dear Mr Keynes

I venture to send you (enclosed) a note of some minor points in your recent book on the Theory of Employment, etc. which gave some difficulty to myself and some other readers, in the hope—though not without hesitation—that it may be of use to you, in preparing a second edition, to have had your attention called to them.

If my acquaintances in the Civil Service are typical, the number of 'eavesdroppers at the debate'[38] is likely to be considerable from the outset (though perhaps some may find themselves a little hard of hearing); you will appreciate the relevance of your book to the practical difficulties we have come up against during the last few years in trying, in day-to-day work, to apply what we know and read of theoretical economics to such Departmental problems as, for example, forecasting.

Yours sincerely,

HUGH TOWNSHEND

P. 44. In the light of the definitions on pp. 15 and 41, should not the first sentence on p. 44 read as follows (the italicised words have been altered):—
  'It follows that we shall measure changes in current output by reference to the *number of hours' labour paid for* (whether to satisfy consumers or to produce fresh capital equipment) on the existing capital equipment, *hours of skilled labour* being weighted in proportion to their remuneration.'

P. 44. Section IV. The function $Z_r = \phi_r(N_r)$ is here defined in a different sense from the aggregate supply function $Z = \phi(N)$ introduced on p. 24 ...the latter being 'proceeds', net of user cost, and the former 'returns', which must cover user cost. If the same definitions were used, some modifications would be involved in Section IV, and the equation of the ordinary supply curve would, I think be

$$p = [\phi_r(N_r) + U_r(N_r)]/\psi_r(N_r)$$

where $U_r(N_r)$ is the (expected) user cost corresponding to a level of employment N_r.

P. 113. The first sentence of Chapter 10 seems to be subject to the implied qualification that nothing happens, or is done, to change the *form* of the propensity to consume, expressed as a function of *aggregate* income in wage-units. If the assumption were made explicit, would it not be clearer that the formal analysis of the first part of the chapter assumes, for

[38] *JMK*, vol. VII, p. xxi.

example, no material change within the period concerned in the rate of public expenditure (in wage-units) on social services financed out of loan or progressive taxation, or in consumers' loan expenditure per unit of income on such things as houses and domestic equipment financed by repayment mortgage or hire purchase?

P. 288. The argument of the last 15 lines, and hence the conclusion at the top of page 289, seems to assume that none of the entrepreneurs in the industry passing through a bottle-neck (pseudopoise-inflation) state, who do not happen to possess products at a relatively advanced stage of production, will (erroneously) *think* that they can attract a share of their luckier competitors' windfall profits by expanding their production, and proceed to expand it accordingly. Should not this assumption be stated, or if material exceptions are possible, the contingency mentioned and the conclusion qualified accordingly?

P. 289. The argument of the first paragraph of Section III seems to assume no change in the physical productivity of employed labour other than that due to the extension of the margin as employment increases—for the postulate of diminishing returns, as is stated on p. 17, applied only to a period short enough for this to be true. But this passage is dealing with the whole progress from any initial degree of under-employment right up to full employment; and the reader taking the passage at the wrong level of abstraction might erroneously infer that a *long-period* programme of expansion of employment *must* continuously depress real wages—forgetting that, at any stage, improving technical efficiency (or even, in theory, increasing keenness for high output per hour on the part of workers) might offset or reverse the fall of real wages.

And does this not perhaps also apply, even in the very short period to some extent, in so far as there may be materially imperfect competition in the wage-goods industries, qualifying the basic postulate of diminishing returns?

To H. TOWNSHEND, *11 March 1936*

Dear Mr Townshend,

It is a great and unusual pleasure for an author to find so close and attentive a reader as you have been! I am very grateful for your corrections, all of which seem to me to be sound.

As it happens, a reprint of the book is now on order, and

I sent off yesterday to the printer some corrections based on your notes which I hope will be in time. The two corrections on page 44 and also that on page 113 I have adopted exactly in accordance with your suggestion. In the case of your comments on page 285 and 289, whilst I agree with you, I am not making a change, since it is not possible without rather upsetting the pages, and also because it seems to me that a reader who is really following the drift of the argument cannot very well fail to see what is intended.

It is evident that you have a perfect comprehension of the whole matter; and indeed it may prove to be the case that, whilst the book is chiefly meant for my academic friends, it may sometimes get easier reception from those outside academic circles, whose ideas are not quite so crystallised.

Yours sincerely,
[Copy unsigned]

On 21 March 1936 a letter from Townshend appeared in *The Economist* discussing that journal's review of Keynes's book on 29 February. In this letter Townshend took up one statement of the reviewer: 'In equilibrium, then, saving must equal investment. If these two tend to be unequal, the level of activity will be changed until they are restored to equality.' He suggested that this statement by the reviewer reflected a misunderstanding of Keynes's definition of investment in the *General Theory* which covered not only capital goods but also stocks of finished goods including consumption goods. On reading the letter, Keynes wrote to Townshend.

To H. TOWNSHEND, *24 March 1936*

Dear Mr Townshend,

Thank you for your letter in Saturday's *Economist*. I was uneasy about the passage in *The Economist* review to which you refer and am very glad that you have dealt with it.

The main point with which you are dealing is concerned, of course, with the difference between Hawtrey and myself.

I gave a good deal of consideration as to whether I should deal with it explicitly, and perhaps I was wrong to decide not to do so. But if once I departed from the definition of investment as an addition to the value of the capital equipment, I should have found myself involved in endless qualifications. It was an immense simplification of my argument to proceed along the line I did; whilst it always seemed to me that an intelligent reader could adapt the argument without difficulty, as you have done, to the position in the very short period.

Once more you have shown a complete comprehension of what I am driving at, and I am very grateful.

Yours sincerely,
[Copy initialled] J. M. K.

From H. TOWNSHEND, *25 March 1936*

Dear Mr Keynes,

Thank you very much for your letters of the 11th and 24th March. I am rather relieved to learn that you approve of my letter to *The Economist*, as I felt when writing it that it might be misconstrued as having a tendentious implication on the controversy about the *causal* importance of variations in stocks—or at all events judged capable of such misconstruction by people who forget that equations of identity cannot distinguish between residual and causal variations in a term capable of both.

As you say, there is hardly scope for any serious misunderstanding about the definitions; and I should not have thought it worth while to write to *The Economist* on such a point, had not the confusion appeared in a review over rather authoritative initials.[39]

I have come up against one difficulty of a more serious kind (unless I have confused myself) in regard to Section I of Chapter 20 and Section VI of Chapter 21 (the generalised quantity theory of money); and unless I can clear it up for myself after some further thought and discussion, I think I will venture to trouble you with another letter.

Yours sincerely,
HUGH TOWNSHEND

[39] The initials were E. A. G. R., the reviewer being Austin Robinson.

DEFENCE AND DEVELOPMENT

From H. TOWNSHEND, *13 April 1936*

Dear Mr Keynes,

The enclosed note is long, and—I am afraid rather tiresome reading. And it probably betrays some confusions.

But in sending it to you, I need hardly say that I do not expect you to be able to find time to undertake the further economic education of an individual reader by replying in detail!

I had been trying to clear up my mind, in re-reading Chapters 20 and 21, on the implications on monetary (as distinct from economic) theory of the double distinction, stressed in the earlier part of your book, between 'effective demand', expected returns gross of user cost, and the total stream of money actually being spent at any moment in the purchase of finished industrial products and services (consumers and producers 'goods' together); and after reading one of your reviewers (in the *Times Literary Supplement*)[40] who inexcusably says that effective demand is 'the *total* stream of money *being* spent on consumers' and capital goods', it occurred to me that you might be prepared to consider dealing with these difficulties in the generalised quantity theory more fully in a later edition.

I am very conscious of not having been able to state the issue clearly, but I think you will agree that there is a real issue.

Yours sincerely,

HUGH TOWNSHEND

Note on the interpretation of Chapter 20 (especially Section I) and Chapter 21 (especially Section VI)

EFFECTIVE DEMAND AND EXPECTED RETURNS

At the beginning of Chapter 20 it is, I think, made clear that the D-symbols, defined as 'effective demand', are not the gross amount of cash (or its equivalent in wage units) which the entrepreneur expects to receive from the sale of his finished product (which must cover his user cost), but the expected returns less the user cost (which last is itself an expectation by definition). That is to say, the D-symbols are anticipated 'proceeds' $(A-U)$, the sum of the expected income of the producing entrepreneur and the incomes which he expects to have to pay out to the other factors (excluding other entrepreneurs).

But in order to retain this interpretation throughout, it seems necessary to interpret all the 'prices' in the algebra of pages 283 et seq. in a special

---

[40] 'Employment and Money: Dilemmas of Saving and Spending', *The Times Literary Supplement*, 14 March 1936, p. 213.

sense, materially different from the ordinary sense of the word 'price', viz, in a way analogous to the definition of 'aggregate supply price', i.e. as the price (in the ordinary sense) less that part of it which may be supposed to be set by the entrepreneur against his user cost.

For otherwise we should not have the identity $D_{wr} = O_r p_r$ on which all the algebra depends.

The difficulty is that the implications of this special interpretation are hard to bear in mind throughout, especially in some parts of the argument, which might in themselves be supposed to relate to the expected flow of cash in final-purchasing (or its wage unit equivalent) in its integrity.

On the other hand, if the p-symbols mean prices in the ordinary sense, the algebra requires the D-symbols to be interpreted as returns, gross of user cost; and the difficulties drawn attention to in footnote 2 on page 24 then crop up. Besides, a further initial assumption about marginal user cost would be needed from page 283, line 3, onwards, as is made clear on page 67. And the argument of page 281 would not, if I have correctly understood it, stand.

The following examples illustrate the point:—

(1) The word 'spent' in line 26 of page 282 does not seem to relate to the whole of the purchasers' expected spending, but only to that part of it which the entrepreneur regards (after having set off the rest against his user cost) as 'spent' in remunerating him and the other factors. Thus e_{er} would seem to be, not the elasticity of the employment to changes in the number of wage units expected to be spent (in the ordinary sense) on the output of the industry, but its elasticity to changes in the income in wage units expected to accrue to the entrepreneur deciding on the output plus the income he expects to pay out to the other factors (but not to other entrepreneurs). This as the independent variable of an elasticity is perhaps rather hard to picture 'physically'. And the other elasticities of the pyramid, containing 'prices' net of their user cost element, seem even harder. One tends almost instinctively to think in these connections of the *total* of cash expected to be spent on the finished product.

(2) On page 284, line 26, a rise of prices in terms of wage units is spoken of as equivalent to a fall of real wages. But is this so, without special assumptions about marginal user cost in the wages goods industries, if 'prices' are to be interpreted in a special sense, net of user cost? (Clearly, the wage-goods industries only are here in question.)

(3) It has been pointed out to me in discussion that on page 302 the *ordinary* price level must be that in question, user cost being there treated

as one of its elements capable of independent variation. This is indeed the way I first read both the latter part of Chapter 20 and Chapter 21 (having, as you advise the reader in a footnote, omitted Section I of Chapter 20 on a first reading). But on re-reading these Chapters, including Section I of Chapter 20, I cannot reconcile my first interpretation either with the opening pages of Chapter 20 or with the algebraic parts of the later argument. Nor can I, on the other hand, restate these last significantly, because of the difficulties of the degree of integration of industry and the duplication of payments between entrepreneurs inherent in the first term of user cost, namely A_1 (user cost $= A_1 - I$).

The difficulty stated above affects the whole of Section I of Chapter 20 after page 282.

The net effect, after several readings and discussion, is that while I think I have got hold of the *trend* of the argument of Chapter 20, in the sense of its general drift, it has lost its precision for me and left my grasp a little insecure on some of the conclusions. For 'the whole pack of perplexities attending the definition of income' kept at bay up to Chapter 19, is once more lurking in the background!

THE EXPECTED INCOME-VELOCITY OF MONEY
AND ITS ACTUAL VELOCITY

It is explained on page 304 that the form $MV = D$ of the simple quantity equation leading up to the final relation between changes in the quantity of money and prices differs from the ordinary quantity equation $MV = PT$ in two minor respects; and these are detailed on page 299, viz. the substitution of expectations for realised returns, and the further substitution of net for gross income.

But are not these differences worth further analysis?

The ordinary equation in its crude form purports to shew in some sense what quantity of money will 'support' a given level of production and employment as a whole, given both the price level and the wage unit, provided the velocity is known. The prices are the actual prices at which products change hands against money, and the velocity, if not at an instant of time at least in a given 'day', is supposed to be measurable, independently of the other terms of the equation, from factual monetary data, if they were available, of actual turnover of balances, etc.

The equation is thus a statement of a kind of theoretical bookkeeping; significant as an identity, though of no economic importance. When the transition is made to an equation of the same form with V representing *income*-velocity and the transactions confined to income-transactions (which is done, I think, with the idea of importing some economic significance into the bookkeeping), the income-velocity is still, I believe, supposed by some at least of those who use the identity in this form to be in theory independently measurable from data of actual happenings.

(In parenthesis, I do not know that this supposition is not an illusion. For example, Mr Durbin tries, I think, in his latest book[41] to say how the banks could *measure* the income-velocity; but, apart altogether from questions of practicability, I cannot [distinguish] between realised results and expectations! The point is that the management take various possible levels of output, including at least in theory zero output, get the corresponding gross expected returns from their sales branch, estimate the relative user and factor costs with the help of *cost* accounting (quite different from the bookkeeper's accounts) and fix output (and prices if they have a monopoly) so as to maximise the excess of the former over the latter. (Strictly, is it not $A - U - F$ which they maximise, rather than the 'proceeds' $A - U$, unless they prefer expansion of employment for its own sake?))

But the bookkeeping results differ radically from these figures, even in a long enough period for fixed plant to be revalued and cash depreciation payments from gross income adjusted—still more in the short period for which alone, if at all, the effects of a single output decision can be supposed to be isolated. They differ, not merely because the expected gross returns and costs are not exactly realised, but (more fundamentally) because the books do not shew *anything corresponding* to the *differential* cost of which one part of user cost (namely, $-I = G' - B' - G$) is the expectation.

It has been pointed out to me that an 'actual' user cost is referred to on page 58. But this 'actual' or realised user cost can never be exactly known—it is not an actuality of bookkeeping. This is in accordance with experience; for when the entrepreneur tries, as of course he does, to check up the correctness of his output decision after the sales results (A) and the *outpayment* costs of production (F and A_1) have become fact, his check is itself dependent on a further estimate; he inevitably finds that his books do not shew him the ('actual') other part of his user cost. For this is a differential cost—the difference between the value of his equipment and stocks as they now are and as they would have been if he had not produced the output which he is costing *post facto*; and obviously after the event the latter item can only be estimated, just as before the event the former could only be estimated.

What is shewn in the books (and that only accurately at long intervals, immediately after revaluations, and not in respect of the consequences of

[41] *The Problem of Credit Policy* (London, 1935).

any individual decision) is, I think, the aggregate of the supplementary and windfall costs, the factor cost and the 'actual' user cost referred to on page 58. But, quite apart from the difficulty of supposing the book results of the complex of overlapping acts of production to be in some way analysed into their component items corresponding to individual output decisions, neither the factual aggregate of costs nor any of its elements, save F, appears at all, even in a derivative form, in the equations of Chapters 20 and 21. I do not think, indeed, that two of the four elements, viz. the supplementary and windfall costs are mentioned anywhere in these chapters.

Thus the management's efforts to do as well as possible (which are what is summarised in the analysis of Chapters 20 and 21) fix employment and output; but these efforts operate, so to speak, over a moving datum-line of plant and stock value, which varies in part from causes outside the management's control and independent of their output (or monopoly price) decisions. Their books give the net result for a period (approximately only, save from one revaluation to another) of their operations (determined partly, in general, in previous periods) and the independent variations in the datum-line; and the management can never precisely distinguish between them. Yet it is surely the transactions shewn in the books, relating as they do to actual movements of money, rather than the economic causes of output decisions, that are relevant to the quantity of money or to changes in that quantity.

A similar argument seems to hold, (with additional complication in regard to the other part of user cost, namely A_1), for industry as a whole, in regard to the relation between prices (as determined by the complex of decisions on output) and money transactions. Surely, therefore, the deterministic connotation of the bookkeeping type of equation is an illusion, and the attempt to give such equations economic significance by such devices as 'income-velocity' *must* perhaps involve radically altering their character. In other words, is not the attempt to produce a quantity equation which shall have at the same time monetary *and* economic causal significance, chasing a will-o-the-wisp?

I think my difficulties about these two chapters can be summed up as follows:—

(1) The p-symbols of the algebra do not seem to mean prices in the ordinary sense. This does not affect the main run of the verbal argument, but does make it hard to be sure that one is interpreting it correctly in some places.

(2) The generalised quantity equation does not seem to have any relation to the flow of cash in the industrial circulation (or to changes in the rate of this flow) as a whole; nor even to the flow of final-purchase expenditure expected by entrepreneurs when taking current decisions on output, unless the difficulties of duplication in regard to entrepreneurs' payments between themselves can be got over (this affects A_1), and also some assumption made about the variation in the other part of user cost, viz. the entrepreneurs' expectations about the differential values of their own equipment and stocks. Thus the generalised quantity theory does not apparently have any positive bearing on monetary policy in the ordinary sense (i.e. roughly, central banking). But I think that perhaps you will agree with this.

I think I appreciate the intrinsic futility, emphasised in the book, of algebraic manipulations of the ordinary type. But they do seem to have acquired a certain temporary importance, not perhaps wholly factitious, through the confused thinking and doctrinaire economic determinism to which they have somehow led (though one would have supposed them to be a harmless amusement!). And besides, the attempt to restate in algebraic form conclusions arrived at by verbal argument (as distinct from the dangerous reverse process) does, I think, sometimes help to bring to light imprecisions which may have crept into the reasoning. And perhaps this justifies trying to analyse them.

To H. TOWNSHEND, *23 April 1936*

Dear Mr Townshend,

Once again I have to thank you for an acute and understanding criticism, with the whole of which, I think I may say, I agree.

It was a great struggle to maintain complete consistency of terminology throughout my book, especially as I was constantly changing it up to the last moment, and was often inclined to forget to bring other parts into complete harmony with the final definitions.

I am inclined to think that your first point relating particularly to Section I of Chapter 20 could be dealt with, though clumsily, by writing $D+U$ in place of D wherever the latter occurs; so that the definitions of the various elasticities will be correspondingly altered. This is undoubtedly rather artificial and does not fully meet your point, but the whole thing is in truth fundamentally artificial. I have got bogged in an attempt to bring my own terms into rather closer conformity with the algebra of others than the case really permits. When I come to revise the book properly, I am not at all sure that the right solution may not lie in leaving out all this sort of stuff altogether, since I am extremely doubtful whether it adds anything at all which is significant to the argument as a whole.

Your point is, of course, a further development, though not so easily dealt with, of the point which you raised at an earlier date in regard to pages 44 and 45 of my book. That point I have dealt with on the lines you suggested in a very slightly revised edition which has just appeared and of which I am asking Macmillans to send you a copy.

Your second discussion concerning the expected income velocity of money and its actual velocity is also, I admit, quite well founded. Here, as you say, it is more difficult to clean the thing up except by rather drastic changes. And here again the trouble really arises from my trying to produce a closer analogy between my terms and those previously employed than the circumstances really justify.

I think there is something suggestive in what I have written; and I were to try to make it quite water-tight in the light of your criticisms it would become so tortuous and complicated as to be worth less perhaps than in its vaguer form. Here again the right solution probably lies in simply cutting it all out. It amounts to very little, contributes nothing to the understanding of the argument and is simply encouraging the reader to waste his time in a rather futile sort of way. I am conscious that this, like a good deal else in the book, is largely the product of the old associations of my mind, the result of always trying to see the new theory in its relation to the old and to discover more affinities than really exist. When one has entirely sloughed off the old, one no longer feels the need of all that. I should like some day to endeavour to restate the whole matter, not controversially or critically or in relation to the views of others, but simply as a positive doctrine.

Criticisms like yours are mainly useful in helping one to get more fully emancipated from what one has emerged out of.

Yours sincerely,

[Copy initialled] J. M. K.

From H. TOWNSHEND, *27 April 1936*

Dear Mr Keynes,

Thank you very much for your letter of April 24th. It was good of you to reply so fully, and I think I have now got hold of the essentials of the matter.

My interest is not altogether academic. For it has been a part of my day-to-day work for the last two years to prepare monthly forecasts of Post Office telephone revenue and similar figures covering a period of a year or two ahead; and these forecasts govern practical decisions on charges and expenditure which affect employment. The demand to be estimated depends to a great extent on outside factors—that is, on the general state of business; and one's estimates must be related to some kind of consistent picture of the influences which govern recovery and recession. I find that discussion of the factual data (in *The Economist* and similar sources) tends to turn largely—too largely—on theories on monetary limits of expansion ('the date of the next slump'). Having in mind Beveridge's recent Report on the finance of Unemployment Insurance,[42] I think you will appreciate my point, and also the difficulty of getting authoritative professional advice on such matters! Yet it is a disquieting thought that a mistake by an amateur on these difficult questions may keep people out of work.

So the appearance of your book, with its synthesis and development of the principles which should lie behind an intelligent expansionist policy, was for me not only a rare intellectual treat, but also the advent of a practical aid. And I am still more indebted to you for the further explanations in your letters.

Yours sincerely,

HUGH TOWNSHEND

[42] Unemployment Insurance Act 1935: Report of the Unemployment Insurance Statutory Committee on the Financial Condition of the Unemployment Insurance Fund on 31 December 1935.

Later in March, Keynes received a draft paper from Gottfried Haberler.

From G. HABERLER, *17 March 1936*

Dear Mr Keynes,

I expect that you are swamped by notes and articles on your new book. Nevertheless I venture to ask you whether you are prepared to accept the enclosed note for the *E.J.* and if so, when it could appear.[43] In the case that you cannot publish it, please let me know it soon and return the note to me.

The note concerns a methodological point which puzzles me again and again and I should like to put it before the English public.

Yours very sincerely,

GOTTFRIED HABERLER

After consulting Richard Kahn to make certain he was not being unfair to Haberler, Keynes replied.

To G. HABERLER, *6 April 1936*

Dear Haberler,

Thanks for sending me the enclosed. But I am a little perplexed as to how to reply to you about it. I see that I am going to be placed in a delicate position, as editor of the *Economic Journal*, in regard to the comments which may be sent me, perhaps in some numbers, concerning my recent book. On the one hand, as editor I should be reluctant to give over much space to discussions of my own work, particularly where I should feel it necessary to make some comment in reply. On the other hand, in declining contributions, it is awkward to be a judge in one's own case.

In regard to your contribution, I should like, if I may, to get a little clearer about your precise point before I come to a conclusion.

That the concept of marginal propensity to consume and the concept of the multiplier are largely alternative ways of

---

[43] The paper was eventually published as 'Mr. Keynes' Theory of the "Multiplier": A Methodological Criticism', *Zeitschrift für Nationalökonomie*, August 1936.

discussing the same subject, I should, of course, agree. I also agree that the reason why I am rather attracted by the marginal propensity to consume is because this directly relates the matter to the psychological motives which lie behind it and determine it. Nevertheless the former depends upon the relation between income and consumption and the term *investment* does not occur in its definition; whereas the latter depends on the relation between investment and consumption.

You seem to suppose that, because aggregate investment is *equal* to aggregate saving, therefore investment and saving have identically *the same meaning*. This leads you to feel free to substitute *investment* where I write *saving*, as though it makes no difference. But the fact that x and y are related does not mean that they are merely alternative notations for the same thing. Again it is untrue to say, as you do on p. 3, that 'the multipler is defined in terms of the marginal propensity to consume'.[44] It is not. Your method would reduce to nonsense all formal reasoning whatever.

On p. 6[45] you charge me with using the term 'marginal propensity to consume' in two different senses, one which represents the same thing as the multiplier and from the other of which the multiplier cannot be deduced. But you say nothing to substantiate this.

Thus, whilst the first five or six pages of the enclosed clearly amount to a grumble, exactly what the grumble is about does not readily appear. Perhaps the major criticisms are meant to come to the front on the last three pages. But what is it that these criticisms amount to? The passage inserted on page 7 points out that when income is changing the propensity to consume does not settle down instantaneously at what will be its eventual figure for the new level of income; and furthermore this is particularly the case if the

44 *Ibid.*, p. 300.
45 *Ibid.*, p. 302.

unit of time employed is a very short one. For my own part, I should get over this difficulty mainly by not using the concept for very small units. But I should not object to its being applied to very short intervals, if anyone wanted to do this. They would, however, have to allow for the fact that when there was an unexpected change in the situation, the propensity to consume would only adjust itself to the new situation gradually. But there is no particular difficulty about all this. What is your trouble?

If the marginal propensity to consume is unity, then, of course, only an infinitesimal amount of additional investment is possible, for full employment will be immediately attained. If when there is a change in the situation marginal propensity to consume is not unity at first, although it is later on, then there is the possibility of a temporary increase of investment. But here again I see no difficulty either logical or methodological.

Again, on the last two pages you seem to think that you have said something devastating when you point out that marginal propensity to consume and the investment multiplier are related to one another. You seem to think that because two things are related, both of them must be nonsensical. But why should you suppose this? Is your criticism here intended to imply that the marginal propensity to consume is a meaningless concept, or what?

I conclude that, whilst I can see clearly that you are grumbling, I cannot see clearly enough what you are grumbling about. Could you not elucidate the matter further?

Yours sincerely,
[Copy initialled] J. M. K.

AFTER THE GENERAL THEORY

From G. HABERLER, *11 April 1936*

Dear Keynes,

Many thanks for your letter of April 6th. I quite understand that you are in an awkward position as editor in regard to communications on your book. Therefore I have decided to publish my note (with some changes) somewhere else.

The logical principle which I wish to illustrate is that one must be careful to distinguish relationships by definition from empirical relationships. If I choose my definitions in such a way that A and B stand in a certain relationship to one another—e.g. $A = 1/(1 - T/B)$—then it is absurd to treat the one as cause of the other or to be surprised to find that whenever there is B, A has the specified magnitude. Such a statement about the relationship by definition is, of course, absolutely exact, but it tells us nothing about the real world but only something about the consistent use of an arbitrarily chosen terminology.

On the other hand, if A and B are said to be empirically related, we cannot prove *a priori* that this must be so in all cases. The statement is not absolutely exact. We can only say, so far as our experience goes A and B stand in the specified relation, but there are cases thinkable where they are not.

My point is now that you must choose. You cannot have the best of both worlds. You cannot say something on the real world and, at the same time make your statement absolutely exception-proof by relating the relevant magnitudes by definition.

Your letter seems to me rather vague. You do not make up your mind about the nature of your theory. You say: 'The concept of marg. pr. to c. and the concept of the multipl. are largely alternative ways of discussing the same subject.' This is not very precise. The truth is that they are related by definition. You go on: 'the former depends upon the relation between Y and C and the term investment does not occur in its def.; whereas the latter depends on the relation between I and C.' This again is ambiguous. The former does not 'depend on...' but *is* the ratio $\Delta C/\Delta Y$ and the latter *is* the ratio $\Delta Y/\Delta I$ and, since $Y = \Delta C + \Delta I$ multiplier and marginal propensity to consume are related by definition. According to your syllogism on p. 63 [*JMK*, vol. VII] saving and investment have identically the same meaning and one term can be substituted for the other. And for the multiplier, according to your definitions, one can always write $1/(1 - \Delta C/\Delta Y)$. If you do not like these consequences then you must change your definitions. By pointing out this I do not, as you say, 'reduce to nonsense all formal reasoning', but I insist on clearness and object against treating as

251

empirically different what is by definition the same. That you shrink from drawing the obvious conclusions from your own definitions, proves again there is something wrong.

You say I do not substantiate my charge that marginal propensity to consume in the formal sense, in which it is closely related, by definition, to the multiplier, is not the same thing as the marg. propens. to consume in the ordinary sense to which our psychological experience refers. I agree, the thing could be elaborated, but I thought, what I said was sufficient and I still believe that a little reflection will make my point clear. I wish you would consider the following: What we know from our own experience and what we see others doing in respect to their income is that *money* income which is being received at certain points of time is being spent or not spent during these intervals. This experience to which you refer in the chapters on 'the objective and subjective factors' and on the basis of which you arrive at certain quantitative estimates about the marg. propens. to consume, do not refer to the latter in terms of wage units and they cannot abstract from the time interval between the receipts of the income. Therefore they refer to something else than the marg. propens. to consume in the formal sense.

You could, of course, try to construct a bridge between the marg. propens. to consume in the psychological sense and the marg. prop. to consume in the formal sense (and thereby between the former and the multiplier) but there again you have to choose whether this indirect connection is to be one by definitions—then it is exact but does not tell us anything about the real world—or an empirical one, then it would tell us something about the world but could not be proved a priori. I hope you will not choose the former procedure, that would amount to lengthening the terminological roundabout way which could only obscure the situation.

I do not think as you want to make me thinking (p. 4 of your letter) [above, p. 250] 'that because two things are related, both of them must be nonsensical'. I only insist on clearness about the precise nature of the relationships and I urge that a relationship by definition should not be treated as an empirical relationship.

Much more could be said to substantiate my criticism, but before I know whether you are prepared to accept the logical principle set out at the beginning, there seems to be no point in elaborating the matter.

Yours sincerely,

G. HABERLER

To G. HABERLER, *30 April 1936*

My dear Haberler,

Of course, I accept as a truism and as a platitude what you set forth on the first page of your letter of April 11th. My difficulty is in seeing any application of this principle to the passage you criticise. The practical significance of what I say about the multiplier and the marginal propensity to consume arises, of course, entirely out of the empirical psychological law, to which I constantly appeal, as to the probable value of the marginal propensity to consume. The formal argument is directed to showing that, if the marginal propensity to consume is determined in accordance with certain broad empirical principles, certain numerical results can be calculated relating to the investment multiplier and the employment multiplier. I do not prove anything about the latter from my definition of the former or vice versa. There are certain formal relations which, given certain assumptions about the real world, allow certain conclusions about the real world to be deduced. But how could I possibly mean anything other than this, and why should you suppose that I do?

When we come to the second page of my letter [above, p. 249], you make a very curious mistake. You apparently believe that I had said 'that saving and investment have identically the same meaning and one term can be substituted for the other.' But where have I said any such thing? On the page to which you refer me I have said that they are *equal*, that is to say, that aggregate saving and aggregate investment are equal, but can you not distinguish between things being equal and having identically the same meaning? Aggregate saving and aggregate investment are equal in the same sense that the aggregate quantity of sales in the market is equal to the aggregate quantity of purchases. It does not follow from this that sales and purchases have identically the same meaning or that one term can be substituted for the other.

For example, an increase of saving by a given individual can be balanced either by a decrease of investment or by dis-saving by another individual. But it is obviously useless for me to elaborate the matter so long as you can see no distinction between two things being quantitatively equal and their having identically the same meaning.

What has come over you? I am perplexed.

Yours sincerely,
[Copy initialled] J. M. K.

From G. HABERLER, *2 May 1936*

Dear Keynes,

The first point which you raise in your letter is the bearing on the multiplier theory of the logical distinction between relationships by definition and empirical relationships. You call it now a platitude to distinguish sharply between the two. It is usually so that such logical rules sound self-evident when stated in so many words, but it seems to be more difficult to apply them in practice; witness your treatment of excess saving and excess investment in your *Treatise*.

Your second point is that I don't distinguish between things being equal and having identically the same meaning. Unfortunately you are putting the problem rather ambiguously. If we put ' = ' between two terms, then they express identically the same thing, if the two terms are so defined that their equality follows from their definition. On the other hand we may mean that the two things are empirically, so far as we know, always equal. Then ' = ' does not signify identity and we are now allowed under all circumstances, to substitute one expression for the other. Now, if I say that according to you saving and investment mean identically the same thing, I refer, of course, to aggregate, net saving. Don't you say on page 63 (1) 'income = consumption plus investment', which is equivalent to '*investment = income minus consumption*' and (2) '*saving = income minus consumption*'? I am at a loss to understand how you can now deny that this means that S and I mean identically the same thing.

It seems to me that I have a right to being perplexed and that it is hopeless to go on arguing on the first point before this confusion is cleared up. It would take too long to explain it in a letter, but if you see Mr Lerner he can tell you that we have reached agreement on more things than you

254

would expect.[46] I am sorry that such differences in language and logic detract attention from more important questions.

Yours sincerely,
GOTTFRIED HABERLER

Your example of the equality between sales and purchases is not any good, because you don't define these terms. Only after having defined them it could be decided whether they are identical or only empirically equal.

In March 1937 Keynes published a note by Hugh Townshend entitled 'Liquidity Premium and the Theory of Value' in the *Economic Journal*. Although there was correspondence at the time, it has not survived. Later in the same month Townshend wrote to Keynes on another matter.

From H. TOWNSHEND, *23 March 1937*

Dear Mr Keynes,

Before writing the review of Mr Hawtrey's interesting but extremely confusing book,[47] I find it necessary to try to be quite clear as to what the *basic* postulate of classical economics is which you have found to be wrong.

I have set out this, as I understand it, on the attached sheet,[48] but it looks too simple to be true; and moreover it is based on the interpretation of your theory of value in my Note in the *Journal* (based on Ch. 17), and I feel a little uncertain from our correspondence whether you agree with this or not. On the other hand, you wrote some time ago that some notes I sent you were 'mainly useful in helping you to get more fully emancipated from what you had emerged out of', and that the new theory had 'less affinities with the old' than a 'good deal' in the *General Theory* would suggest; and you say in the Preface that what you are saying *is* really simple. *If* I am on the right lines, a brief statement of the point in the review might help to remove the intolerable shoal of red herrings which—so it seems to me—are being thrown, both in Mr Hawtrey's book and elsewhere, across the trail. But I am anxious to avoid adding another one; and I should be most grateful for a hint on the subject.

Yours sincerely,
HUGH TOWNSHEND

[46] See above, p. 214.
[47] R. G. Hawtrey, *Capital and Employment* (London, 1937). Townshend's review appeared in the *Economic Journal* for June 1937.
[48] This has not survived.

P.S. Incidentally, I don't think Mr Hawtrey's own monetary theory and his account of the short-term rate of interest is consistent with the classical postulate, or with his theory of the long-term rate based on it. But that is another matter—though I think it follows from my argument.

To H. TOWNSHEND, *25 March 1937*

Dear Townshend,

I am glad to hear that you are reviewing Hawtrey. The way you are tackling the question in the enclosed seems to me to be right. It is certainly interesting. Though perhaps you were rather explaining what assumption is required to justify the classical postulate than stating what the classical postulate is.

On what you have actually written, however, I have one important criticism. You have inserted in the middle of the first page in ink 'the assumption that they knew what is going to happen implies that all rates of interest are zero'. I am not clear that this is right. The implication is, I suggest, that *inactive balances are zero,* so that *any* reduction in activity or wages necessarily reduces the rate of interest sufficiently to restore either activity or wages to the level at which all balances are required actively. This is quite a good way of expressing the classical postulate, and I am not sure that Hawtrey does not somewhere suggest something very like it himself. On the other hand, the classical economists would scarcely recognise this as representing their basic assumption. Unfortunately they have not thought it worthwhile to state their premises. But I should be inclined to say that the above is not so much their premise as that it lies behind their premise and is required to justify it, if only they knew it. I have made various suggestions in the course of my book as to what their premise may be; all my suggestions amount to the same thing, though expressed in different ways. The form of the premise which they are semi-consciously making is, I fancy, much more like Say's Law. They assume, that is to say, that the demand price for aggregate output is always equal to the supply cost, whatever the level of output.

I think, however, that you are tackling Hawtrey's argument in quite the right way, though no one could accuse Hawtrey himself of being a classical economist. His mistake is a different one, quite peculiar to himself.

Yours sincerely,

[Copy initialled] J. M. K.

From H. TOWNSHEND, *7 April 1937*

Dear Mr Keynes,

Thank you for your letter of March 25th, which clears up the main point I had in mind. I see that the assumption that the inactive balances are zero may be regarded (like Say's Law, full employment, etc.) as one of the alternative forms of the classical postulate.

But I am feeling more and more doubtful whether the position would not be more precisely stated, in accordance with the theory of value implied in Chapter 17 of the *General Theory*, by the proposition that no consistent theory of profit and interest based on any of these postulates is *logically* possible. That is to say, the arguments which appear to be based on them seem to me to involve in their deeper origins the same kind of difficulty as Marshall's conception of a money of constant purchasing power; one cannot strictly 'prove' that in the real world the purchasing power of money in general is not constant, (however obvious this may seem—to some of us!), because there is no such thing as that, the constancy of which is being 'postulated'. In other words, I suggest, we have to deal in the last analysis, not really with an unstated postulate which does not happen to hold good, but with a logical confusion—an elusive thing which no one states because it cannot strictly be 'stated' at all.

I won't try to 'state' this at length; you will, I think, see what I mean if I suggest (1) that your theory of value in its most general form shews that it is not true that the price of *any* durable asset (not merely the rate of interest) is determined by the equations of supply and demand for the others—so that *all* dynamic equational theory must be abandoned (this follows from the effect of expectations in the second-hand market—the exchange of *existing* assets), and (2) that all the forms of dynamic classical theory which I know seem to me to be trying to describe a world in which *risk exists without uncertainty*. The economic man is supposed both (a) to know

257

the future and (b) not to know it, at the same time. It can surely only be because of (a) that he keeps no inactive balances and because of (b) that he earns profit by risk-taking (cf. Knight [*Risk, Uncertainty and Profit*]).

On this view, parts of the *General Theory* should be read as indicating stages of your thought in which you are approaching the most general theory of Chapter 17, but have not quite 'emerged out of' (viz. in regard to the theory of value of durable physical assets) the classical idea of determinacy (at the margin of production), which you shew from the outset to be untenable in the case of money-debts (the rate of interest). I rather gathered from an earlier letter of yours that something like this may perhaps be the position. You will forgive me if I am wrong.

Yours sincerely,

HUGH TOWNSHEND

P.S. I did not mean to suggest that Hawtrey was a classical economist! But he does seem in his latest book (to my surprise) to have one foot in the (pre-Marshallian) classics. The other remains in his own cash-monetary theory. *Both* (I think) neglect the idle balances; but apart from this, they are surely inconsistent with each other?

To H. TOWNSHEND, *11 April 1937*

Dear Townshend,

I have your letter of April 7th. On second thoughts the assumption which I ought to have attributed to the classical economists is not that inactive balances are zero, but that they are inelastic in response to changes in the rate of interest, so that a tendency of the active balances to decline has the effect of lowering the rate of interest by whatever extent is necessary to restore them to their previous figure.

I think there is a great deal to be said for your view that the classical theory is not valid on any assumptions, and that you have put your finger on the spot in saying that they are trying to describe a world in which risk exists without uncertainty. But all this, of course, goes a bit beyond what Hawtrey is dealing with or has in mind.

I agree with you, in this new book Hawtrey is surprisingly on classical lines, particularly pages 102 to 104. I have been reading Hawtrey in the last few days, and I should be interested if you would give your mind to the question of the consistency of pages 102 to 104 with the definitions which come to a head on pages 159 to 160.

According to these latter definitions, saving is equal to the increment of wealth which is equal to capital outlay plus the addition to working capital. Thus an excess of saving over capital outlay is the same thing as an addition to working capital. It is difficult, therefore, to know what Hawtrey means by idle savings or the like; though he makes a further distinction, I think, between a designed augmentation of working capital and an undesigned. Idle savings should mean the same thing as an undesigned addition to working capital.

But on pages 102 to 104, he is practically assuming Say's Law, and an appropriate fall in the rate of interest whenever there are idle savings in the above sense.

In other passages, on the other hand, he implies that there is no remedy for a depression except a reduction in the short-term rate of interest, which will cause the designed stocks of commodities to increase. Apparently, he holds either that an increase in permanent investment can do no good or that an increase in permanent investment will be brought about by a designed increment in stocks of commodities. However, I cannot extract out of it anything which to me makes sense.

Yours sincerely,
[Copy initialled] J. M. K.

In April 1937, Keynes received an interesting note from Gunnar Myrdal.

From G. MYRDAL, *24 April 1937*

Dear Mr Keynes,

Professor Ohlin wrote me in a letter that you were looking for quotations proving that Wicksell knew of the only indirect relation between saving and investment. I am sending you some remarks on the question although I don't think they will tell you anything new. Ohlin must have misunderstood you.

We remember all your pleasant appearance in Sweden and would like to see you here again.[49]

With kind personal regards, I remain

Sincerely yours,

GUNNAR MYRDAL

The idea that there is only an indirect relation—via changes in the money rate of interest and the whole price structure—between saving and investment is so fundamental in Wicksell's theory of money that it is, indeed, very difficult to point out specific quotations, where he is stating it expressively. The whole theoretical problem which Wicksell is trying to solve is, however, what happens to prices, incomes, etc., because of the very facts that the savers are not the same persons as the investors, and that the decisions of those two groups of individuals are governed by quite different motives and only by chance—or on account of a stabilising monetary policy—in harmony with each other. Wicksell used to stress the distinction by making the assumptions of no investment of one's own money and no private borrowing:

> In order to make a clear distinction between the roles of capitalists and of entrepreneurs, we may imagine that the latter work entirely on borrowed money and that they derive this money, not directly from the capitalists, but from a special institution, a bank. (*Interest and Prices*, London 1935, p. 137).

The most clear statement I can find by just running through the content of his 'Lectures' is the following:

> Finally, as regards the statement that increased entrepreneurial activity may lead to higher prices, this is often true, but only on the assumptions which we have already indicated and which we shall examine more in detail at a later stage. In itself the increased 'spirit of enterprise', i.e. the increased employment of capital in the service of production, only creates an increased demand for certain raw materials which are necessary for the creation of almost all fixed capital, especially iron and steel, bricks, timber, etc., and these are in fact the goods which at the beginning of so-called 'good' times first rise in price.* But whether this

---

[49] Keynes had lectured in Stockholm in the early autumn of 1936. See *JMK*, vol. XIV, p. 100.

* The American statistics given by W. C. Mitchell's *Business Cycles* [Berkeley, 1913] do not seem entirely to confirm this view, especially as regards pig iron. I will not for the moment discuss how this contradiction is to be explained or whether it is only apparent.

rise in prices will be followed by a rise or a fall in the prices of other commodities cannot be determined in advance. It depends on whether the money market itself has participated in stimulating the spirit of enterprise. If the moneys from which the increased demand for fixed capital, or its components, proceeds are the fruits of *present* savings, then there will be a corresponding decrease in the demand for ordinary consumption goods, and their price should accordingly fall. The case is quite different where the necessary money capital is partly supplied from metallic reserves which were accumulated and lay idle during previous 'bad' times or where they are created by extended credit, in other words, by an accelerated velocity of circulation of money. (*Lectures on Political Economy*, [vol. II], pp. 158–159.)

Important are also the following passages:

In the foregoing I have merely wished to point out the folly of supposing that circumstances in which, as in the case of concrete commodity prices, there is an essential relation between two things—goods and money—can ever be satisfactorily explained from the point of view of the changes undergone by only one of them, in this case goods, without reference to the other, money. It is, moreover, evident that it would be useless to dwell on the question at all if this view were not in fact so widespread, not only in business jargon but also in scientific literature, especially German.

In one respect, however, this view is justified and serves a purpose in more detailed investigations into the causes of price changes. Every rise or fall in the price of a particular commodity presupposes a disturbance of the equilibrium between the supply of and the demand for that commodity, whether the disturbance has actually taken place or is merely prospective. What is true *in this respect* of each commodity separately must doubtless be true of all commodities collectively. A general rise in prices is therefore only conceivable on the supposition that the general demand has for some reason become, or is expected to become, greater than the supply. This may sound paradoxical, because we have accustomed ourselves, with J. B. Say, to regard goods themselves as reciprocally constituting and limiting the demand for each other. And indeed *ultimately* they do so; here, however, we are concerned with precisely what occurs, *in the first place*, with the middle link in the final exchange of one good against another which is formed by the demand of money for goods and the supply of goods against money. Any theory of money worthy of the name must be able to show how and why the monetary or pecuniary demand for goods exceeds or falls short of the supply of goods in given conditions. [*Lectures on Political Economy*, vol. II, pp. 159–60.]

To G. MYRDAL, *16 June 1937*

Dear Dr Myrdal,

Many thanks for your letter of April 24th concerning the doctrines of Wicksell. I think, however, that there is a misunderstanding about my enquiry.

In his article in the *Economic Journal* for March 1937 (page 55) Ohlin wrote the following passage:—

Already Wicksell had stressed that consumption purchases are governed by that part of individual incomes which people want to consume, whereas investment purchases are not directly governed by the part of income people want to save. The decisions to save and the decisions to invest are taken largely by different individuals, and there is no mechanism which guarantees that the volume of savings and of investment will always be equal. This is the very essence of the Wicksellian approach. Wicksell goes on to investigate what role the rate of interest can play in making them equal, and what happens when they are not made equal.

This took me by surprise and I asked Ohlin to let me have some references where I could see Wicksell's actual wording on these matters. His letter to you presumably arises out of this question. There is not, however, very much connection, I think, between the quotations you have sent and the passage Ohlin gives. Is not Ohlin reading into Wicksell a much later order of ideas?

I do not doubt that Wicksell held the normal old-fashioned view that saving and investment must be equal and that he investigated the mechanism by which, as he supposed, the rate of interest made them equal. Whether he also investigated, as Ohlin alleges, what happens when they are not equal I am not aware. But in any case this is diametrically the opposite from my approach as I have explained in my article in the June *Economic Journal*, and diametrically the opposite to Ohlin's own view as explained at the commencement of his article in the June *Journal*, since Ohlin and I agreed in supposing that it is not the rate of interest which makes saving and investment equal, since they are equal *ex definitione* whatever the rate of interest.

Yours sincerely,

[Copy initialled] J. M. K.

On 9 October 1937 Keynes received from J. W. Angell a note concerning D. H. Robertson's review of his *The Behaviour of Money*.[50] He thought Robertson had misrepresented parts of his evidence and his deductions from it and he was also disposed to take issue with Robertson on some matters of principle. Accordingly, he enclosed a rejoinder. Keynes was initially inclined to break his rule over the publication of rejoinders to reviews, but was persuaded by Austin Robinson, his Assistant Editor, not to diverge from established policy.[51] However, as Angell had sent him a copy of his contribution to the Irving Fisher *festschrift*,[52] the correspondence moved on to other matters.

From a letter to J. W. ANGELL, *7 January 1938*

Many thanks for sending me a copy of your paper in the Irving Fisher volume. I should like sometime or other to write out more fully my views on liquidity preference and the other matters you discuss, for I agree that the discussion of them in my *General Theory* is far from complete. I do think, however, that I have dealt with some of the points you raise. My object throughout has been to distinguish one thing from another, and particularly changes in the marginal efficiency of capital, changes in the estimation of the risk of a given contract being carried out, and the pure rate of interest. Liquidity preference, on my definition, relates to the pure rate of interest only. But this does not mean that I under-estimate the relative importance of fluctuations in the other factors. Indeed, I should agree without hesitation that fluctuations in the marginal efficiency of capital (which

[50] (New York and London, 1936.) The review appeared in the *Economic Journal* for June 1937.
[51] E. A. G. Robinson to J. M. K., 4 November, 1937.
[52] J. W. Angell, 'The General Objectives of Monetary Policy', in A. D. Gayer (ed.), *The Lessons of Monetary Experience: Essays in Honour of Irving Fisher*, (London, 1937).

embraces the risk of disappointment from expectation as distinct from contractual risk) are as a rule far more important than fluctuations in liquidity preference. All the same, particularly on certain occasions, fluctuations in liquidity preference are capable of being decisively important. I wish some time you would read what I have written again, looking at it from the point of view which you have now reached in your own mind. In the case of a good many readers, I have found that they have only read my book at a time when their own attitude towards the problems discussed was much more different from mine than it became subsequently, and in such cases the impression left on their minds as to what I have really said is often quite erroneous. I have a feeling that, if you look again, and bear in mind precisely what my definitions are, you will find that there is much less difference between us than you are sometimes suggesting.

I enclose reprints of two recent articles of mine in the *Economic Journal* bearing on these matters.[53]

From J. W. ANGELL, *22 January 1938*

Dear Mr Keynes,

Thank you for your letter of the 7th and the reprints.

I have not as yet had opportunity to re-read all the relevant parts of your *General Theory*, but I am quite prepared to find that when I do the differences between your view and mine will seem—as you suggest—less than it did when I wrote the article for the Fisher volume. It is doubtless inevitable that when trying to clarify one's own mind, one should exaggerate differences.

With reference to your letter, however, it is not yet clear to me that all the factors you refer to are really as separate as you suggest. Thus the 'estimation of the risk of a given contract being carried out' is surely one of the elements of 'expectation' that get into the marginal efficiency of capital and affect its numerical size; and so does the rate of interest when viewed as an element of prospective cost. Again, I agree that fluctuations

[53] These cannot be identified with certainty.

in liquidity preference may at times have decisive importance. But surely the thing that governs liquidity preference itself is chiefly (speaking loosely) the state of expectation with respect to the future, or some function thereof. In other words, what we are dealing with is a complex set of *inter*-relations between factors, many of which are 'effect' seen from one angle but equally 'causes' seen from another.

It is for these reasons, among others, that in my article I attempted to broaden and generalise, as it were, on your line of analysis. By making both the marginal efficiency of capital and liquidity preference dependent in part on the state of expectation, and by making this last some function of changes in national money income (*not* of consumption alone), I obtained the outline of what seemed to me a more comprehensive and more satisfactory picture. I hope you may find time at some point to comment on my general argument here. (It needs the addition, of course, of some propositions relating to the differences in durability of different kinds of goods and the effects thereof, to the acceleration principle so-called, and to certain other relations.)

I have also sent you a reprint of another article, which despite its tedious mechanics I hope may interest you.[54]

Mr Robertson has just sent me a copy of a reply he had prepared to my proposed Note, which makes me wish still more it had been possible to print both.

I expect to be in England this summer, and shall hope to see you.

Sincerely yours,
JAMES W. ANGELL

To J. W. ANGELL, *7 February 1938*

Dear Professor Angell,

In response to your letter of January 22nd, I fully agree that the points we are discussing do need further consideration and analysis. When one is separating for purposes of analysis elements which are seldom or never discoverable in isolation in the real world, there is an arbitrary element, and one must be governed by what seems most instructive and helpful in understanding the substantial issue.

The object of my distinction—I do not say that I have

[54] Presumably 'The General Dynamics of Money', *Journal of Political Economy*, June 1937.

successfully accomplished it—was to separate the three following elements in the state of expectation:

1. The expectation of income from a physical asset,

2. The expectation of the future rate of interest for different terms of years (which, as I have shown, determines the current rate of interest for any given period), and

3. The expectation of 'moral' risk, that is to say, the failure of the contracting party to keep its engagements. But I do not mean to deny that these elements interact on one another. In particular, the expectation of income from a physical asset depends on the expectation of the scale of output of that type of asset, and this in turn is not independent of a future rate of interest.

Yours sincerely,
[Copy initialled] J. M. K.

Early in 1938 Keynes was again involved in discussions as a result of a book review in the *Economic Journal* by someone else, this time Gottfried Haberler who took strong objection to Richard Kahn's review of his *Prosperity and Depression: A Theoretical Analysis of Cyclical Movements* (London and Geneva, 1937).[55] In this case Keynes accepted Haberler's comments and a rejoinder by Kahn;[56] but in the process of editing he became involved in controversy.

To G. HABERLER, *6 February 1938*

Dear Dr Haberler,

Thank you for your paper in answer to Kahn's criticism which we shall be glad to print in the *Economic Journal*. It has reached me, I am sorry to say, just too late for publication in the March *Journal*, especially as I think it is better that you

---

[55] Kahn's review appeared under the title 'The League of Nations Enquiry into the Trade Cycle' in the *Economic Journal* for December 1937.
[56] Both appeared in the *Economic Journal* for June 1938.

should see a galley proof. It will, however, appear in the issue of the *Journal* to be published on June 1st.

When the proof reaches you, I should be grateful if you would compare your first sentence with the actual passage in my article from which you are quoting.[57] You will find that I have promised, not to give up using the term 'classical economists', but only to remember that there is a variety of other errors!

Would you let me know if you have any objection to our letting Kahn see a proof of this article before it appears, so that, if he persuades us to let him make a further rejoinder, it can appear in the same issue. We shall certainly not encourage him to reply—editors do not like controversies of this sort dragging on, though you, of course, have a clear and undoubted right in such a case as this—and we should press him, in any case, to keep very brief. But, since we shall have in any case to consider whether a reply is to come, there would be an advantage, if there is one, that it should appear in the same issue.

As I am sending off the article to the printer forthwith, I have not done more than glance rapidly at its contents. It will certainly help to minimise disagreement, if we can all get quite clear as to how we are using terms. I am glad to note, therefore, the explicit way in which you make it clear that by an increase in hoarding you mean exactly the same thing as a reduction in the velocity of circulation, so that there may be an increase in hoarding, even though the amount of inactive balances has decreased; and that by an excess of investment over circulation [saving?] you mean exactly the same, and no more than that income is increasing. But these

[57] Haberler's sentence ran as follows: 'In response to a complaint from Mr Robertson, Mr Keynes has promised no longer to clap the label "classical economist" or "classical theory" on to "the vacuous countenance of some composite Aunt Sally of uncertain age".' The Keynes passage referred to was from p. 663 of his 'The "Ex-Ante" Theory of the Rate of Interest', *Economic Journal*, December 1937 (*JMK*, vol. XIV, p. 215).

terms certainly are not exempt from other suggestions than these, and I should have thought you would have found it awfully difficult to keep up these uses consistently.

Many thanks for your good wishes. I am beginning to get better, but I am still not right.[58] I have not yet returned to Cambridge and still have to spend a good deal of my time in bed resting.

Yours sincerely,

[Copy initialled] J. M. K.

Haberley's reply contained marginal comments by Keynes which appear as numbered footnotes.

From G. HABERLER, *17 February 1938*

Dear Mr Keynes,

Many thanks for your letter of February 6th. I am glad that I have a chance of seeing the galley proofs. Rereading my manuscript it seems to me that at some points my criticism of Kahn's paper is perhaps a little too strongly worded and I shall take the opportunity of correcting the proofs to tone down these passages somewhat. For that reason I would prefer that Mr Kahn did not see the original manuscript. I do not want to hurt his feelings.

(You say that you are glad 'to note the explicit way in which I make it clear that by an increase in hoarding I mean exactly the same thing as a 'reduction in the velocity of circulation, so that there may be hoarding, even though the amount of inactive balances has decreased'. Now, I think that hoarding has always been understood as implying a decrease in the velocity of circulation. But I do not define it as exactly the same thing, because I say that V may change *for other reasons* too, which we do not usually classify as hoarding. 'Hoarding' is the species and 'change in the velocity' the genus proximum.[59] The important thing is that there can be hoarding though the amount of *total* balances remains constant (what is denied by Mr Lerner and Mr Kahn) and even if it decreases. A decrease in *inactive* balances, however, implies *ceteris paribus* an increase in V (provided that the total amount of balances remains unchanged or even if it decreases by the full amount of the decrease in inactive balances). Hence if we define an increase in hoarding as implying a decrease in V,

---

[58] Keynes had been ill since the spring of 1937.

[59] As you were! I remain, thus, fogged as to what Hoarding is. Hoarding implies decreased velocity, but decreased velocity does not imply hoarding. I suppose he might mean changes in habits and customs.

a decrease in inactive balances is incompatible with an increase in hoarding.

I think you will agree that the concept 'inactive balances' implies the velocity concept, because one must specify how long a balance is to remain inactive in order to belong to the inactive kind. In a very short period all balances are inactive. In a longer period all of them are active, that is are turned over. Without the concept of some sort of an average rate of turnover, you cannot make your distinction between active and inactive balances precise.

(I think you are right that it is sometimes difficult to use consistently the definition of an excess of I over S as implying an increase in Y. Nevertheless, it seems to me clearly to express what those writers who used this terminology without bothering much about the definitions had in mind. An excess of I over S 'is financed by inflation', they say. And does inflation not imply an increase in Y?[60]

I am glad to hear that you feel better and hope that you will have soon completely recovered.

Yours sincerely,
GOTTFRIED HABERLER

P.S. I once more considered your proposal to publish Mr Kahn's reply, if there is to be any, in the same issue as my answer to his original criticism. I should like to say quite frankly, that I should prefer to have it published only in a subsequent number of the *Ec. Journal*. This might also give me a chance to discuss the matter with him, if, as I hope, I can go to England next June. That might save him from further misunderstandings.

G.H.

From a letter from G. HABERLER, *23 March 1938*

As regards the quotation from your article in the first sentence of my note to which you object I should like to say this: I understood you to have promised not to use the term classical economist any more, because it covers a multitude of different views; the admission, in other words, that what you called the 'classical theory' covers a number of heterogenous propositions—erroneous ones in your opinion—carries with it, I thought, the promise not to call all these different views indiscriminately 'classical'. In this assumption I am evidently mistaken, and I have accordingly changed the first paragraph of my note as indicated on the enclosed paper.[61]

[60] God's eyes! Does an increase in Y imply inflation?

[61] Haberler's revised sentence ran 'In a recent contribution to this *Journal*, Mr Keynes admitted the validity of Mr Robertson's complaint that his condemnation of classical economics is tantamount to "shying at a composite Aunt Sally of uncertain age".'

I should like to have your reactions to my remarks in my letter of February 17th on the hoarding problem.

To G. HABERLER, *3 April 1938*

Dear Dr Haberler,

I have your letter of March 23rd, enclosing a revised version of the first paragraph of your article. I will substitute that and be content with it, though it does not really meet my point.

It does not meet my point because I have not in any way changed my use of the term 'classical economist'. The passage which has misled you meant to be saying ironically that, after reading all the articles in the *Economic Journal* in question, I did indeed have to admit that the classical theory was not by any means the only form of error. But I am afraid that one cannot rely on one's irony, any more than one's arguments, being always understood by everybody.

I mean by a 'classical economist' one who, whether he knows it or not, requires for his conclusions the assumption of something in the nature of Say's Law. For example, the concept of the rate of interest being determined by the interaction of the demand for new capital with the supply of saving is a good example of a classical theorem.

Before the war we were all classical economists. I taught it myself to Robertson, undoubting and unrebuked. But, in recent times, I have never regarded Hawtrey, Robertson or Ohlin, for example, as classical economists. Indeed, they have all been pioneers in the other line of approach; though Robertson (not the other two) seems constantly trying to make out that he does still hold the classical theory as well as one of the newer versions. Pigou, on the other hand, was certainly a classical economist up to last year; though whether he still is to-day it would not be quite easy to say. Practically all the more senior and reputed economists in America are classical. Why the term, which is a very convenient and appropriate one, makes people so angry I have never been able to fathom. Why should it be thought so outrageous to say that there was a compact and coherent pre-war theory of economics to which most senior economists still subscribe?

As regards hoarding, you will find in the June *Economic Journal* a short article by Mrs Robinson on the various uses of this term, to which I completely subscribe.[62] There will also be, in addition to your article and one from Robertson, an analysis of the different theories of the rate of interest by A. P. Lerner,[63] which also expresses views which I share.

As your proof reached us in excellent time, we have been able to pass your article on to Kahn in time for him to prepare a short rejoinder for the June number.

Yours sincerely,
[Copy initialled] J. M. K.

From G. HABERLER, *16 May 1938*

Dear Mr Keynes,

Many thanks for your letter of April 3rd. I hope you don't assume that anybody could overlook that you wanted to be ironical. Only the exact meaning of your irony is open to doubt. As it stands and in view of Mr Robertson's remark to which it refers, your passage says that what you called 'classical economics' covers a multitude of *different* errors. That you reserve the word 'classical' for one of them was not clear.

I am glad that you interpret 'classical economist' now in such a broad sense. If Hawtrey, Robertson, Ohlin are not classical economists, then Wicksell isn't one either, nor Pigou in his *Industrial Fluctuations*, and not even Marshall in many passages. Everybody is then classical and non-classical at the same time. In business cycle theory Say's Law is quite out of place and there is no doubt that cycle theory has more and more encroached upon general economic theory, relegating full-employment equilibrium to a special case.

On your definition I do not regard myself as an adherent of the classical school. It seems to me that the difference between your theory and of writers which you call classical, is still smaller, if a number [of] purely verbal

[62] J. Robinson, 'The Concept of Hoarding', *Economic Journal*, June 1938.
[63] A. P. Lerner, 'Alternative Formulations of the Theory of Interest'.

misunderstandings are removed—of which an almost complete collection is contained in Mr Kahn's paper on my book.

There is one further point: Would you agree that an equilibrium with involuntary unemployment is incompatible with perfect competition in the labor market? If namely competition there were perfect, money wages would fall all the time so long as unemployment existed and any conceivably desired level of liquidity could be reached. If that could be agreed upon—and I think you say it yourself in a later part of your book—most classical economists would agree with you, because nobody denies that unemployment can persist, if money wages are rigid.

I enjoyed very much your criticism of the tactic[s] of the present British government in their dealings with the dictators and wish it would influence public opinion profoundly.[64]

I shall be in England during the second half of June and there may perhaps be a chance of seeing you.

Very sincerely yours,

GOTTFRIED HABERLER

To G. HABERLER, *25 May 1938*

Dear Dr Haberler,

I have your letter of May 16. If you will look again at my article you will see that you are still in error as to what I said, which was that the classical theory was not the only form of error. In regard to the last paragraph on your first page,[65] I have as you say answered it in my book. If a decline in employment is associated with an increase in the quantity of money in terms of wage units *ad infinitum* a compensatory factor comes into force: though even so it does not follow that involuntary unemployment can be avoided any more than it can be avoided by increasing the quantity of money indefinitely, keeping money wages unchanged. If classical economists have always meant that a sufficient increase of money in terms of wage units would be a compensatory element, well and good. I am not aware of any passage written before the

---

[64] A reference to 'A Positive Peace Programme', *The New Statesman and Nation*, 25 March 1938 which appeared as 'A British Peace Program' in *The New Republic* of 13 April (*JMK*, vol. xxi).

[65] Above, p. 271.

publication of my book, in which anyone in the classical tradition has said this or anything remotely resembling it. I have always understood that they favoured a reduction in money wages because they believed that this would have a direct effect on profits, and not one which operated indirectly through the rate of interest. But you are more learned in these matters than I am, and I await a reference from you to a passage where a classical economist has indicated a theory of wages resembling mine in the above respect.

You remind me of that passage in the first paragraph of my preface, where I say that 'those who are strongly wedded to what I shall call the classical theory will fluctuate, I expect, between the belief that I am quite wrong and the belief that I am saying nothing new'! I am not quite sure whether you are in the phase of gradually passing from the first belief to the second, or whether perhaps you hold both.

Yours sincerely,
[Copy initialled] J. M. K.

With reference to the 2nd page of your letter I quite agree that very few 'classical' economists have managed to be entirely consistent when writing in other contexts.

As a postscript to the Keynes–Haberler correspondence, we should note that when the second edition of *Prosperity and Depression* appeared in 1939, Keynes reviewed it anonymously for the *Economic Journal*. He wrote his note on the book while at Royat and sent it on to Austin Robinson with a covering note.

To AUSTIN ROBINSON, *28 August 1939*

My dear Austin,

I enclose a note for you on Haberler. I am clear that this is enough and that a new review (which would add little to this note unless it was controversial) is most unnecessary. If any part of it seems to you too obviously ironical, let me know.

It is an odd book. He has taken the greatest pains to be scrupulously fair and in my opinion he has succeeded. Indeed the truth is that he has come the whole way round and swallows the book bait, hook and line. But his digestion tells him that it is all very familiar diet. His method of showing this is to demonstrate that not everything said hitherto is false, at any rate garnished with the proper qualifications, and that such previous remarks and explanations as are, properly qualified, can be shown to be compatible with my theory,— with all of which I cordially agree!

Also it is all very skilful and clever.

Better, perhaps, to type the enclosed out correctly before sending it to the printer.

Yours,

J. M. KEYNES

From The Economic Journal, *September 1939*

HABERLER (G. VON). *Prosperity and Depression.* Geneva: League of Nations (Allen & Unwin), 1939. 9½". Pp. xix+473. 7s. 6d.

This is a revised version of the first edition of 1937, considerably enlarged by an additional chapter of nearly 100 pages, entitled 'Some Recent Discussions relating to the Theory of the Trade Cycle'. The text of the first edition had been substantially completed before the publication of Mr Keynes's *General Theory of Employment, Interest and Money,* and the new chapter aims at dealing systematically with this book and with other recent literature emanating from it. A considerable part of it is occupied with a discussion of differences in terminology. Prof. Haberler prefers Prof. Robertson's definition of saving because in that case a state of inflation (corresponding to an excess of investment over saving) means precisely, no more and no less, that to-day's income is greater than yesterday's, which is, he says, just what an unsophisticated person means by inflation. As regards hoarding he prefers a definition in terms of velocity of circulation to one in terms of the quantity of money held. When he comes to more sophisticated issues he shows how various trade cycle explanations can be formulated in Mr Keynes's terms and along the lines of his theoretical scheme. Generally speaking, Prof. Haberler accepts the broad line of Mr Keynes's theory as valid, but finds nothing significantly new in it except the insistence on the relationship between hoarding and the rate of interest. 'Apart from this,' he concludes (p. 237), 'we have not as yet discovered any essential differences between Mr Keynes's theory and that of the other recognised authorities...as represented by, say Prof. Pigou's *Industrial Fluctuations*, Prof. Robertson's writings or the synthesis attempted in Part II of the first edition of this book.' As regards Mr Keynes's theory of employment and his chapter on 'Changes in Money Wages', Prof. Haberler 'on closer analysis' finds 'that there is no fundamental difference between Mr Keynes's results and those reached by more orthodox writers such as Prof. Pigou in his *Industrial Fluctuations*'. This part of the discussion is rather lacking, however, in precise references to earlier writings. Nor is it made clear whether all the conclusions of earlier writers are in accord with Mr Keynes's *General Theory*, or only some of them. The chapter ends with an important discussion of the distinction between so-called 'static' and 'dynamic' theories. Prof. Haberler threads his way through complicated controversies with great skill, and his *resumé* is much enriched by very full (and extremely up-to-date) references to the relevant periodical literature.

In March 1938 Keynes also became involved in a discussion with E. S. Shaw, then on leave in London from Stanford University. The paper which Shaw sent to Keynes, at D. H. Robertson's suggestion, has not survived but it dealt with Keynes's contribution to the December 1937 issue of the *Economic Journal*, 'The Ex-Ante Theory of the Rate of Interest' (vol. xiv, pp. 215–23).[66] On receiving the paper Keynes replied.

[66] Parts of Shaw's paper found use in his 'False Issues in the Interest-Theory Controversy', *Journal of Political Economy*, December 1938.

To E. S. SHAW, *25 March 1938*

Dear Dr Shaw,

Many thanks for letting me see the enclosed, which I return to you in case you want to keep Mr Robertson's observations.

My own view of it is that it is impossible to get clear about this problem so long as there is a confusion between the supply of savings and the supply of money or its equivalent. They are not *in pari materia* and could not be added together in the sort of way which you seem to do on the top of page 7. I suggest that this becomes obvious when you reflect that for the purpose of restoring liquidity consumption is just as good as saving. The phenomenon we are discussing has nothing to do with saving and investment as distinct from consumption, but with providing financial security in the interval between planning and execution. This applies just as much to the production of consumption goods as to the production of investment goods. When income is created by the expenditure of the 'finance', it is a matter of indifference in this connection whether the recipients save it or spend it. In either case liquid resources are increased by the release of the 'finance' which has been temporarily held up.

Yours very truly,
[Copy initialled] J.M.K.

From E. S. SHAW, *29 March 1938*

Dear Mr Keynes,

Thank you very much for your response to my note. May I reply very briefly, on the understanding that this is not a move to exact still more asistance from you?[67] I appear to be at the mercy of an insidious urge for the last word.

There are two articles of faith expressed in your letter with which I can heartily agree. First, it is certainly true that finance is required just as much for the production of consumption goods as for the production of

[67] I.e. further comments.

investment goods. There can be no doubt that an increase in investment, whether in capital goods or in stocks of consumption goods, tends to exert pressure on the rate of interest. Second, and even more important, flows ('supply of savings') and stocks (your 'supply of money or its equivalent') are not *in pari materia* and cannot be added together. Confusion over the time dimension has, of course, been the chief obstacle to a definitive solution in interest theory.

The remainder of your note is extremely instructive, I think, of the sources of dispute between yourself and your critics. You are using one technique of analysis, your critics another. To a certain extent both parties employ the same terminology, but, because of the difference in technique, the terms have different connotations. May I develop this thesis very briefly?

Your position is that one should analyse variations in the rate of interest by means of a series of snapshots. Each snapshot exposes an instantaneous situation; the volume of money and demand schedules for cash to hold. There is no place in this picture for a flow, whether of savings or investment or consumption or anything else. Only stocks, and preferences, are relevant. Mr Robertson, Mr Ohlin and others have preferred to analyse the problem of interest, not by the instantaneous approach, but by an approach that utilizes the notion of flows or rates. Stocks are irrelevant for them, and when they speak of the supply of money they are not thinking of balances but of the volume of money-to-lend moving to the capital market per period of time from specified sources.

Your *dictum* that there can be a shortage of cash but not a shortage of savings means one thing for you and something quite different for the others. By savings you mean what Ohlin chooses to call *ex-post* savings, the gross difference between income and expenditure on consumption. By cash you mean cash stocks. For Mr Robertson, for example, savings mean not this simple mathematical difference but what Lerner and Lange have called savings decisions or what Ohlin has called *ex-ante* savings. Whichever of the two terms is used, the substance is that portion of the total flow of loan capital, or money-to-lend, which is the product of (a) the receipt of income and (b) the determination to spend it on securities or in the repayment of bank loans. Cash is taken by your critics to mean not stocks but the flow of loan capital which [is] the product of bank lending or dishoarding. In our replies to your recent article, Mr Robertson and I were not confusing stocks and flows: we were using the terminology you had reserved for stocks to describe a flow. In the instantaneous approach there is no place for a shortage of *ex-post* savings. In the flow approach there is no place for a shortage of balances.

Your critics prefer their line of analysis. But Mr Robertson and I have indicated to you that, in our opinion, identical results may be achieved by the two methods, *if* the same fundamental determinants are employed, and *if* the definitions are consistent with the method. We are convinced, too, that each method is useful in throwing a peculiarly strong light upon some of the determinants. In some respects each method is more instructive than the other.

May I develop Mr Robertson's point that you have attempted to hybridize the two methods of analysis? In your letter you mention two processes by which liquidity is restored. One is the expansion of cash balances consequent upon entrepreneurial expenditure of finance. This is an instantaneous phenomenon. A snapshot of cash balances taken immediately after the receipt of income reveals balances in excess of previous non-speculative requirements by exactly the amount of the finance. On your assumption that no change has occurred in speculative requirements between the moment of the snapshot and the moment before, speculative balances bear the brunt of the new cash, the rate of interest declines and finance is liquidated.

The second process of restoring liquidity is a flow phenomenon: '...consumption is just as good as saving' (two flows) for the purpose of facilitating repayment of bank loans or diminishing the rate of flow of bank credit to the market. The course of events is, I presume, as follows: either by selling securities (flow) or by selling consumption goods, the entrepreneur obtains the cash stream he requires to cover disbursements in loan repayment. The time dimension of this process is entirely distinct from the time dimension of the first process.

I am troubled over your interpretation of the instantaneous or stock method of analyzing the restoration of liquidity. The assumption that all expenditures of finance must be credited *at once* to the speculative balances of income recipients is questionable. It requires that the liquidity preference calculus be used to rationalise the holding of receipts. Is it not more realistic to assume that the reason for holding, at the instant of receipt, may be complex? May not one visualise a sharp momentary shift upward in the demand schedule for active balances, succeeded eventually by a gradual and almost, but not quite, complete recession? The transactions demand for cash is stable only as an average over a series of moments in time. This is, I believe, the essence of one of Mr Robertson's criticisms of your recent article, and it is precisely the point I had in mind when I suggested that the entrepreneur must not anticipate the final swings of the multiplier.

My inclination is to minimise the immediate reduction in the margin of liquidity preference. But there is an additional criticism. At the moment of receipt a period closes in which saving takes place. It is followed by a period of dissaving, as the receipts are spent. It appears to me that you have interpreted this analytical necessity to mean successive phases of rising and falling liquidity preference. In other words, you have come dangerously close to confusing the supply of ex-post savings and the stock of money balances.

Your description of the second process of restoring liquidity is almost equally disturbing. You remark that consumption is just as good as saving and that the phenomenon we are discussing has nothing to do with saving and investment as distinct from consumption. But doesn't consumption restore financial security *via* the process of disinvestment (also a flow)? If the entrepreneur uses the proceeds of his sales of consumption goods for repaying bank loans, he cannot also use them for maintaining his stocks or keeping up with replacement requirements. He must do one *or* the other. The decision to consume is not the crucial fact, but rather the decision to disinvest. The phenomenon we are discussing is, when it is analyzed by the flow technique, a matter of saving (properly interpreted) and investment. Finance is retired and the interest reduced, not by consumption but instead as the result of a decline in the rate of investment.

This latter process of restoring liquidity can be reinterpreted in terms of the instantaneous technique. At the instant in which cash finds its way into the hands of the entrepreneur (not the income recipient), the margin of liquidity preference is reduced (by assumption). As a result the 'public's' demand for securities at prevailing prices (the effective desire to repay bank loans at current rates) is increased. After purchases of securities (loan repayments), the prices of securities rise (bank loan rates fall) to a new equilibrium level.

The two methods of analysis lead to the same result. Furthermore, there is real point in using both of them: motives and processes become all the more clear. The decision to disinvest releases cash from transactions balances into speculative balances. Disinvestment and balances are not *in pari materia*, but they can be used with their respective peculiar complements of analytical tools for the same purpose.

These notes are merely a preliminary attempt to prove the compatibility of the two analytical techniques. I hope that eventually I may be able to submit a more complete verification.

Sincerely,

E. S. SHAW

To E. S. SHAW, *4 April 1938*

Dear Dr Shaw,

Thank you for your interesting comment of March 20th. Without wishing to deprive you of the last word, I add one or two remarks.

1. I should myself claim that I deal sometimes with flows and sometimes with stocks, but not with both at the same time. At any rate, that is what I try to do.

2. I am not concerned with instantaneous snapshots, but with short-period equilibrium, assuming a sufficient interval for momentary decisions to take effect.

3. I should much doubt whether Mr Robertson means by 'savings' what Ohlin has called 'ex-ante savings'. At any rate, he has not said so. May I refer you again to what I said about ex-ante savings in my *E.J.* article.[68] Of all the very bad ideas which have been advanced in this connection I consider that much the worst.

4. I am inclined to agree with you that the whole controversy is becoming about very little indeed, and largely a question of expression. But you must remember that it did not begin that way. When my book first came out, the theory of liquidity preference was entirely repudiated by practically all my critics; and, whilst many of them were already holding theories not really consistent with the classical idea of the rate of interest being fixed by the interplay of the demand for new capital with the supply of savings, they were nevertheless clinging to that idea as having substantial validity. By a long series of easy stages a point has now been reached when there is indeed very little in it. My recent article in the *Economic Journal*[69] did no more than emphasise a little more than formerly, in the hope of helping some of my critics, the fact

[68] 'Alternative Theories of the Rate of Interest', *Economic Journal*, June 1937 (*JMK*, vol. XIV, pp. 201–15).
[69] 'The "Ex Ante" Theory of the Rate of Interest', *Economic Journal*, December 1937 (*JMK*, vol. XIV, pp. 215–23).

that the finance required by the planning of activity was one of the ways, by no means negligible, in which changes in the level of activity affected the demand for liquid resources, a factor which had always played a prominent part in my theory. Substantially my theory is exactly what it was when I first published my book.

5. On the question of flows and stocks, and indeed on the whole problem, perhaps I may refer you to an article by Lerner which will appear in the June *Economic Journal*.[70] It seems to me that this really puts it all in a way as clear as daylight, which to my way of thinking is entirely acceptable. I should be much interested to know whether, when it appears, you differ from it.

Yours very truly,

[Copy initialled] J. M. K.

From E. S. SHAW, *7 April 1938*

Dear Mr Keynes,

You were very kind to reply to my last crop of comments. I have only a backhanded way of repaying you—to send another and bulkier crop![71]

I am looking forward to Mr Lerner's article. You will note that some of his concluding remarks in a recent contribution to the *Quarterly Journal of Economics* draw fire (misfire?) in this latest set of notes.[72]

Sincerely,

E. S. SHAW

To E. S. SHAW, *13 April 1938*

Dear Dr Shaw,

I am afraid that I cannot get much sustenance out of the enclosed. But I suppose I am prejudiced! At any rate, there is a good deal in it which I cannot accept as anything like an accurate version of what I am driving at. For what I do mean may I refer you to two contributions to the next *Economic*

[70] A. P. Lerner, 'Alternative Formulations of the Theory of Interest'.
[71] These have not survived. [Ed.]
[72] A. P. Lerner, 'Savings Equals Investment', *Quarterly Journal of Economics*, February 1938.

Journal, namely Lerner's article and my reply to Robertson?[73] Meanwhile, you will not expect me to enter into details.

I confess that I find this sort of controversy dreadful[ly] barren. When *A* criticises *B* on the basis of attributing to *B* meanings which *B* does not accept, there is nothing for *B* to do, if he is to [do] anything, except to pursue the matter sentence by sentence, the final result being of little use to anyone and certainly extremely boring to the reader. Why not attempt a constructive statement of the correct theory, as you see it. Then whether I am right or wring, that would be valuable to the *reader,* and *I* should have a chance of seeing whether or not there is substantial difference between us. But the enclosed, as it stands, looks to me more like theology than economics!

One point I do agree with. I do not consider that the conception of 'finance' makes any really significant change in my previous theory. It is, as you say, no more than a type of active balance which I had not sufficiently emphasised in my book. I described it as 'the coping stone' and attached importance to it in my article mainly because it seemed to me that it provided a bridge between my way of talking and the way of those who discuss the supply of loans and credits etc. I thought it might help to show that they were simply discussing one of the sources of demand for liquid funds arising out of an increase in activity. But, alas, I have only driven them into more tergiversations. I am really driving at something extremely plain and simple which cannot possibly deserve all this exegesis.

Yours sincerely,
[Copy initialled] J.M.K.

Another set of letters concerns J. T. Dunlop's 'The Movement of Real

[73] See above, p. 171 and '"Mr Keynes and Finance": Comment' (*JMK*, vol. XIV, pp. 229–33).

and Money Wages'[74] which along with another paper by Lorie Tarshis stimulated Keynes to tackle another aspect of the *General Theory*.[75]

From J. T. DUNLOP, [*April 1938*]

Dear Mr Keynes,

I am wondering if you may be sufficiently interested to take a little time from your strenuous program to glance over the enclosed. It first took form as a paper to the Research Students in Cambridge last term. Since last August I've been in Cambridge on a Social Science Research Council Fellowship working on 'The Role of Wage Rigidities in the Business Cycle'. Six weeks were spent in Manchester with Professor Jewkes and now three weeks in London on the empirical data. Files of trade union periodicals and records of arbitration awards and negotiations have been worked through in addition to a number of interviews with trade union secretaries and officials of the Ministry of Labour. Professor Bowley has also discussed some of the more strictly statistical problems with me.

Mrs Robinson suggested the importance of correcting the English data for changes in the terms of trade. Recently the index of A. K. Cairncross[76] has been used to correct the data; the corrected results show no significant change. From the historical point of view the Inquiry of 1867 gives considerable evidence of the importance of changes in the cost of living in wage negotiations for that period. Neither of these points has been included in the enclosed.

The enclosed is but a single phase of a more extended program which has tried to (a) survey the literature on wage reductions (b) study the 'structure of wage rates', i.e. the margins between skilled and unskilled, women and men, adult and juvenile, overtime and time, industrial and geographical margins, etc., in the cyclical setting (c) [study the] relation between *changes* in the level of employment and the *levels* of employment (Mrs Robinson's essay)[77] to wage rates (d) construct a model sequence analysis in which to study the effects of wage rate changes on various assumptions, etc. I should therefore be extremely grateful for any suggestions you may care to make on the enclosed as it is related to this larger field of interest.

[74] Subsequently published in the *Economic Journal*, September 1938.
[75] See *JMK*, vol. VII, Appendix 3.
[76] Data from his 1935 Cambridge Ph.D. dissertation 'Home and Foreign Investment in Great Britain 1870–1913'. Much of this was subsequently published as *Home and Foreign Investment 1870–1913: Studies in Capital Accumulation* (Cambridge, 1953).
[77] J. Robinson, 'Full Employment', in *Essays in the Theory of Employment* (London, 1937).

The point of departure of the enclosed is your question about the comparative movements of real and money wage rates in the *General Theory*. Should you not have time to go over all of it, sections i, ii, and v are by far the most important I believe... I am also wondering if you would regard the subject matter and the approach of the enclosed of sufficient importance to be worked eventually into an article.

For your further information I lectured at Stanford University last year and hold an instructorship at Harvard for the coming year.

Very truly yours,
JOHN T. DUNLOP

To J. T. DUNLOP, *9 April 1938*

Dear Mr Dunlop,

I have read the enclosed with a good deal of interest. I think you undoubtedly have material worth working up into an article and, if you were to do so, I should be glad to consider it for the *Economic Journal*.

In considering the relation of your statistical results to my, perhaps rash, generalisations in the *General Theory*, it is important to be clear just what it was that I was saying and subject to what conditions.

My first concern, of course, was to deny the theory that conclusions about real wages could be turned without material alteration into conclusions about money wages. I then proceeded to argue that money wages were as a rule a function of activity (though, of course, I did not mean this to cover the great inflation periods), tending to rise and to fall with the level of employment. I argued further that the proportion of the product going to profits also tended in the short period to increase with activity, owing to the normal prevalence of increasing cost in short-period conditions. In so far as these two conditions are fulfilled, my result followed, subject only to a possible frictional disturbance.

In addition, however, to the assumption that money wages tend to rise and fall with activity and that the proportion of the product going to profits also tends to rise and fall with activity, there were certain other assumptions implicit in the argument. In the first place, it is assumed that real wages consist in the wage product produced by the labour in question; in the second place, trend has to be eliminated; and, in the third place, it is, of course, hourly wage rates, and not aggregate earnings, which are in question.

In my *obiter dicta* relating my theory to the real world, I assumed that trend had been eliminated and that hourly wage rates were in question, but I did assume that the general conclusion would not be much disturbed by the fact that real wages may not consist solely of the wage goods currently produced. In so far as the system is not a closed system, changes in the terms of trade have to be allowed for, and the cost of living may include items such as rent which are more or less fixed except for longer periods than those in view.

In your treatment I am not quite clear how far you are dealing in aggregate earnings and how far in hourly wage rates, and only here and there, so far as I can see, has trend been eliminated.

If you care to make use of some such fuller statement as I have given above of what I am trying to say, please feel free to do so; though I should like to see any use you make of the above before it is printed.

Yours very truly,
[Copy initialled] J. M. K.

From J. T. DUNLOP, *10 May 1938*

Dear Mr Keynes,

Thank you very kindly for your letter of April 9th with comments on my discussion of 'The Movement of Real and Money Wage Rates'. Your suggestions did much to clarify my own ideas and I have subsequently discussed the various problems with Mr Sraffa, Mr Robertson, Mr Kalecki and with Professor Bowley.

As per your suggestion I am wondering if you would consider the enclosed for the *Economic Journal*. The paper may be too long but in that event some of the material in footnotes—of which there is considerable—

might be deleted. In any event I should be very appreciative of any comments you may care to make on the subject matter—as I feel it is both interesting and not unimportant.

Very truly yours,
JOHN T. DUNLOP

To J. T. DUNLOP, *30 May 1938*

Dear Mr Dunlop,

I like this article very well in its revised form and shall be glad to accept it for the *Economic Journal*. Before I send it to the printer, however, I should be glad if you would consider the following points:—

1. First of all as regards length: As you rather feared, it is really too long for us. I do not want to decline it on that ground, but I think that if you read it through you could cut it by about 15 per cent by small adjustments here and there without doing it any injury—indeed the contrary. Section II is, I fancy, particularly susceptible of reduction; and, as you say, some of the footnotes could be curtailed or deleted. It would be easier, I think, to make the reduction by numerous adjustments here and there than by cutting out a whole section.

2. I feel rather strongly that you will help those who come after and make it much easier both to check and to use your work if you give actual tables instead of merely describing the outcome of your investigations. For instance, the summaries you give on pages 2 and 3 and generally throughout Section I give the reader no indication of the magnitude of the changes; nor can he check how they are associated with three- or four-year periods of recovery and depression. Why not print a table for the whole of the period you are considering, giving in the first column money wages, in the second column the usual cost of living index, in the third column this index corrected according to your own ideas, in the 4th column real wages on this basis, in the fifth column the same corrected

for the terms of trade, and in the last column the same with trend eliminated. This will have the great advantage of giving a real picture to the reader and enabling him to have a much more detailed picture than you give him at present, and something which he can use for his own purposes without doing all your work over again. At first sight this may seem to add to the length of the article, and possibly it may do so a little. On the other hand, with this table to support you you should be able to curtail considerably the number of words used in summarising your conclusions derived from it.

3. I assume that you are using throughout wage rates for the same job and as nearly as possible hourly rates rather than an index of earnings. There is a little danger here, since for the purpose of studying the progress of the wellbeing of the working classes one needs something different. If more men are employed on a higher paid class of jobs and if earnings are increasing faster than rates, that obviously improves the wellbeing of the working classes, though it is irrelevant for your particular discussion. If in any case you are not able to get comparable statistics for rates for the same class of job this should be indicated. If, on the other hand, you are able to observe this condition that should be emphasised.

Yours very truly,
[Copy initialled] J. M. K.

From J. T. DUNLOP [*about 13 June 1938*]

Dear Mr Keynes,

Thank you very kindly for your letter of two weeks ago with the suggested points of change for the article on real and money wage rates. I am returning the article to you having attended to the points you raised. As to length: the earlier draft had 38 pages; this has 31 including the three pages devoted to the table you suggested. The reduction in length is thus of the magnitude (15 per cent) that you suggested.

I decided to set the table up with links—in spite of the additional work—as I thought this form would be more useful to the reader. Table 2 takes care of comparisons in the cyclical setting, and adds somewhat I think to the presentation of the argument. I have summarized the results of Table 1 in the text on the grounds that a long table might not be examined. I have not indicated any definite insert for Table 1 in Section I but suppose the set-up of the pages will indicate a convenient place.

I shall be leaving England on July 13th and am therefore wondering if it would be more convenient for the *Journal* to have the proof examined—if it were possible—before that date. Mr Sraffa suggested that I should mention this matter to you.

On an entirely different matter, Mr Kalecki suggested to me that you were especially interested in 'the degree of monopoly'. Because I was convinced that most of the current discussion in American journals on 'rigidity' lacked theoretical orientation I attempted to calculate the 'degree of monopoly' for a number of American industries in the post-war period. I was interested in the cyclical changes; and took the ratio of price to average prime costs (materials and labour, weighted in a proportion indicated by the Census of Manufacturing). It is interesting to note the contrast in the cyclical swing of this measure for steel, paper manufacturing, boot and shoe, and tobacco on one hand and cotton, wool, and agricultural machinery on the other. I am wondering if you would have any suggestions for further work along these lines.

Very truly yours,

JOHN T. DUNLOP

The final exchange in this Volume carries us back to Keynes's earlier concerns, even earlier than the 1913 paper which began Volume XIII.

To H. TOWNSHEND, *27 July 1938*

Dear Townshend,

The enclosed has been sent to me.[78] I have not yet seen your review of Shackle's book,[79] or how far you there deal with the same problem.

The matter you are tackling is a very important and interesting one often in my mind. But the enclosed treatment seems to me still too much half-baked. I fancy one has to tackle

---

[78] This has not survived, but was presumably a paper.
[79] Townshend's review of G. L. S. Shackle's *Expectations, Investment and Income* (London, 1938), appeared in the *Economic Journal* for September 1938.

it on the basis of 'equivalent certainties'. But, above all, one wants a few rather clear and striking examples. I doubt if your example of the St Petersburg paradox is good in this connection, since it is too extreme. But a main point to which I would call your attention is that, on my theory of probability, the probabilities themselves, quite apart from their weight or value, are not numerical. So that, even apart from this particular point of weight, the substitution of a numerical measure needs discussion.

Moreover the economic problem is, of course, only a particular department of the general principles of conduct, although particularly striking in this connection because it seems to bring in numerical estimations. One arrives presumably at the numerical estimations by some system of arranging alternative decisions in order of preference, some of which will provide a norm by being numerical. But that still leaves millions of cases over where one cannot even arrange an order of preference. When all is said and done, there is an arbitrary element in the situation.

Yours sincerely,
[Copy initialled] J. M. K.

From H. TOWNSHEND, *25 November 1938*

Dear Mr Keynes,

Thank you for your letter of July 26th.

I recognise that my notions about the logic of probability are half-baked; but I have thought about it for a long time and hardly expect to be able to get any further in isolation. I know of nothing of any value recently written on the subject; and people seem very unalive to its existence. But I am quite content not to rush into print if I may call your attention to what I believe to be a point relevant to the economic side of the story.

First, may I correct a misunderstanding? I had not overlooked the non-numerical nature of the probabilities of ordinary life—though I see I expressed myself very badly about this. I have been alive to this point ever since I read your *Treatise on Probability* a good many years ago. But on re-reading what I wrote, I see that the way I tried to put my point won't do.

I will confine myself to economics and put my point in a different way, as follows:—

Those who, following on the appearance of the *General Theory*, are trying to develop further an expectational economic analysis, seem to me to be proceeding on two alternative lines. (Shackle, in particular, adopts both, in different places.)

(1) The first line bases a doctrine of equivalent certainties on the hypothesis that probabilities *are* numerical. The unanalysed judgments of the future on which the economic man acts are supposed, in each case, to lead him to take the same action as he would have taken if he had assigned their numerical probabilities to the various alternatives foreseen as possibilities. I *think* that this type of analysis is *also* forced either to neglect the weight of the evidence altogether or to treat it as a (numerical) probability of a (numerical) probability; but my present argument does not depend on this—the non-numerical nature of the probabilities themselves suffices. In my review of Shackle I have demurred to this line of approach.

(2) The second, and more usual, line appears at first sight to avoid this difficulty; and my point is to shew that it does not really avoid it, but illegitimately evades it by an incorrect analysis of the time-factor. This method is to envisage a short interval, and to suppose that the speculator (since the existence of a market gives him the possibility of reversing his transaction at the end of the interval, *however short it may be*, and he knows this beforehand) is governed by the values (not probabilities) which he expects all the various assets, in which (as an alternative to money and to each other) he can hold his wealth, to take at the end of the short interval. (It is in this way that, e.g. Shackle arrives at what he calls a startling conclusion about the effect of the speculation-motive, taken in isolation, on the rate of interest; but he is not alone in using the method—I think it lies behind both Hicks' and D. H. Robertson's ideas).

This method seems to me wrong. I don't think it is legitimate to abstract from the *length* of the interval, or rather from its 'inside', its time-content. As I see it, the reluctance to part with liquid money—the property of liquidity which gives it exchange value and enables people to obtain interest by parting with money under contract—has its origin in the doubts of wealth-owners as to what may happen to values *before the end of any interval, however short*; and I suggest that the basic cause of interest is bound up with this. Also since a speculator (defined as one who buys for a rise) must (in doing so) become less liquid, I suggest that the speculative motive may properly be regarded as the converse of the motive of liquidity preference and therefore like the latter tied up with the doubt about what may happen in the subsequent interval.

(In parenthesis, I would point out that doubt about what may happen *within* a finite future interval is the only source of insecurity attaching to the ownership, instead of money, of a debt issued by a debtor of 'perfect' soundness and repayable at the end of the interval—the kind of asset which is supposed to earn 'pure' interest. But I don't suggest that 'pure' interest is a precise concept).

No one would deny that doubt is always in fact entertained about what may happen during a finite future interval; and I think that, if one bears this in mind, an analysis of method (2) leads to the following dilemma.

The short interval in question in any analysis must be conceived of either (a) as finite (i.e. in possessing a time-content during which the unforeseen may occur and expectations be revised in the light of events) or (b) as indefinitely short (i.e. of *negligible* length and therefore *negligible* time-content).

(a) On the one hand, if one tries to take into account the speculator's ideas about what may happen *before* the end of a *finite* interval *at or before* the end of which he expects to be able profitably to reverse his transaction (should he, when the time comes, wish to do so in the light of his then revised expectations), one is led back to method (1); and so (unless some *alternative* doctrine of equivalent certainties can be devised) to the illegitimate assumption of numerical probabilities. For his actions must in such a case be governed, not by a single set of values which various assets are expected by him to take at one definite instant of future time, but by a series of time-schedules representing respectively the expected course of these values throughout the interval, associated with alternative events of various probabilities, each carrying the probability of action *during* the interval; and no way has been found (I suggest) of assessing arithmetically from such data a determinate course of maximum apparent profitability, save by assigning numerical values to the probabilities of the alternatives to the expected values at each point on each schedule, so as to be able to discount the gains and losses that would accrue from acting on alternative revised expectations during the interval based on them for the appropriate times, to get comparable (e.g. present) values. *The elimination of the probabilities depends on the elimination of all instants of future time but one instant.*

(b) On the other hand, the notion of an *indefinitely short* interval (in the precise sense of an interval such that happenings within it may be neglected without introducing material error), *at* the end of which (and not before) transactions are supposed to be expected to be reversible, seems to me illegitimate. I think this can be shewn as follows. It seems impossible to conceive of anyone contemplating the exchange of money for other capital assets and *vice versa* at more than a certain speed—e.g. every few minutes—without the *certainty* of incurring expenses exceeding the *anticipated* value of any possible gains. Incidentally, to assume this 'friction' away seems to be to assume away an essential feature of the illiquidity which all assets other than money possess. But, however this may be, friction (delay and/or cost) in realisation does always occur and is therefore always expected *with certainty* to occur. This fact implies that speculators' calculations of expected profit must be conceived of as always allowing for a *finite* time (a kind of indefinite, but finite, minimum time) expected to elapse before realisation (so that profits in excess of the cost of realisation may have time to mature). This in its turn implies that their anticipations must allow for the possibility that *within* this term something may happen to force *premature* realisation at a loss (absolute, or relative to their expectation) and so to upset the expectation—even if the asset purchased is a debt payable in full by a 'perfectly' sound creditor at the *end* of the short term.

This is the nearest I can get to an analysis of the part played by the factor of confidence in the rationale of interest. I believe that its further logical analysis at a deeper level of generalisation is connected with the part played by the weight of evidence in your theory of probability; but I cannot see just how. The connection in my mind comes about through the contrast with the conditions of the mathematical theory of probability appropriate to timeless games of chance, where in some way conditions *not indefinitely repeatable* are abstracted from. But this is probably unintelligible. I think I have got as far as this: that in discerning interest as a monetary phenomenon, e.g. as a function of the value of time-debts, to analyse real time into a succession of very short intervals *during each* of which nothing unforeseen is supposed to be expected (as the beginning of each) to happen, is to assume away an essential feature of what is being discussed.

The 'practical' bearing of the above seems to me that it implies, if it is correct, that neither of the methods hitherto used for expectational economic analysis is quite valid; in particular, to subdivide away—so to speak—the length or content of the period in the short-period expectational analysis of value is to assume away, in a peculiarly subtle manner, the phenomena of liquidity and interest. Yet it is becoming customary to do just this. That is the point I wanted to make.

All this, of course, leaves open the question whether, as you suggest in your letter, it may not be possible to develop a logical doctrine of equivalent certainties free from the assumption of numerical probabilities, and perhaps of wider than economic application. I am only maintaining that this has not yet been done. It also leaves out of account the element of arbitrariness in judgments of probability, to which you refer. I think that this last, in its economic aspect, really implies a criticism, or at least calls for further analysis, of the basic concept of the economic man, defined as *determinately* motivated by (his) judgments of maximum (in some sense) anticipated profitability. I tried to touch on this in my review of Hawtrey's *Capital and Employment*.[80] (Incidentally, he thought it worth while to publish a rejoinder in which he confuses the assumption that a determinate set of decisions exists, such that, if all the entrepreneurs took them, their profits would be maximised individually, with the assumption that the entrepreneurs actually take such a set of decisions!)[81] I do not really believe that anything more can be hoped for in economics from the sort of abstract reasoning in which I am indulging (with others!) than the negative result of exposing current fallacies. My present point is to expose what I think to be one such. I hope I have succeeded in disentangling this point from deeper logical issues on which I am not clear; and that I have not bored you with this long letter.

Yours sincerely,

HUGH TOWNSHEND

To HUGH TOWNSHEND, *7 December 1938*

My dear Townshend,

I am interested that you are still pursuing the elusive problems discussed in your letter of November 25th. There is very little in that letter from which I want to differ.

In particular, I agree that intervals must be regarded as finite, and that doubt as to what may happen within the interval is a factor of which we must take account. As regards my remarks in my *General Theory*, have you taken account of what I say at page 240, as well as what I say at page 148, which is the passage I think you previously quoted. I am rather inclined to associate risk premium with probability strictly speaking, and liquidity premium with what in my *Treatise on Probability* I called 'weight'. An essential distinction is that a risk premium is expected to be rewarded on the average by

---

[80] See above, pp. 255-9.

[81] See R. G. Hawtrey's 'Alternative Theories of the Rate of Interest III', *Economic Journal*, September 1937, pp. 441-3.

an increased return at the end of the period. A liquidity premium, on the other hand, is not even expected to be so rewarded. It is a payment, not for the expectation of increased tangible income at the end of the period, but for an increased sense of comfort and confidence during the period.

I think it important to emphasise the point that all this is not particularly an *economic* problem, but affects every rational choice concerning conduct where consequences enter into the rational calculation. Generally speaking, in making a decision we have before us a large number of alternatives, none of which is demonstrably more 'rational' than the others, in the sense that we can arrange in order of merit the sum aggregate of the benefits obtainable from the complete consequences of each. To avoid being in the position of Buridan's ass, we fall back, therefore, and necessarily do so, on motives of another kind, which are not 'rational' in the sense of being concerned with the evaluation of consequences, but are decided by habit, instinct, preference, desire, will, etc. All this is just as true of the non-economic as of the economic man. But it may well be, as you suggest, that when we remember all this, we have to abate somewhat from the traditional picture of the latter.

Yours sincerely,
[Copy initialled] J. M. K.

APPENDICES

Appendix I

THE NOTATION OF THE *TREATISE*
AND THE *GENERAL THEORY*

A Treatise on Money

B—the value of the current account balance

C—the volume of net investment

E—the total earnings or costs of production (includes the normal remuneration of entrepreneurs)

e—the coefficient of efficiency

G—exports of gold

I—the value of investment

I'—the cost of production of investment goods

I_1—the value of home investment $= (I - B)$

I_1'—the adjusted cost of home investment $= (I_1 - Q_2)$

L—the value of foreign lending

M—total deposits

M_1—income deposits

M_2—business deposits

M_3—savings deposits

O—the volume of total output

P—the price level of consumption goods

P'—the price level of investment goods

Q—total profits (the difference between actual remuneration and the normal renumeration of entrepreneurs)

Q_1—profits on the production and sale of consumption goods

Q_2—profits on the production and sale of investment goods

R—the volume of consumption goods coming to market and purchased by consumers

S—savings

S_1—$S - (L - G)$

W—the rate of earnings per unit of human effort
W_1—the rate of earnings per unit of output
w—the proportion of cash deposits to total deposits
V—velocity
Π—the price level of output as a whole

The Fundamental Equations

(a) in a closed economy

$$P = \frac{E}{O} + \frac{I'-S}{R} \qquad \Pi = \frac{E}{O} + \frac{I-S}{O}$$

(b) in an open economy

$$P = \frac{E}{O} + \frac{I_1'-S_1}{R} \qquad \Pi = \frac{E}{O} + \frac{I_1-S_1}{O}$$

The General Theory of Employment, Interest and Money

A—the value of entrepreneurs' sales of finished output to consumers
A_1—the value of entrepreneurs' purchases of finished output from other producers
a—the percentage appreciation or depreciation of an asset in terms of itself
B'—entrepreneurs' expenditure on maintenance and improvement
C—consumption
D—aggregate demand
D_1—expected consumption
D_2—expected investment
E—the wages and salaries bill
G—the value of capital equipment
I—investment
k—the investment multiplier
k'—the employment multiplier
L—liquidity function
l—liquidity premium
M—the stock of cash
M_1—the stock of cash held for transactions and precautionary purposes
M_2—the stock of cash held to satisfy the speculative motive
N—the volume of employment
O—the volume of current output
P—the price level of current output (except in Chapter 20, when it is expected profit)

Q—the yield of an asset
q—the yield of an asset in terms of itself
r—the rate of interest
S—savings
U—user cost
V—supplementary cost (except in Chapters 15 and 21, when it is the income velocity of money)
W—the wage unit
Y—income
Z—aggregate supply

Appendix II

LIST OF CORRECTIONS TO VOLUMES XIII AND XIV

VOLUME XIII

page	line	correction
xiii	1	For 'three' read 'five'
1 n.1, l.2		For 'S. J.' read 'J. S.'
43	20	For 'xxiv' read 'xviii'
113	19	For 'finest' read 'first'
126	6	For '1931' read '1930'
176 n.2, l.1		For '*Wessen*' read '*Wesen*'
189 n.1, l.1		Add the words 'drafted by Keynes' between the words 'questionnaire' and 'ran'
193	29	For 'assuring' read 'assuming'
208	28	For 'exces ssaving' read 'excess saving'
213	36	For 'papers' read 'paper'
246	19	For '129' read '219'
269 n.1, l.1		For '*Theory*' read '*Economics*'
321 n.1, l.1		For 'should have' read 'Shove had'
337	9	After the word 'did' add 'in his December 1931 letter to Kaldor (above p. 243) and'
342	6	For 'vi' read 'v'
376	3	For '244' read '299'
399	25	For the second 'ΣP_2' read '$\Sigma P_2'$'

APPENDICES

VOLUME XIV

CORRECTIONS

VOLUME XIV—INDEX

page	column	line	correction
549	2	42	For '435' read '435–6'
549	2	43	For '77' read '77–8'
550	1	19	For '406' read '412'
550	2	32	For 'XIII' read 'XIV'
551	2	18	For 'The General Theory' read 'Mr Keynes' The General Theory of Employment, Interest and Money'
551	2	51	For '430–8' read '436–44'
552	1	13	For '557' read '558'
552	2	53	For '163' read '162–3'
553	1	50	For '484' read '118'
553	2	6	For '340–7' read '340–1'
553	2	40	For '175' read '176'
553	2	54	For '457–71' read '457–68'
554	2	16	For 'XIII' read 'XIV'
554	2	34	For '278' read '277'
554	2	51	For '531' read '513'
555	1	35	For '520' read '524'
555	1	36	For '635' read '633'
555	1	50	For '647–9' read '647–50'
555	2	10	For '87–101, 223–8' read '87–100, 223–9'
556	2	2	For '175' read '176'
556	2	17	For '375' read '373'
556	2	23	For '311' read '211'
556	2	24	For '26' read '36'
556	2	34	For 'III' read 'XIII'
557	2	44	For '394' read '400–1'
558	1	35	For 'The General Theory' read 'Mr Keynes' The General Theory of Employment, Interest and Money'
559	2	2	For '73' read '72'
560	1	36	For '447' read '453'
560	2	32	For '400–1, 406–7' read '406–7, 411–12'
561	2	41	For '265' read '266'
562	1	21	For '406' read '405'
562	1	25	For '372' read '371'
562	2	30	For '489' read '490'
562	2	34	For '498' read '504'
563	1	9	For '295' read '294'

CORRECTIONS

page	column	line	correction
565	1	36	For '175, 223' read '174, XIV, 223'
565	2	2	For '493' read '498–9'
565	2	28	For '407' read '413'
565	2	29	For '373' read '377'
566	1	6	For '242' read '243'
566	2	11	For '266' read '267'
566	2	17	For '376, 378' read '381, 383'
566	2	18	For '476' read '482'
566	2	30	For '28' read '28–9'
566	2	31	For '405' read '412'
567	1	7	Before '*Poverty*' add '*The Burden of*'
567	1	10	For '464' read '465'
567	1	20	For '151' read '150'
568	1	3	For '108' read '107–8'
568	1	44	For '270' read '271'
568	1	49	For '373' read '377'
568	2	7	For '51' read '41'
569	1	42	For '441' read '446'
569	2	2	For '116' read '166'
569	2	41	For '425' read '431'
572	2	29	For '66' read '59'
573	1	22	For '484' read '490'
573	2	5	For '201–3' read '201–2'
573	2	9	For '306–7' read '306–9'
574	1	9	Omit '1'
574	1	11	For 'II' read 'I'
574	2	13	For '72' read '73'
574	2	35	For '*Theory*' read '*Economics*'
575	1	46	For 'Joan Robinson' read 'Kahn'
576	2	52	For '114' read '115'
577	1	16	For '*Wessen*' read '*Wesen*'
577	1	47	For 'XIII, 268, XIV, 302, 313' read 'XIII, 268, 313, XIV, 302'
577	2	11	For '339' read '338'
577	2	15	For '359' read '358'
578	1	3	For 'XIV' read 'XIII'
578	1	4	For '431' read '421'
579	1	54	For '370' read '371'
579	2	13	For '381' read '387'

APPENDICES

page	column	line	correction
579	2	39	For 'XIII' read 'XIV'
580	2	44	For '308' read '306'
581	2	8	For '341' read '343'
582	2	40	For '353' read '352–3'
582	2	45	For 'XIII' read 'XIV'
583	1	6	For '284' read '285'
583	1	9	For '292' read '282'
583	1	38	For 'XIII' read 'XIV'
583	2	4	For '390' read '490'
583	2	32	For '404' read '40'
584	1	5	For '473–4, 475n, 477' read '479–80, 481n, 483'
584	1	6	For '476, 478' read '482, 484'
584	1	26	For '432–4' read '431–5'
584	2	14	For '281' read '291'
584	2	31	For '420' read '422'
584	2	34	For 'XVI' read 'XIV'

DOCUMENTS REPRODUCED
IN THIS VOLUME

Where documents come from the Public Record Office, their call numbers appear before the date.

DOCUMENTS REPRODUCED IN THIS VOLUME

DOCUMENTS REPRODUCED IN THIS VOLUME

DOCUMENTS REPRODUCED IN THIS VOLUME

ACKNOWLEDGEMENTS

We should like to thank Professor Richard Keynes, Keynes's nephew, for making this new material available so promptly, and many readers of Volumes XIII and XIV for their comments and corrections. We should also like to thank Professors Richard Kahn, Don Patinkin, Joan Robinson and Lorie Tarshis, as well as Victoria Chick, Michael Danes and Susan Howson for comments and advice, and Coral George for typing. The Canada Council and the Humanities and Social Sciences Research Council of Canada provided financial support.

309

INDEX

Acceleration, principle of, 265

Accountants, 195n, 197n; bookkeeping, 242–4; cost accounting, 243; depreciation accounts, 195

Accounting period, *see* Period of production

Adam Smith Prize, 4

Adarkar, B. P., 13, 15

Advertising, 139

Aggregate, *see under* Capital; cost of production; costs; demand; disbursement; effective demand; employment; expenditure; income; output; propensity to save; quasi-rent; saving; saving and investment; supply; supply function; wages

Agriculture
  agricultural machinery (U.S.A.), 288
  stocks of agricultural commodities (U.S.A.), 202, 203, 204; total output of agricultural products (1933), 205

'Alexander', *see* Kahn, R. F.

Algebra: of *General Theory*, Townshend on, 240–5; reply (JMK), 245–6

Allen, Maurice, Fellow of Balliol College, 23

America, *see* United States of America

American Economic Review, articles on JMK's theories, 177

Angell, J. W.
  The Behaviour of Money, reviewed by Robertson (*Economic Journal*, June 1937), 263, 265
  Contribution to Irving Fisher *Festschrift* (1937), 263, 264–5
  'The General Dynamics of Money' (*Journal of Political Economy*, June 1937), 265
  list of letters, 304

Annuities, 111

Appreciation
  of assets, 296
  and interest, theory of, 83, 84

Art or *technique*, 116. *See also* Technique

Assets
  appreciation and depreciation, *General Theory* a, 296
  capital, 14, 292; and quasi-rent, 111–17; calculation of value, 113–14, 119–20
  income-yielding, 141–2; in *General Theory* notation, 297
  physical, expectation of income from, 266
  purchases of, by the public, 93–4, 141
  and saving, 14, 15–16, 104
  scarcity of, 116–18
  speculation in, 290, 292
  also mentioned, 134

Assumptions, 40
  in classical theory, *see under* Classical theory
  in *General Theory*: on output and income, and on income and expenditure, 39, challenged in the 'Manifesto', 42–5; on over-supply of machines and men, 50–1; on savings and investment, 56; on propensity to spend, 135–6, 137
  in generalised long-period theory, 57
  Lindahl's, 130
  Pigou's, 31, 32, 33
  'simplifying' assumptions, 143, 145, 149
  in traditional rate of interest theory, 118–19, 270

Austrian school of economists, 156

'Automatic' forces leading to equilibrium between saving and investment, 56, 103, 107, 137; Wicksell's view, 262

Entrepreneurs (*cont.*)
   mistakes, 136, 137, 138, 211
   notation for, in *Treatise*, 295, in *General Theory*, 296
   profits, 5
   and rate of interest, 7
   self-interest motive, 132
   see also Business; Firms
Equations
   to be based on gross figures, 58
   for determination of employment, 65
   fundamental, 36; in draft contents of *General Theory*, 63; draft chapter on (1933), 68–73; of *Treatise*, 4, 73; notation for, 296
   Lindahl on, 122–3, 126–8
   of price, relation to *Treatise* terms, 71–2, 73
Equilibrium
   disequilibrium, 7, 33–4, 101
   economic equilibrium, 150; Lindahl on, 129
   equlibrium level of employment, 137
   between holding money and other forms of wealth, 83, 142
   between investment and saving, 129, 137, 147–8
   long-period, 51, 54–5, 56–7, 72; short-period, 136–7, 158
   marginal efficiency a concept of, 112–13; between marginal efficiency and rate of interest, 115, 118, 141, 143, 144, 148
   neutral, 91–2, 137, 158–9
   optimum, 92, 99; below optimum, 57
   and production period, 155, 156
   re-establishment of, after increase in quantity of money, 131
   of relative prices, 221
   between saving and consumption, 103
   and scarcity of assets, 117
   stable, 138; unstable, 40, 43
   in the stock-exchange market, 11
   in an unclosed system, 95n
   between wages and output, 157, wages and prices, 159
   also mentioned, 26, 32, 98n, 212, 272
Equilibrium economics
   long- and short-period, 35
   orthodox, 220; divergence of *General Theory* from, 101, 132–3, 215
Equities, 114

'Equivalent certainties', 288–9, 290, 291, 292
Ex ante and *ex post*
   concepts of saving and investment (Lindahl), 127; *ex post* quantities, 130
   Ohlin's *ex ante* and *post ante* savings, 277, 280; *ex ante* theory of rate of interest, 164, article by JMK on (*Economic Journal*, December 1937), 164, 165, 170n, 267 n57, 269, 275, 280
Exchange, mechanism of, in *Treatise*, 9
Exchange market, 145; rates, 145, 146; restrictions, 145
   see also Foreign exchange
Expansion, policy of, 233–4, 235, 247
Expectation
   correspondence with J. W. Angell on, 264–6
   entrepreneurial, 89–90
   expectational economic analysis (Townshend), 291–3
   expected consumption (D_1), investment (D_2), 296
   expected returns, 240, 243
   expected variable cost, 101
   of future value of assets, 134
   long-period return to capital, 72
   manufacturers', 74–5
   and propensity to spend, 135, 138
   in relation to prices, 120–3
   risk and, 264, 266
   role in demand for investment goods, 139; for money stocks, 142
   also mentioned, 150, 233
Expenditure
   aggregate and aggregate cost, 90, 91–2, 99
   on consumption, 136
   creates its own income, 81
   defined, 134, 135; in definition of investment, 138
   entrepreneurs', 13, 90; control of, in an entrepreneur economy, 95
   increases in, and employment, 136, 144, 149
   loan expenditure by government, 95, 237
   maintenance expenditure, 139; in capital formation, 188, 190, 191, 196, 200
   relatively to costs, 94, 95
   rises with rise in income, but not in same proportion, 137

331